Steering by Starlight

HOW TO FULFIL YOUR DESTINY, NO MATTER WHAT

MARTHA BECK

piatkus

PIATKUS

First published in Great Britain in 2008 by Piatkus Books
This paperback edition published in 2009 by Piatkus Books
First published in the US in 2008 by Rodale

A CIP catalogue record for this book
is available from the British Library

ISBN 978-0-7499-2931-2

Book design by Christopher Rhoads

Data manipulation by Phoenix Photosetting, Chatham, Kent
www.phoenixphotosetting.co.uk

Printed in the UK by Clays Ltd, St Ives plc

Papers used by Piatkus are natural, renewable and recyclable
products sourced from well-managed forests and certified
in accordance with the rules of the Forest Stewardship Council.

Piatkus
An imprint of
Little, Brown Book Group
100 Victoria Embankment
London EC4Y 0DY

An Hachette UK Company
www.hachette.co.uk

www.piatkus.co.uk

CONTENTS

ACKNOWLEDGMENTS v

INTRODUCTION ix

CHAPTER 1

The End   1

CHAPTER 2

Wizard versus Lizard: The Battle for Your Brain   25

CHAPTER 3

Digging out of the Dungeon   49

CHAPTER 4

The Ring of Fire   75

CHAPTER 5

Dreaming Your Star Chart   97

CHAPTER 6

North Star Mapmaking   123

CHAPTER 7

Hear, Here   147

CHAPTER 8

Working Miracles: The Pathfinder's Progress   169

CHAPTER 9

Leading Your Life   189

CHAPTER 10

The Beginning   213

To you, whenever you're walking in the dark.

ACKNOWLEDGEMENTS

There are only so many ways to say "thank you," so these acknowledgements will be rife with repetition. Trying to express the gratitude I feel toward everyone who contributed to this book, and who shored me up during its writing, is like trying to capture a sunrise by drawing with a stick in the dirt. As many "thank you's" as there are here, each is different to me; they have their own colors and brilliance, and each is unique.

That said, I first must thank my clients, whose courage and determination to live their destinies inspire and motivate me every day. Without their example, and their willingness to trust that we'll find their destiny together, I could never have developed the strategies or imagine the stories recounted in this book.

Thanks to my editor redoubtable Leigh Haber, Nancy Bailey, and all the good people at Rodale who were there to support the labor of writing, to hold the baby manuscript once it arrived, and care for it until it could stand on its own feet.

My fabulous literary agent, Suzanne Gluck, is a phenomenally concentrated source of intelligence, wit, heart, and savvy. It's a privilege to work with and learn from her. Amy Gray and Bill Stankey, agents in other fields, have put enormous energy into the work we've done together. Deep thanks to all of them.

More gratitude for the amazing people at O, The Oprah Magazine, including (but not limited to) my kind, longsuffering, and talented editor Mamie Healey, the inimitable Amy Gross, the irrepressible Gail King, and the incomparable Oprah Winfrey. I would never have dared dream that I'd be associated with a team, so gifted, impressive, and kind.

Betsy Rapoport's brilliant mind and sparkling, steadfast spirit have shaped my writing and my life for over a decade. I don't even want to imagine what my world would be like without her friendship. Annette Rogers is not only one of the best authors and editors I know, but a dauntless companion always ready to offer wisdom, compassion, and generosity. Ruth Killpack and Rita Edmonds are always ready with listening ears, deep insights, and endless kindness. To them, and to my other friends (oh, God, did I leave anyone out?) my most heartfelt thanks.

I can't begin to express my gratitude for the amazing people who've come to be trained in my life-coaching methods. They are very sweet to me, and very salty, as in "the salt of the earth." I'm so proud and happy our paths have crossed, and continue to do so. My coaching tribe is an incredible blessing, and I love you all. Specifically, my life-coaching colleague Brooke Castillo is one of the most talented, compassionate, and ethical people I've met in any business. Meadow DeVor's combination of high humor and laser insight changed my life. Yvonne Morier is as dependable and trustworthy as sunshine. I'm inexpressibly grateful to be working with them.

Koelle Simpson, gifted coach, horse whisperer, and all-around shaman, shares my passion for animals and has taught me so much through her gift for working with animals and humans, separately or in combination. Thank you, thank you.

Deep appreciation and amazed gratitude go out to all my friends in South Africa: inspired master coach Judy Klipin, Alex van der Heeber, the whole astonishing Varty family, the personnel at *The Oprah Magazine* in SA. The magnificent Jane Raphaeli and Thami Ngubeni are not only colleagues, but shining warriors of peace, using the pen rather than the sword to bring peace where there might be war.

The wonderful people at Piatkus Books, especially Judy Piatkus, who has been a stalwart champion, brilliant colleague, and understanding soul through many adventures. Also to those at Penguin South Africa, including but not limited to Karen Lane and Michelle McGrane, who have kindly and patiently dealt with logistical obstacles, travel schedules, and my own jet-lagged incompetence. I doubt they can know how much I appreciate them.

Stacey Shively, Al Preble, and especially Kim Barber, have also devoted themselves to figuring out how adults learn, change, and find their own North Stars. I loved the time we spent working together, and look to them for new insights, theoretical advances, and applications as life coaching develops in the coming decades. They are ground-breakers who've already touched thousands of lives, and will continue doing so. Again, I am so, so grateful.

John, Joni, and Joseph Parker have been a gentle and blessed presence in my life. John's spirit, care, advice, selflessness, and enormous compassion put me back together when I'm frazzled into fragments.

Lydia Nibley, Russell Martin, Megan Nibley, Sylvia Nibley, have been willing to swim in the end of the gene pool where I paddle around. My gratitude for this leaves me speechless—and as my loved ones know all too well, I am rarely speechless.

Most of all, I must thank my wonderful, patient, loving, accepting, wise, supportive family: Kat the wizard, Adam the angel, Elizabeth the practical magician, and especially Karen the soul-guide, without whom I could never have learned to steer by starlight myself. If we really are commingled with everything in the universe, as physicists tell us we are, then my love for all of you permeates every star in the cosmos. It certainly feels that way.

INTRODUCTION

I know a man—let's call him Gus—whose nose is continuously attempting to turn itself into an ear. Gus's original nose was crushed in a car accident, and plastic surgeons rebuilt it by taking cartilage from one of his ears, sculpting it into the shape they needed, and grafting it to his nasal bridge. Their skill was amazing; you'd never notice anything unusual about Gus's remodeled schnozz.

However, that little bit of cartilage never forgot what it started out to be. Ever since the surgery, it's been trying to re-create the ear from which it was harvested. Gradually, as the years go by, it morphs into a delicate aural whorl, and Gus's doctors have to go back in and whittle it down again. But the cartilage is not discouraged. Before the procedure is over, it's already continuing its humble, inexorable ambition to regenerate its original form.

I can empathize with Gus's nose. I suspect you can, too. The fact that you're reading these words suggests that you're looking to find and follow the life you were meant to have: your highest and happiest possible destiny. This wouldn't be an issue if you already felt fully "on purpose" or if you lacked any sense of destiny at all.

I'm betting you're like many clients I've coached, people who feel that they aren't quite themselves, who continuously sense that they are trying to regain their true form but who have only the faintest inkling of what that might be. My goal in writing this book is to help you find your deepest sense of purpose—to give you back to yourself, since you are the ultimate arbiter of your own fate. You don't need a book to do this. Whether or not you're consciously following your destiny, your destiny is always following you. But this book may well make the process quicker, cleaner, and easier.

Why This Book May Help You Fulfil Your Destiny

Let me explain a little about why I venture to offer you advice about your life, which you know far better than I ever can. I'm a "life coach," part of a profession that popped up like a mushroom in the last few years of the twentieth century. There's no standardization or regulation for life coaching. I have no idea what most people who go by that title actually do. I think of myself as the behavioral equivalent of a personal trainer. A therapist, like a physician, works with unwell people to restore them to health. I work with healthy people to help them achieve maximum "fitness"—that is, well-being and quality of life.

Oddly enough, I knew my life-coaching destiny subconsciously even when I was young and life coaching hadn't been invented. At age sixteen, I filled out a scholarship application that asked me for a single-sentence summation of my mission in life. My younger sister suggested that I write, "My mission in life is to learn how to say, 'Hey, sailor, want to get lucky?' in every living language." But we lived in Utah, and I feared this would not be well received. So instead, I tossed out a random thought: "My mission in life is to help people bridge the gaps that separate them from their true selves, from one another, and from their destiny." Today, approximately four hundred years later, I don't think I'd change that description. Our right lives ride in our cells, in our DNA, and they pop up to speak to us in idle moments, when we think we're just shooting the breeze.

My Adventures in Life Design

A year after filling out that scholarship application, I took a big old detour from the clear self-perception of innocent adolescence. I went off to

Harvard and got sucked into the culture of the Ivy League (unofficial motto: "If you aren't incredibly smart, just kill yourself."). I stuck around Harvard long enough to earn three degrees: a bachelor's in East Asian languages and civilizations and my master's and Ph.D. in sociology. I spent time in Asia, learning some Chinese and Japanese and absorbing a philosophical tradition that would profoundly influence all my future thinking.

I also got married and had myself three rug rats, demonstrating the sound life-planning skills of a meth addict who goes bungee jumping without a cord. My middle child, Adam, was diagnosed with Down syndrome two months before he was born. This forced me to face a few little questions, like "What makes a human life worth living?" and "What is the reason for our existence?" and "How do you use American Sign Language to tell a baby, 'I'm changing your diaper,' while simultaneously changing the diaper?" In other words, real life invaded my ivory-tower education and smacked me around, hard, until I had to admit my own total ignorance about everything that really matters. And this, as Plato says, is the beginning of wisdom. Not wisdom (I don't claim that), but its beginning.

After that, I steered my whole education toward understanding how to build a life that would be worth living. I worked on a twenty-year study of career patterns at Harvard Business School, wrote a dissertation on role conflict among working women, and spent hundreds of hours doing interviews in which I asked people to describe their lives. My "researcher" status was really just a duck blind I used to coax the truth into the open. What I really wanted were ideas about how to cope, how to be happy, how to find and fulfil my own purpose.

I also did a lot of teaching, in a weird variety of subjects: social psychology, Caribbean culture, studio art. Eventually, I found myself teaching business at the American Graduate School of International Management, which goes by the nickname Thunderbird. My T-bird students weren't like the MBAs I'd known at Harvard. They wanted adventures, not just money. They wanted to matter. Some of them asked me to talk to them about their lives outside of class—and they offered to *pay* me for it. "What the hell," I thought, "it beats working."

And so I began teaching what I'd learned from all those endless hours of thinking, hurting, reading, hoping, interviewing, longing, teaching, and gradually discovering how humans can follow their bliss. I'd begun life coaching, though I wouldn't call it that until I read an article in *USA Today* that called me "the best-known life coach in the country." I was thrilled to learn that there was a name for what I do. I felt stunned with gratitude to be doing it. I still feel that way.

How to Use This Book

So, as you read this book, I want to be *your* life coach. I'll tell you everything I've learned about finding and fulfilling your destiny, in the briefest, simplest possible way. An ancient Chinese text says, "The way to simplicity lies through complexity." I've learned that fulfilling your best destiny is a startlingly simple process—but that doesn't mean it's easy. You may have to go through some complex thoughts and experiences in order to absorb and utilize the surprisingly straightforward methods that can liberate us from everything that doesn't serve our right lives.

You don't have to be smart to do this—in fact, book-smarts may actually hinder your progress. Another Asian saying is "The mind is a wonderful servant, but a terrible master." Your mind can understand parts of your search for destiny, but it can't grasp some of the most powerful truths. These must be experienced to be understood. If something you read in the upcoming chapters sounds so simple you figure you don't have to bother with the accompanying exercises, think again. *Don't dismiss any of the ideas until you have actually done the exercises.* Not every exercise will work for you, and that's okay. *But if you think reading is enough and doing isn't required, none of them can work.*

This is because the knowledge of your destiny isn't in your mind. It's in a deeper part of you: the awareness of the true self, the soul—call it whatever you want. This deep part of you is like Gus's nose/ear. It always remembers what it is meant to be and never stops trying to be what it is, no matter what happens to it. Trying to force the mind to do the soul's job is like trying to whittle your ear into a nose—it can work, sort of, but you'll find yourself continuously yearning away from what you've forced yourself to become. Your true self is vastly more intelligent than your mind; in fact, it is limitless. The exercises I'll suggest will help you tap that infinite intelligence.

A Word about Examples

I'll tell a lot of true stories to show you how I arrived at my theories and methods. In the ten years I've been coaching, I've focused intensely and intimately on the lives of literally thousands of people. I've heard stories that would startle you, amaze you, make your hair stand on end. I'll use some of the most extreme of these stories as I talk about destiny. You probably haven't experienced such extremity. I'm assuming you fall somewhere in the middle of life's big bell curves—that you aren't, for instance, as wealthy as the rich people I've coached (who own things like the copyright to the law of gravity) nor as poor as my poorest clients (like the homeless heroin addicts at the methadone clinic where I sometimes do volunteer coaching).

The way to benefit from these extreme examples is to contrast them with your own (probably less dramatic) experiences. "Wow," you might think, "if the homeless person in that example can start living her destiny, then maybe I can, too, even though I'm barely making rent." Or "Huh. If a world-famous millionaire is still afraid of going broke, maybe getting a million dollars isn't all I need to feel secure."

That said, I want to assure you that all the stories in this book are true. Aside from changing names and surface details that might identify my clients, I'll give you the facts as I know them, without distortion. There may be unwitting errors in some of the tales, but there are no deliberate falsifications or exaggerations of factual reality. As you read, I encourage you to use a social science method called "bracketing." Anthropologists might use it to study, say, an obscure jungle-dwelling tribe that believes God speaks to them through frog droppings. The scientists would imagine putting up a mental bracket like this: { and willingly suspend their disbelief in the tribe's religion. When the period of study was over, they'd close the bracket: } and analyze events from a logical perspective.

You might need to keep up mental brackets throughout this book because much of what I'll describe may sound incredible. Every so often, when I introduce a theory to consider rather than a simple fact, I'll warn you to "bracket up." I won't ever tell you to put your brackets down—you can do that when you're finished reading. Then you can decide which of my ideas seem most true to you. I urge you—I beg you—to discard all those that don't.

In one of my previous books, I used the phrase "your own North Star" as a metaphor for your right life, in order to avoid using the word *destiny* and its mystical nuances. But since writing that book, I've worked with well over a thousand clients, and I've seen that once they commit to following their own North Stars, the word *mystical* is a tame description of what actually unfolds. I'm skeptical of religion and superstition, and I believe there's a scientific explanation for everything. But I also know from much experience that current science can't begin to explain the things that will happen to you if you begin steering your life by starlight.

Manifest Destiny

Here's an example of what I mean. I was in Washington, D.C., serving on an advisory committee to the makers of the children's TV show *Sesame Street*. Another committee member was an absolutely delightful woman named Rosario Marin (she isn't a client, so I'm using her real name).

Rosario was one of those people with so much charisma they practically glow in the dark. We were both on Pacific Coast time, which meant that the meeting started when our body clocks said 5:00 a.m. By midmorning, we were both staring at our agenda sheets, slumped and slack-jawed and too sleepy to blink. So we sneaked off to find a Starbucks and bathe ourselves in caffeine. Once we'd absorbed enough coffee to regain the power of speech, we began to chat.

"You know," said Rosario, "I've always thought I'd live here in Washington someday."

I felt something like a mild electric shock. Every hair on my body bristled. This is always my own true self's reaction when someone is nearing the truth about their destiny.

"Rosario," I said, "I think you're right."

Rosario didn't strike me as a weepy person, but suddenly her eyes filled with tears. "I can't figure out why I feel this way," she whispered. "Sleep deprivation, right?" She belted back half a triple-shot latte, fighting to control her emotions.

"No, Rosario," I shook my head. "It's not sleep deprivation. It's whatever you're supposed to do. You're not letting it be big enough. It's big. Very big." Pulses of electricity kept sweeping over me like waves on a beach.

With obvious difficulty, Rosario fought back her tears and regained her usual jovial composure. "Oh, well," she said. "I guess time will tell."

"I guess so," I said.

I didn't see Rosario again for a couple of years. The next time we met was in London, at a meeting for the board of Special Olympics International. Rosario gave me a huge hug. I asked how her family was doing.

"We're great," she said. "The move to D.C. wasn't easy, but we're settling in now."

"You moved to Washington?" I asked.

She gave me an odd smile. "Oh. I guess you haven't heard."

"Heard what?"

Rosario said, "I'm the Treasurer of the United States."

Later that day, she gave me a one dollar bill that bears her signature. If you're carrying American currency right now, you probably have a few such bills in your wallet or purse. Any time you need to be reminded that intimations of destiny can be real, pull out some paper money and look for the name Rosario Marin in tidy handwriting next to the portrait of the dead president. I call these bills my North Star Bucks (get it?). Every time I use a Rosario Marin–approved bill to buy a cup of coffee, I'm reminded that the magic of destiny, though still a mystery to me, is real. We align ourselves with it every time we find ourselves in darkness. All we have to do to get magic on our side is to look up at the stars.

Becoming the Stargazer

I used to think of the human psyche as having two sides: the "essential" (or genetic) self, which determines our talents and preferences, and the "social" self, which predisposes us to respond to other people's influence. Over the past few years, I've also come to believe there is a third self, one that goes beyond the boundaries of both the genetic and social selves. Buddhists call this "no-self," a confusing term meant to focus our attention on something the intellect can't grasp. Other traditions call it the great Self, an identity that is shared by everything that exists. I'm going to call it the Stargazer because it never loses sight of your own North Star, your destiny.

I used to help people dig through their social roles (for example, "I'm a mother, a firefighter, a good Christian, an intellectual.") to their inborn personalities or essential selves ("I'm talented, sensitive, loving, tough."). Nowadays, that's not enough for me. Your genetically determined essential self is closer to your destiny than your social self, but as we'll see, even your genetic self is highly vulnerable to things that knock it off the path of your right life. The genetic self is subject to mental illness, dementia, and death. Above all, it is afflicted by fear, in all that emotion's manifold guises. The

Stargazer within you is unaffected by any of these problems. It extends beyond your brain, beyond your personality. It's so deep and vast that nothing can ever disturb it.

I'm going to give you fair warning: Learning to live as the Stargazer can be a wild ride. If you don't want to have any strange and possibly mystical experiences, turn back now. Find another self-help book. There's no guarantee that magical things will start happening to you if you do all the exercises necessary to become the Stargazer, but I'd say the likelihood is around ninety per cent. You'll have premonitions, unaccountable knowledge, experiences that go so far beyond statistical likelihood that to call them "coincidence" would be irrational. The very fabric of reality will seem compelled to help you when you set out toward your North Star, and the more time you spend Stargazing, the more magic you'll experience.

This is not any sort of tribute to my methods, only to the fact that mystical experiences are an innate part of being human. We tend to deny this because modern cultures repress magic in much the same way Freud's culture repressed sex—with similar results. When they're denied or repressed, our mystical drives get warped and misguided, turning us neurotic or overly gullible. This may lead to bizarre religious fundamentalism and various forms of magical thinking (which doesn't work) as opposed to actual magic (which does).

You are a natural mystic. All humans are. But given our culture, it's likely that every time your being starts to assume the gentle curve of the mystic's soul, something else—your peers, your parents, your own rational mind—slices into you like the scalpel slicing into Gus's cartilage, forcing you back to the rational shape you're "supposed" to have. The exercises in this book are meant to set you free from all forms that are not your deepest nature. As this occurs, you may become unrecognizable to many people who are important to you, including your present ego. You will become the person your best destiny calls you to be.

Still with me? Brackets still up? Excellent. In that case, let's preview the process of learning to steer by starlight.

The Three Stages of Steering by Starlight

Learning to live from the Stargazer's vantage point requires three basic stages, which I call "dissolving," "dreaming," and "daring." Here's a preview, so you'll know where we're headed.

Stage 1: Dissolving (Your Non-Stargazing Obstructions)

To say that you can "find" your destiny is misleading because it never goes anywhere. Your destiny is closer to you than your own beating heart (literally: I've heard this from people whose hearts stopped beating and who realized during the ensuing "near-death experiences" that they'd known their destinies all along). The reason many of us feel that we've "lost" our destinies is that we spend a lot of time putting on blinders.

We make these blinders of a highly opaque substance: thoughts. Our thoughts are then rendered sticky by emotions, so taking off the blinders can be extremely difficult. Unfortunately, the central premise of all rationalist cultures is that we can think our way out of any problem. This is like trying to put out a fire with kerosene. Our subcultures of therapy and the arts suggest that when thinking doesn't work, exploring our emotions will. This is like trying to extinguish the kerosene fire with gunpowder. While thoughts and emotions are wonderful parts of an authentic life, they don't free us from pain; used incorrectly, they intensify it. The way to find your own North Star is not to think or feel your way forward but to *dissolve* the thoughts and feelings that make you miserable. You don't have to learn your destiny—you already know it; you just have to *un*learn the thoughts that blind you to what you know.

We can be blinded by many different types of thoughts. Sunny thoughts can hide the stars because they glare so brightly: "I've got a great job, a cool car, and red-hot monkey lust; now, if I can just get that promotion and put a few more bucks in the bank, I'll finally feel complete." Other thoughts cloud the sky so that no light of any kind, let alone starlight, can get through: "I'm trapped. This whole damn world is against me. There's nothing I can do but lie here and drink." No matter what our thoughts, if they obscure our sense of joy and purpose, they're always inaccurate. Your mind won't see this right away (or possibly ever). Your emotions will follow your mind wherever it goes. The only part of you that cannot be blinded or misguided is the Stargazer.

Mental Metamorphosis

As you go through the exercises in the first section of this book, gradually learning how to unlearn, you will see that the obstacles and problems you once thought insurmountable begin to disintegrate like rice paper in the rain. What happens inside your head during this stage is similar to what happens when a caterpillar metamorphoses into a butterfly. Caterpillars don't just hunker down inside their cocoons and sprout wings. For many species, the first thing that happens inside the cocoon is a total meltdown. The caterpillar literally dissolves, so that if you cut open the chrysalis, you'd find nothing but liquid, a goop of undifferentiated cells.

That's what it feels like to release all the thought structures and emotional habits that keep you from seeing your destiny. Depending on how tightly you're attached to your favorite blinding thoughts and feelings, your entire ego may fall apart during this stage of fulfilling your destiny. Both the social and essential selves may strongly resist the process, because these small selves are *made* of thoughts and feelings. When mind structures dissolve, the ego goes with them, and egos just hate the thought of not existing.

My clients virtually always want to skip the "dissolving" stage of fulfilling their destinies. "I don't like this," they'll say. "Can't we just get to the part where I have the perfect spouse and a ton of money?" Sadly, no. As Joseph Campbell said, "You must give up the life you had planned in order to have the life that is waiting for you." The caterpillar that goes into the cocoon never makes it out alive. The You that fulfils your destiny cannot be the same You that's blinded by false beliefs.

The only part of your awareness you can never dissolve—because it is nothing (no thing)—is the Stargazer. This aspect of you doesn't feel like an individual ego but only an integral part of a completely interconnected universe. It's so passionately in love with your destiny that it never gets sunblind or befogged. Nor does it mind the mistakes your ego has made. It's happily amused by all your errors and will always kindly set you back on the life course you are meant to have. That is its entire function and purpose, the nature of its being. When various forms of blindness send you off track—and they will—knowing how to access the Stargazer allows you to return to the path of your best destiny *instantly*. As you learn to stay on that path for longer periods of time, you'll develop such clear night vision that you'll start seeing magic.

Stage 2: Dreaming (Envisioning Your Future Destiny)

Once a caterpillar has totally dissolved into a glop of random-seeming cells, the DNA in those cells tells them how to rearrange themselves into a totally different animal. It's as though you built a life-size version of the Taj Mahal out of Legos, then took them all apart and rearranged precisely the same number of Legos into a life-size replica of the Lincoln Memorial. Miraculous! This is what happens to our lives when we fully dissolve our mind-structures. We begin to see flashes of our own North Stars and realize that whatever we thought should happen to us, whatever we wished would happen, isn't half so wonderful as what's meant to happen. As your "dissolving" stage ends and the "dreaming" begins, you'll start to see a map of your destiny forming where you thought everything was chaos.

I call stage two "dreaming" because, at first, it feels like a dream—in fact, you may experience it first in night dreams. Protected from the mind by sleep, your Stargazer self will begin handing over hints, premonitions, inexplicable urges, overwhelming feelings. When you wake up, you'll find yourself drawn to your North Star by a force that feels like magnetism. The map of your right life will draw itself as you watch.

Eventually, you will begin to experience things in your waking life that are so inexplicable you may think you're still dreaming. That's what happened to Rosario and me that morning in the D.C. coffee shop (perhaps it helped that we were half asleep). Idle thoughts, half-formed dreams, flashes of insight will begin making the jump from the world of your imagination to the world of material objects and events. Circumstances beyond your control will begin aligning as if to facilitate your actions.

I've seen this so often it should no longer surprise me, but it always does. I have no explanation for the magical things I've seen happening as my clients begin making maps of their future lives. Some have literal dreams come true—things they've seen in their sleep turn up in reality. Many others find that the people, information, or supplies they need seem to drop into their lives, out of nowhere. And I can't begin to describe all the synchronicities and "coincidences" that have reassured my clients they're mapping out the destinies they were meant to experience. The same force that assembles the butterfly from caterpillar soup seems to build each person's best destiny out of the shambles of our preconceptions.

Our culture explains all these inexplicable events very simply: It insists that they don't exist. This is very convenient, like any absolutism, but if you begin to watch your life from the perspective of the Stargazer, you'll find that simple materialism is pitifully inadequate to describe your own experience. Fortunately, many other cultures have given more recognition and respect to practical magic than ours.

The middle section of this book will give you methods for mapping the path of your best destiny with one foot planted in the Stargazer's mystical realm and the other in material reality. The methods I use for doing this are cherry-picked from all sorts of intellectual trees: some from ancient wisdom traditions, some based on recent science, some that emerged spontaneously from the people I've coached. They'll help you chart a course that combines inspiration with perspiration, which is fortunate because you'll need both to make it through the final stage of fulfilling your destiny.

Stage 3: Daring (to Live Your Best Destiny)

As the path of your best destiny begins to appear in what we call "the real world," you must learn to *work miracles* on a daily basis. Notice that there are two words in that phrase. The second is *miracles*. The first is *work*. Don't be deceived into thinking that just because magical things begin happening to you, your whole best destiny will be manifested by magic. The Stargazer within you is a wizard, but wizards still have to *do* the magic they have learned.

One of the best life coaches I've trained started her training by saying serenely, "I believe that if God wants me to do this, He'll make it easy and comfortable." She then embarked on the most uneasy, uncomfortable days of her life. The "easy and comfortable" clause seems to have been omitted from God's contracts with anyone who's ever made any significant contribution to the world. You'd think the Almighty would've smoothed the path for Moses or Joan of Arc or Winston Churchill or even Tina Turner, but no. To paraphrase Churchill himself, the destiny of world-changers tends to be "just one damn thing after another."

I compare this phase of living your destiny with the struggle a butterfly encounters once it's fully formed and ready to leave its chrysalis. This is a difficult, dangerous process; the butterfly is a damp, shriveled little thing, soft and vulnerable as it cuts the top off the cocoon and pulls itself into the air. Often, a butterfly will stop and pant for hours, apparently exhausted, before it continues its daring escape. However, if you "help" the butterfly by cutting open the cocoon, the creature will die. In fact, the longer it struggles to be free, the stronger it becomes and the longer it lives. True, the Stargazer's steady vision makes for less inner conflict as we live out our destinies. But that doesn't make the path easy to travel.

For one thing, when you begin following your North Star and veering off well-travelled roads, the people on those roads (often your nearest and dearest) are almost certain to see you as wrongheaded, insane, pernicious, and/or stupid. Your mother probably won't like it when you quit your dental practice and begin flying rescue helicopters. Your spouse may throw a fit when you stop playing your role at family gatherings and start speaking your mind instead. Your coworkers will stare daggers at you when you suddenly start outperforming them or quit the job you all hate and become successful on your own.

In addition to this social resistance, you may find yourself facing tasks and logistical problems that often seem overwhelming. What looks like a straight, simple path on your internal map may require you to cross Mount Everest and the Gobi Desert. Things will take longer and be more complicated than you think they should. These problems won't shrink to psychological insignificance just because you know you're fulfilling your destiny—in fact, the very authenticity of your path can make you feel more vulnerable. When J. R. R. Tolkien sent off the manuscript of *Lord of the Rings*, he told a friend, "I have put up my heart to be shot at." Your destiny *matters*, matters deeply and almost painfully. You could fail. You could be disappointed. No, scratch that—you *will* fail and be disappointed. Many times.

If I could make this phase of living your destiny quick and cozy, I wouldn't. I tried that with many unfortunate clients, and it never helped any more than yanking a butterfly out of its chrysalis. What I've learned to do instead of trying to make the process easy is to help you enjoy living out your destiny—not in spite of the fact that it's often difficult and scary but because of that fact.

The last section of this book will tell you everything I've learned about following your purpose through logistical difficulties and aggressive social resistance. We'll talk about ways to handle relationships with people who may not be into Stargazing and who want you to stay in *their* world, follow *their* maps. No matter how long you've been following your destiny, no matter how good you are at steering by starlight, you have to use these strategies (or something like them) to move on to the next phase. Right up to the end of your life—right *through* the end of your life—you have to dare.

You Are the Star

Ultimately, everything you read in this book is just a reminder that you—and only you—possess total knowledge of, and capacity to create, your right life. I can't steer you into it; I can only teach you the ways of steering I happen to have learned. In my own life, I've made infinite mistakes and landed in infinite numbers of circumstances that were at odds with my own happiness. But some unfathomable part of me never stopped trying to turn me into what I was meant to be, like Gus's nose ceaselessly, dauntlessly growing ear-ward.

The same thing is happening to you, right now. No matter what life has made of you, no matter what problems, people, and situations have conspired to rob you of your right life, your own North Star is still shining—in outer space and in inner space. You can see it if you begin paying attention. You were born to follow it. So begin right now. Put this book down and find the still point inside you that is already guiding you toward your best destiny. If you see nothing, or something that scares you, don't worry. You're in good company.

Just turn the page.

CHAPTER 1

The End

"The first guy to go in always carries a shotgun," says Kirk Fowler. He's not a big man, for a law enforcer; in fact, he's not much taller than I am. This is a quality I appreciate in a martial arts instructor. Kirk is my *sensei*, and in the middle of a lesson, he's telling me how he used to serve warrants on suspected drug runners and *coyotes*, con artists who take would-be immigrants' money, then load them into trucks and abandon them in the desert to die.

"These are really violent people," Kirk says, "and they have an intense fight-or-flight reaction at that first sight of the officers. They're usually doing drugs as well as selling them, and that makes them about as violent and unpredictable as humans get. You're never in more danger than when you're walking into a room to serve a warrant. It's scary as hell."

It's hard to imagine Kirk terrified. He's a master of aikido, a martial art that focuses more on inner peace than on physical power. I'm learning aikido because it works like magic. Literally. An aikido master gently touches your head, and suddenly you're on the floor. You try to slug him, and you can barely lift your arm. These effects feel almost supernatural, but given a few minutes, anyone can use them well enough to see that they're real. So it isn't surprising that Kirk's aikido training was very helpful when he worked for the Border Patrol. What is surprising is the *way* it helped.

"One day when I was serving a warrant, I decided to try going in with my energy totally calm and relaxed, instead of high adrenaline. The suspects were in a motel room, wired, scared, and well armed. To reach a place where my energy was calm, I had to imagine that all of them were already dead.

"So I went into that room feeling really quiet and respectful, the way you'd feel going to a funeral. And when I opened the door, no one did anything. The suspects just looked at me as though they'd invited me to a summer picnic. They cooperated with the officers through the whole arrest. Even to me, that was *weird*.

"From then on," Kirk concludes, "I kept my energy tuned that way whenever we served a warrant. I still had the shotgun. But I never needed it. Over and over, people who should have fought or run simply started cooperating."

I know this makes no kind of sense. It sounds like an exaggeration, if not an outright lie. But I don't think it is. I've seen and felt Kirk's energy change the atmosphere in the room without his moving a muscle.

"In my mind," he says, "the fight's already won. You begin where you want it to end. That's most of the battle."

Most people will never discover this because it contradicts everything we're taught to expect. We have a linear view of progress: We start at the beginning of a task, and we work our way to the end. This is a useful way to look at things, but it isn't the only way. Especially when you're seeking to fulfil your destiny, the best way to succeed is to begin at the end.

A Quick Trip to the Observatory

By the time you finish this book, you should be able to identify and dissolve most of the mind clouds that keep you from seeing your own North Star. This is a process you'll continue all your life. It's a very specific and disciplined way of thinking (although it's easy and delicious once you're used to it). It will bring you inner peace and also help you build your outward empire. But it takes a while to make all that happen, and I've never been a fan of deferred gratification. So right now, even if you're a homeless junkie who found this book in a dumpster and is planning to eat it, I want it to give you access to the end of your journey, the fulfillment of your best destiny.

Think of the techniques in this chapter as ways you can visit a celestial observatory in your head. The observatory has powerful telescopes that you can use to get a clear look at the stars. For a moment, as you look through those telescopes, your own North Star will shine like a floodlight. You'll feel as though your destiny is a done deal—until something pushes your mind out of the observatory and back into its typical patterns, the well-worn trails ground into your life by repetition and habit, and you go back to feeling as though nothing in your life will ever really work.

You may have experienced this after hearing a powerful speaker or watching an uplifting movie. "I can do anything!" you feel. "Nothing can stop me now!" Then you get home from the convention hall or the movie theater, and everything goes to hell in a handbasket. Your spouse yells at you, the mail is full of bills, the cat has eaten the steaks you left out to thaw and is now experiencing bouts of diarrhea in parts of your home you didn't even know existed. Abruptly, you lose your connection to your Stargazer self and slam back into your cold, cruel, earthbound daily life.

Upcoming chapters will help you learn how to keep this exhausting emotional vacillation from smacking you around. You'll learn to live in your Stargazer self, which exists beyond the reach of what Chinese philosophy calls "the ten thousand joys and sorrows" of ordinary life. But right now, from the word go, I want you to be able to run back to the observatory and look through the telescope whenever you need reassurance. This can help you stay motivated as you learn the sometimes baffling work of becoming a full-time Stargazer. So, as they never told you in school, last things first.

Step 1 on the Path of Your Destiny: Getting Whatever You Want

Screenwriters tell us that all movie plots begin with a character who wants something very, very much and is having a lot of trouble getting it. We viewers identify with that character immediately, because that's us up on the big screen. That struggle to get what we want is the story of our lives.

Identifying Your Wants

Right now, you probably have a mental list of things you want very, very much. You may be working toward these things, buying Lotto tickets in bulk, praying in every living language as well as interpretive dance. In the space below, write down a few of the things you *most* frequently wish you had: a bigger house, loving friends, more time to meditate, a boyfriend with fewer than twelve pitbulls. List up to five of these things.

Some Things I Really Want

Thing 1: _____

Thing 2: _____

Thing 3: _____

Thing 4: _____

Thing 5: _____

No offense, but if you're like most people, the things you just wrote down probably aren't what you actually want. More likely, each thing is a means to an end. Remember King Midas? When he got his wish—that everything he touched would turn to gold—he found himself surrounded by cold metal objects that used to be his bed, his favourite horse, his wife, and his children. Obviously, this didn't feel nearly as good as he'd expected. The moral: What we think would bring us happiness often won't do the trick. What we're really after when we yearn for something is a *feeling state*.

Look back at the list you just made and imagine that you already have each thing on the list. Try to feel as you'd feel if you had millions of dollars or a perfect lover or a gorgeous body that never gets tired or sick. Pay attention to the feeling state you'd get from this dream come true. In the spaces below, write a word or two that best describes the feeling state you'd get from having each of the things you want.

How I'll Feel When I Have What I Really Want

When I have Thing 1, the sensation I'll feel is: _____

When I have Thing 2, the sensation I'll feel is: _____

When I have Thing 3, the sensation I'll feel is: _____

When I have Thing 4, the sensation I'll feel is: _____

When I have Thing 5, the sensation I'll feel is: _____

I've found that while people's desires seem endlessly varied, the feeling states we all desire are few, simple, and universal. They include peace, security, belonging, comfort, love, joy. We think we'll get these feelings by nabbing anything from an Olympic gold medal to our parents' approval. I hear a lot of statements like these.

Popular Lies about Destiny

"If I could find that special someone, I wouldn't be lonely anymore."

"When I get that promotion, I'll finally know I'm good enough."

"If my spouse stopped being critical, I'd be able to relax."

"What I really need is a job in television. That would be so exciting."

"I need my mother to say she loves me; then I'll be happy."

"I'd have plenty of confidence if only the right mentor would show up."

"Once I'm at my goal weight, I'll feel great about dating."

"Building my dream business would be easy if I had an MBA."

If you can't see that all these statements are false assumptions, you haven't been sitting in my life-coaching chair for the past ten years. From my vantage point, you'd have seen many, many people who are deeply loved and still lonely, beautiful and still horribly self-conscious, professionally successful and still so terrified of failure that their nocturnal tooth-gnashing could crush diamonds. Here's something you'll need to hold in your mind, at least temporarily, if you want to get a good look at your own North Star: *External circumstances do not create feeling states. Feeling states create external circumstances.*

Here, let me show you.

Testing the Causal Direction of Desire and Destiny

It's easy to see that in everyday human interactions, most situations come from feeling states rather than feeling states coming from situations. Consider these scenarios.

1. You're an employer looking for someone to hire. Two clients apply. One is desperate and frantic. "Please, please, I need

this job; you've got to help me," he begs. The other candidate is calm and confident. He asks, "How can I help you?"

Which one would you rather hire?

2. You're shopping for clothes. In one store, a salesperson dogs you, pressuring you to buy more expensive merchandise, *now!* In the other location, you get a cheerful "Hello," and then you're allowed to try on outfits without pressure.

Where do you feel more comfortable making a purchase?

3. You meet your friends Pat and Chris for lunch. You haven't seen them for weeks. Pat is relaxed and happy, eager to catch up. Chris, on the other hand, keeps putting in passive-aggressive digs at you, the absentee friend: "I wish you'd made it to the concert, but I know you're too busy for insignificant folks like me."

With whom do you want to spend more time?

Unless you are truly an epic codependent, you probably feel more like cooperating with the people who behave as though their needs are already being met. This is simply how human psychology works: When we push, grab, manipulate, or pursue people, they start to feel as though we're huge mutant versions of the bird-flu virus. For this reason, if no other, you'll experience far more success in all areas of life when you dwell in a sense that your goal has already been achieved. (It's also true that when you reside in a calm future-self, even inanimate objects like money seem to seek you out—but that's a level of magic we'll talk about later on.)

Quick Stargazing Exercise for Beginning at the End

Try this: Think of someone whose approval you covet. It might be your lover, someone else's lover, your boss, a celebrity who may never even meet you, or (if you happen to be an approval whore like me) every single person you ever meet. Get all those needy feelings front and center. Let them fill your whole mind. Now imagine that you get to spend an hour with the person whose approval you seek. Can you feel the desperation, the grasping, the sick sense that this hour isn't nearly enough? Excellent.

Now, begin at the end. Imagine that you already have this person's approval, that they *adore* you, that nothing on God's green earth could ever diminish their total approval. You are *awash* in approval. You couldn't possibly in a million years soak it all in. Letting this mental position fill your mind, picture interacting with your hero again. Can you feel the freedom, the ease, the humour that's suddenly available to you? Can you feel yourself start to smile without trying? Can you tell that this version of you is way more likely to get approval than the version who's always desperately seeking it?

If so, you have just visited the observatory in your head and focused briefly on the truth as your Stargazer self knows it. If not, try again. Sometimes it takes a while to focus the telescope, but you'll get there with a bit of trial and error.

Once you can do this exercise in your head, try it in a public place. My favorite social venues are coffee shops, so that's where I do most of my experiments, but you might choose another location: a bookstore, a shopping center, a rock concert, exercise time in the yard. Just choose a place where there are lots of people milling about.

For Trial One, walk into such a place thinking, "I need these people to like me! I need them to do what I want! I need their help!" Notice how people interact with you. For Trial Two, go into the same place the next day. This time, prep yourself by thinking, "These people love me. They think I'm clever, handsome, talented, and gracious. I rock their socks." If you can keep such thoughts in mind, you'll notice that you move differently, talk differently, smile in a different way as a sock-rocker.

Do this exercise several times, and you'll start to notice how differently other people act around you. The more desperate you feel, the more they'll move away. The more sure you are of their adoration, the more positive interaction you'll get. If you want extra validation, have a friend precede you into the space you're using for the test and observe the way other people interact with you.

I've supervised this experiment with clients who have very low self-esteem, including some juvenile delinquents and ex-convicts. The results are amazing. In a self-critical, fear-based mindset, the clients seem to physically repel people—everyone in the space literally moves away, some slightly, others dramatically. But when my clients manage to hold on to thoughts of being worthy and lovable, others move toward them, usually smiling, appearing to relax as they get closer. No one seems to be doing this deliberately; it's like watching a field of tall grass bend one way, then the other, as the breeze changes.

When Kirk went to an end-state mindset by imagining that the fugitives were very calm—as in dead—they became so docile that even Kirk was a little freaked out. I don't know if I'd have the nickel-plated guts to stake my life on beginning at the end, but I've seen and felt enough to know that it works a lot better than beginning at the beginning.

Achieving Your Heart's Desire, Now

Here's something you may or may not have noticed: As you worked through the steps above (and I'm going to fill my mind with the belief that you actually did it), you voluntarily suffused your consciousness with the very feeling states you plan to get by pursuing all the things you want. By using your imagination to go to an end-state (for example, imagining the security of having megabucks or the bliss of being in love or the peace of being totally safe), *you have already given yourself exactly what you long for.*

Remember, what you're after is a feeling state, not an object or event. When you're in that feeling state, using imagination as your "telescope," you are experiencing life from the perspective of the Stargazer. You haven't created an illusion that life is good and your real dreams will come true; you've dispelled the illusion that life is a bitch and then you die. Go there again, and this time, linger for thirty seconds. For that half-minute, feel the prosperity, the adoration, the svelteness, the joy.

That's all it takes to get what you want.

Some people feel cheated by this exercise. "Well, if I just wanted to feel good by deluding myself, of course I could do it," a client told me once. "Anyone can feel good. What I want is to get ahead." If this is your position, if you agree that it is better to look good than to feel good, be my guest— stay miserable. But please bear in mind that as a miserable person, you'll have a much harder time getting ahead.

If you're ready to make your journey to happiness easier and much more pleasant, know that the observatory door is always open. You can skitter on in for a peek through the telescope any time you're willing to visit the end result of your destiny rather than wandering blindly around the beginning. And the more you do this, the more you will notice something very odd: You'll feel yourself aging backward.

Next Step: Learning to Live Backward

It's very strange to watch a roomful of people picturing the fulfillment of their dreams. As they preview what they'll feel when they get what they want (which, in fact, actually gives them exactly what they want most), people literally look different. The lines on their faces disappear. Their spines straighten. Their skin begins to glow. For some individuals, this is so pronounced that when a small group of my clients meet for the second day of a seminar, they literally aren't recognized by the group. Everyone tells them the same thing: "You look so much *younger!*"

People who've had a lot of therapy often doubt that this can happen as quickly and easily as it actually does. They're half right. It doesn't take any time at all to get to the feeling state you most want. It does, however, take a lot of practice to *stay* in this state if you're not used to it.

Neurologists like to say that "what fires together, wires together." This means that when we make mental associations, we form literal paths in our nervous systems that create clusters of thoughts and physiological changes. As we grow, learn, and get bombarded by the slings and arrows of outrageous fortune, most of us develop clusters of fear, rage, or sadness that become deeply "hardwired." *We aren't born with these negative feelings.* Human infants have only two natural fears: the fear of loud noises and the fear of falling. Every other fear is learned. But the harder our lives, especially in childhood, the more deeply and unconsciously negative reaction-clusters are etched into our brains and bodies.

I was thirteen when I read that the brain is basically fixed and rigid after age five. I remember looking in horror at the pages, thinking, "Damn, damn, damn, I'm already hopelessly screwed up, and I have my whole life ahead of me!" It wasn't until I'd reached middle age that psychologists finally developed tools sophisticated enough to watch the brain working and found (surprise, surprise!) that it keeps changing, growing, morphing, and regenerating throughout life.

In other words, the negative reaction-cluster—the stress reactions, the emotional pain, and the physical weakness that are wired together in your brain and body—can be rewired. The associative learning that makes us feel depressed, anxious, and old can be unlearned. The brain can drop its fears, "aging backward" toward its virtually fearless original state. And though our bodies will keep aging until they die, you'd be amazed how much younger you can feel if you rejuvenate your brain.

You can achieve this by doing deliberately what the brain-body is always doing by default: creating associations that fire together and therefore wire together. The trick is to form, and then hold, positive associations instead of negative ones. It's literally like driving a car down a rutted road but refusing to let the tires skid into the old ruts. You have to deliberately steer yourself into positive associations in order to wear new ruts, or strong neuron pathways, into your brain. But once you do this, the effects are astonishing—and empirically testable. Scientists have found that Tibetan lamas who do something called "loving-kindness meditation" have thicker-than-average neuron development in parts of the brain associated with happiness. Meditation has also been shown to lessen heart disease, high blood pressure, infectious illness, and many other indicators of both health and aging.

I stumbled across ways of doing this when I was suffering from multiple diseases (interstitial cystitis, fibromyalgia, granuloma annulare), all of which are progressive and incurable. Just to relieve my constant pain, I learned to do the exercise you ran through briefly above, when you imagined what it would feel like to have what you want. At this writing, my diseases have been running in reverse for several years. In my forties, I'm far healthier, more active, and vigorous than I was in my twenties. The main practice that has wrought this change is a form of meditation I call "treasuring."

Treasuring the Future—Now

To do this exercise, take a ten-minute break from the rest of your life and sit in a quiet place. Alternately, you can do it while driving (alone, without the radio on), walking, or jogging. A bit of solitude and quiet is all you need.

At the beginning of this ten minutes, choose one item from your list of heart's desires and once more vividly imagine that you've already got it. Create a detailed fulfilled-desire scenario in your mind and preview the way that scene will affect each of your senses. Feel the warmth of your soulmate's arms around you. Taste the fresh trout you'll catch and cook when you're living in your Rocky Mountain log cabin. Smell the downy head of your longed-for baby. Go through it methodically, by sense: How does this scene sound, look, smell, feel, taste?

Once you've created a vivid image of your dream come true, simply continue to experience it for ten minutes. *And I mean at least ten minutes—* by the clock. You'll find that your mind skitters out of its treasuring mode and into your usual fears and stressors almost immediately. Gently notice this and re-create the experience of a fulfilled desire by tapping back into your fantasy scenario with all five senses, one at a time. *Focus on "treasuring" your heart's desire ten minutes per day for a full month.*

I can always tell which of my clients are actually doing this exercise because their appearance changes. The radiance of their skin, the good posture that comes from improved muscle tone, the general vigour of having a strong immune system begins to transform their bodies, as well as their brains, even when they aren't doing their "treasuring" exercise. (It's also true that magic starts happening to them—but we'll get to that later.) When brain mapping became available to the general public, I had my brain "mapped" before and then during this exercise. The scientists who wired up my head were able to physically demonstrate that my brain showed less stress-indicating beta wave activity after doing it. In other words, my brain was losing its fear, erasing the dread-ruts I'd been building since childhood.

The Magic of Backward Living, the Backward Living of the Magician

Living backward happens to be a common trait of the "magical" people in many traditional cultures, part of the smorgasbord of traits that goes with the status of shaman, medicine woman, witch doctor. For example, in ancient Britain, druids like the wizard Merlin supposedly aged backward. Across the puddle in America, the shamanic *heyoka* of the Lakota people walked and rode horses backward, bundled up in midsummer, and streaked about nearly naked, complaining of the heat, during blizzards. In China, Lao-tzu instructed his students, "To move forward, go backward." In the Middle East, Jesus advised us to rise above all things by going below all things, and the mystical Sufi celebrated "holy fools" who reversed all the rules of normal society.

Anthropologists call these people "contrarians" and write many boring theories about them in academic journals. "The contrarian strengthens social norms by standing outside them, embodies the balance between custom and innovation, blah blah blah." What no rational scholar will tell you is that people who see life backward may actually perceive it more accurately than anyone else. You won't read in any academic journals that the words *wizard* and *wisdom* come from the same root, because the backward-living contrarian often sees magical truths unavailable to people who can only look forward. But I believe this is so.

Contrarians and Their Complications

It's not an easy thing to be a born contrarian. The young people I coach who have run afoul of the law, have gotten hooked on drugs, or simply live in a state of constant angry rebellion often see things "backward" when compared with their more placid peers. But I've found that the contrarian instinct, the "wrong" reaction, the socially unacceptable statement is often the seed of destiny struggling to germinate. If you remember feeling painfully unacceptable, especially during your youth, you might want to explore those memories for truths your subsequent socialization thrashed out of you.

"You're ruining your future, young lady!" snapped Jennifer's fifth-grade teacher. It was a lecture Jennifer had heard many times before from other teachers, the principal, her parents.

"This class clown behavior may seem cute to you now," the teacher continued, "but being glib and back-talking won't help you survive in the real world!"

At this, Jennifer forgot her attempt to disappear and squinted up at her teacher in genuine perplexity. "Are you crazy?" she said, exhibiting the bluntness that had earned her rock-bottom citizenship grades since preschool. "In the real world, everyone's going to listen to me." She honestly didn't mean this as an insult or a challenge. To her, the future was as evident as her desk. Her words to the teacher weren't meant to be "glib." They were simply honest. She was too young, and too clear sighted, to pretend they weren't. Not surprisingly, Jennifer went on to bomb the fifth grade. But today, at thirty-nine, she's one of the most successful talk-radio DJs in the country.

When Bruce quit his job in Silicon Valley, his father threw a fit. "All that work to get the only great job you'll ever have," he shouted, "and you threw it away! You'll be broke your whole life. How do you expect to make a living?"

Bruce had no answer. He remained silent, just as he'd done every other time his dad screamed at him. (Bruce didn't talk much as a kid.) Anyway, he didn't quite know what to say, since he wasn't sure how he was going to build, patent, and sell the devices he constantly imagined, most of which used digital technology to make old-fashioned machinery more efficient. Bruce could *feel* them working already, in some pocket of time that was as real to him as the present moment, and nothing his father said could destroy that feeling. The year he turned forty-eight, Bruce the inventor paid more money in income tax than he'd earned in ten years at his "only great job."

Eileen was a sickly child, born with a clubfoot, asthma, and a weak immune system. "Everyone always expected me to have a small life," she says. "Everyone but me. I'd lie there, deathly sick, and see myself having adventures all over the world. That future wasn't theoretical to me. It was absolutely real."

Today, Eileen leads eco-tours for nature lovers. She's river-hiked the wilds of New Guinea, climbed Kilimanjaro, traversed the tree canopy of the Amazon rain forest. She's the healthiest person in her astonished family.

Jennifer, Bruce, and Eileen are born contrarians. As children, they were called uncooperative, oppositional, delusional, stupid; there's no place for living backward in our culture. But even unjust punishments and crushing criticism couldn't shake their faith in their best destinies, because these three people can't help seeing the end from the beginning. Instead of checking their North Stars in brief, temporary visits to their mental observatories, they steered their lives by starlight continuously. Most of us aren't born with that much contrarianism in us, and many more have had our backward-vision squelched. The following exercise is meant to help you regain the "backwardness" that was actually your destiny struggling to become conscious.

Reviving Your Backwardness

Think of three situations in your past life where you felt like a fish out of water—you didn't fit, you couldn't make yourself understood, nothing worked right. Three places I felt this way are PTA meetings, junior high school gym class, and Harvard wine-and-cheese parties. Yours might be summer camp, prison, and church or perhaps cosmetology school, dog shows, and the floor of the Senate. List them here.

Three Places I Did Not Fit In

Setting 1: _____

_____

Setting 2: _____

_____

Setting 3: _____

_____

Choose the setting that was most uncomfortable to you, that caused you the most grief. Now, painful as it is, return to that situation in your mind. Allow the awful feeling of being out of place and misunderstood to grow large, to fill your whole awareness, to reveal its spiky texture and awkward weight. Now, finish the sentences below *as childishly as you can, without censoring yourself at all.* Even if you were an adult when you actually experienced this unpleasantness, let yourself express your inner brat.

Speaking the Contrarian Truth

1. I don't fit in this situation, in this place, with these people, because I am not _____
   _____!

2. I hate these people because they can't see that I _____
   _____!

3. If I were in my right environment, with people like me, everyone would realize that I'm _____!

4. I'd be so much more comfortable around people who don't ____
   _____!

5. It's so frustrating that these people expect me to _____
   _____!

6. Compared to everyone here, I'm much more _____
   _____!

7. This situation is way, way too _____
   _____!

8. I can't wait to get away from people who _____
   _____!

9. I want to scream in this situation because _____
   _____!

10. I'm so angry because no one here wants to let me _____
    _____!

17

Now, read over your responses. If they still shock you, you're very much at odds with your contrarian side. As your *ad litem* life coach, I can tell you that such continuing horror means you'll have to focus very intensely on the process of "dissolving" that we'll be learning in the upcoming chapters. But it's more likely you'll see that the "contrarian" thoughts arising in situations that were wrong for you are simple, direct statements about who you truly are and what your right life is supposed to be like.

Ironically, the less disapproving you are of your most contrarian impulses, the less angry, spiteful, and resistant you will act toward others. I was once assigned to write a magazine column about "embracing your inner brat." It was my editor's idea, and I thought it was wonderful. I thoroughly enjoyed writing the article. But it got a scathing review from a reader of the magazine. She found it "shocking" and "appalling" that anyone would ever connect with any childlike, contrarian part of herself.

It was, frankly, one of the brattiest letters I've ever read.

Moral: By embracing your contrarian or bratty self, you actually calm down your inner child; repress your brat, and you act it out no matter how old you get. The calmer your inner child, the more joy and simplicity you'll bring to the process of following your bliss. Emotionally and behaviorally, you'll be aging backward into the healthy, innocent self-love of a happy child. In case the very phrase "happy child" has pitched you into the gloom of contemplating your horrible childhood, the next exercise in living backward will help.

Telling Your Life Story Backward

This exercise requires that you reverse a habitual pattern: your way of describing and explaining your own life. Instead of thinking about your life from beginning to end, you need to get used to thinking of it from end to beginning.

In the spaces below, write down three of the best things in your life: relationships, situations, or objects without which your world would feel significantly bleaker.

Three of the Best Things in My Life

Thing 1: _____

Thing 2: _____

Thing 3: _____

Look over this list and circle your favorite of the three items. Though it's impossible to say which aspect of your life is "best," for now we'll call the thing you just circled your Favorite Thing.

Now recall a positive turn of events in your life that enabled you to have this Favorite Thing. For example, if your Favorite Thing is your significant other, recall how you happened to meet him or her. Maybe you worked together or got a lucky hit on match.com, or maybe, like so many couples, you were pinned under the same circus tent when it was downed by rogue elephants. If your Favorite Thing happens to be your fabulous car, recall what enabled you to get it: conscientious behavior, a winning raffle ticket, your God-given talent for armed robbery. Write it down in the spaces below. This is a "proximate cause," something that directly linked to your Favorite Thing about your life at this moment.

Happy Event That Contributed to Having My Favorite Thing (Proximate Cause)

_____
_____
_____
_____
_____

Now, go back a step further in your life history. Read over the event you just described and describe something *else* that happened to make *that* event possible. If you want to get fancy, you could call this an "antecedent to the proximate cause." For instance, say your Favorite Thing in life is your dog, Robert Redford (I love Robert Redford; I would name my dog after him in a New York minute). Perhaps the event that led to your owning Robert Redford (the proximate cause) is that he wandered onto your porch one night, unclaimed and starving, and you took him in. But this wouldn't have happened if you still lived in the city, because your building had a "no pets" policy, and Robert Redford would have had to take an elevator ten floors to wander anywhere near you. Therefore, "moving out of the city" might be one event that made Robert Redford's presence in your life possible—an antecedent to the proximate cause. Write down the thing that led to the thing that led to your Favorite Thing.

Prior Happy Event That Allowed the Proximate Cause Event to Occur (Antecedent to the Proximate Cause)

_____

_____

_____

_____

What we've done here is reversed the storytelling order of your life, so that the mental momentum runs from future to past rather than vice versa. Now you're thinking like a contrarian. Keep it up: Follow your chain of life events backward until you can *think of one piece of "bad luck" that helped your Favorite Thing come into your life.* This could be damage far back in your childhood that made you a crusader for justice, a health condition that forced you to think carefully about how you use your time, or a financial disaster that led to a career change.

For example, I get to write books—for money!—partly because my son was prenatally diagnosed with Down syndrome, giving me the material for a memoir that eventually became a bestseller. It also helped that when I was a kid, my family didn't have a television, which meant I had a choice between constant reading and chronic boredom. And then there were the dreadful years when I was clinically depressed and unable to afford therapy. To cope, I poured out all my feelings into journals, unwittingly conditioning myself to sit and write for hours and hours and hours.

Once you get started, you'll see that you, too, can list many "bad" incidents that became links in the chain leading to your Favorite Thing. Jennifer, for instance, is dyslexic—a core reason for her constant disruptive behavior at school. If she'd been "normal" or had spent an hour less in study hall, she might not have developed the wicked sense of humor and deep empathy that make her a smash hit on radio. If Bruce hadn't been mercilessly criticized by his father, he might never have escaped into computer-world, where his million-dollar ideas were born. If Eileen hadn't been forced to lie down and handle pain for so long, she might not have developed her unstoppable commitment to adventure—or the high pain threshold that's made her a successful explorer.

By now, I'm hoping you've thought of at least one "bad" thing that helped support the best thing in your life. Write it down in the space below. If you can think of two or three more, this exercise will work even better.

Supposedly "Bad" Event That Eventually Supported My Favorite Thing

_____

_____

_____

_____

Now you're ready to tell at least part of your life story—the story of your Favorite Thing—from the backward perspective of the Stargazer. The process is one of simple substitution. Instead of saying, "This bad thing happened once, but then later, some good thing happened," tell the story this way: "My destiny was to have my Favorite Thing. Therefore, this bad thing happened in order to make my Favorite Thing possible."

For example, instead of writing, "I was born with dyslexia, so I flunked out of school and went into radio," Jennifer would write, "Because I was destined to be in radio, I was born with dyslexia and hated school." Bruce might say, "I was destined to be a wealthy entrepreneur, so I got a father who chased me into the computer world." Eileen's story could be: "I was meant to roam the wild places of the earth, so I had a lot of health problems early that taught me to handle pain and love freedom above everything else." To tell your first backward story, fill in the blanks below.

The Story of My Favorite Thing, Stargazer Version

I was destined to have [list your Favorite Thing] _____

_____

Because of this destiny, something negative happened [write in the Supposedly "Bad" Event you identified above] _____

_____

Fortunately, this led to [write the Antecedent to the Proximate Cause] _____

_____

And that helped this other thing to happen [note the Proximate Cause] _____

_____

And that, sports fans, is how destiny brought me my Favorite Thing.

Life in the Observatory

If you did this exercise (and I hope you did; the view from the observatory is well worth the effort), you simply created a *post hoc* interpretation of your life as a wonderful process where bad things are always meant to create good things. Please realize that *this is no more arbitrary than creating a* post hoc *interpretation of your life as a meaningless parade of events that usually end badly.* The personal history in your head is always a fictional story crafted to match your biases, as will become abundantly clear in upcoming chapters. A negative, nihilistic version of your history is no more verifiable than an optimistic, creative one.

What does differ significantly between a forward-looking story and the Stargazer's backward version is the effect on you, the storyteller. An earth-bound version of life can be sorely oppressive, burdened with suffering, and doomed by entropy. This is true even for the most beautiful, successful, wealthy people in the world. The contrarian's viewpoint, the worldview of the wizard, literally transmutes your past—even the worst of it—into the path of your best destiny. That's why the Spanish poet Antonio Machado wrote that as he lay sleeping, he dreamed of a beehive in his heart, where "golden bees/ were making white combs/ and sweet honey/ from my old failures."

This is the way we may sometimes see our lives in the night, as we lie sleeping. During the bright, sunny times of our lives, the consensus of sighted beings and the sunny glare of good fortune help us feel confident that time's arrow flies only one way, that good is good and bad is bad, that backward-aging wizards are either nonexistent or completely nuts. But when darkness comes—and it always does—it's nice to know we can go straight to the observatory in our minds and connect with the Stargazer.

"You know," says Kirk reflectively, "there are a lot of times in life when it feels like you're walking up to the motel room door to serve an arrest warrant. There are always dangers. You're always vulnerable. And it always helps to find a place inside you where the problem is already solved—solved so completely there's absolutely no way for anything to go wrong. You go to that place—you *live* in that place—and darned if everything doesn't start inviting you in to the picnic. This is what I've

learned: Everything always passes, and everything is already okay. Stay in the place where you can see that, and nothing will resist you."

Then he touches me gently on the head ("Like a butterfly landing," he says), and I fall like a sack of wet sand. Lying there on the floor, seeing stars, it's hard not to wonder where this whole way of thinking is going to take me next.

CHAPTER 2

Wizard versus Lizard: The Battle for Your Brain

L ouise, an investment banker, was deathly afraid she'd run out of money and end up a bag lady. She confessed this phobia in a tremulous voice, plainly convinced that it was unique, impressive, and exceptionally horrifying.

I yawned. I just couldn't help it.

Virtually every client I've ever coached, including the men, has voiced the Bag Lady Fear. If all these people's dire predictions about their finances actually came true, the world supply of bags would run out within minutes, and we'd all have to sit around terrified of becoming rock ladies or mud ladies or whatever bag ladies become when they hit a financial downturn.

"No matter how much I earn," said Louise, picking nervously at a slub in her raw-silk Armani suit, "it's never enough. My expenses keep going up, and I'm always barely in the black or even a little in the red."

Like many people who have told me similar stories, Louise didn't appear impoverished. She drove a Hummer, owned a gorgeous house, and had her nails manicured and her legs waxed at least once a week. Yet she lived in a state of genuine panic, utterly convinced that those expensively depilated legs were running just one short step ahead of poverty. Once, I tried pointing out that Louise lives in more luxurious circumstances than the vast majority of humans who have ever hit this planet. This had no effect on her fear.

"Oh, sure, I'm getting by all right just now," she said, waving her hand dismissively, "but I could lose my job any time, you know. There are a lot of people who want it. I'm swimming with the sharks." She rubbed the loose thread on her suit until I feared it might burst into flames.

"Once I've saved twenty million dollars," Louise muttered, "I'll be able to relax. Well, not relax, exactly, but dial down the pressure a little, because the second twenty million dollars comes a lot easier than the first. Of course, then I'll have a bunch of sycophants trying to milk me dry. People can smell money. I have to remember that. I'll have to take precautions."

If I hadn't known what was going on in Louise's brain, I would have found her unbearable, like Marie Antoinette having a tantrum because the peasants had served her the wrong kind of cake. But I knew I wasn't talking to Louise at all, just the most fear-bound and primitive layer of her gray matter. The real Louise, the cheerful, fun-loving, high-achieving woman, had disappeared. In her place, entrenched in its purely materialist world-view, swaddled in its expensive silk suit, squatted Louise the reptile.

Your Inner Lizard

One of the deepest layers of your brain is a neural structure that first evolved in early vertebrates—specifically, reptiles. Because of this, scientists call it the reptilian brain. It's wrapped around your brain stem, deep in the center of your head, like the serpent twined around the knowledge tree in the Garden of Eden. In fact, I've often wondered whether the biblical serpent is a metaphoric version of our brain structure, because the reptilian brain, like the serpent in the garden, is constantly talking us into ignoring what I'm calling the Stargazer, the connection with a fearless and infinite benevolent power.

The entire purpose of your reptilian brain is to continuously broadcast survival fears—alarm reactions that keep animals alive in the wild. These fears fall into two categories: lack and attack. On one hand, our reptilian brains are convinced that we lack everything we need: We don't have enough love, time, money, *everything*. On the other hand, something terrible is about to happen. A predator—human or animal—is poised to snatch us! That makes sense if we're hiding in a cave somewhere, but when we're home in bed, our imaginations can fixate on catastrophes that are so vague and hard to ward off that they fill us with anxiety that has no clear action implication: The Republicans (or the Democrats) are trying to ruin our lives! Our feet are full of toxins, which can be removed only through the diligent use of coffee enemas! Every person's fears are unique, but the themes of lack and attack are drearily repetitive.

Because the reptilian brain is so thoroughly hardwired in place and because (as medical psychologists recently determined) there is no way to stop it from broadcasting fear impulses, *lack and attack fears are the major sources of the smog that keeps you from steering by starlight.* You can't simultaneously be both the serpent and the Stargazer, the inner lizard and the inner wizard. What you can do is choose to ignore the former and tune in to the latter.

The next several pages will walk you through this process. You'll start by clarifying how your inner lizard "thinks." Then you'll name your own personal set of justifications for your reptile fear. Next, you'll begin distancing from your fear-based thinking by seeing it as separate from your core consciousness. This leads spontaneously to my favorite part of the lizard-to-wizard transition: realizing that survival fears are virtually always not just harmless but hilarious. As this whole process becomes familiar to you, the dark fears that have beset you on so many sleepless nights will simply make you laugh.

Know Your Enemy, Step 1: The Lack-and-Attack Syndrome

Louise the investment banker was a thoughtful, introspective person who enjoyed reading philosophy and writing poetry. Her inner lizard, on the other hand, was as subtle and sophisticated as a wooden club. *"Be afraid!"* it shouted all day long and into the night. *"Lack is here! Attack is near! Be very, very afraid!"* For Louise, this showed up as an obsession with running out of money at some point in the indefinite future. When I train life coaches, they often have trouble getting clients beyond this fear because they experience it as acutely as the clients do. The terror of "not enough money" appears to be virtually universal among Westerners. But there are exceptions—exceptions that helped me dispel the fear of poverty in my own mind.

Compare and contrast Louise with Alyssa, a woman who, on the surface, seems to have a similar life. Alyssa is a successful attorney, a partner in a prestigious law firm. She's also one of the few people I've coached who have no fear whatever about going broke. Is this because Alyssa is so wealthy she knows the money will never run dry? *Au contraire, mon cher.* Alyssa grew up in the projects of Chicago, the fourth child of an unwed, unemployed mother. Her memories of childhood include many occasions when she and her siblings helped their mother go through the sofa cushions or scour the streets looking for pennies, with the goal of gathering ten cents so that her mother could change the pennies for a dime and use a pay phone to call a relief agency that would feed the family that night.

"I've been poor," says Alyssa, "so I'm relaxed about it. Running out of money is like getting in the deep end of a swimming pool. It's scary until you realize you can swim out of it, that there are multiple ways to solve every financial problem." This confidence makes Alyssa a tower of strength and calm for her clients—and it's also helped make her a rich woman.

Alyssa is rare in having no scarcity fears whatever, and for a long time, I thought her brains and her natural resiliency were what allowed her to escape poverty. Then I began doing volunteer work with heroin addicts at a methadone clinic. Many of them are homeless, have recently been released from prison, and seem totally justified in their fear of "not enough money." So I was stunned to learn that each of them spends an average of $180,000 every year on heroin alone. Even if they're making every cent of that $180K through robbery and prostitution, those are some very hard-working robbers and prostitutes. They can't make rent or afford food, so how do they come up with so much cash for drugs? As one of them told me, "You just don't give yourself an option about that. You don't doubt yourself. You just decide to get that money, and then you go out and get it."

In other words, when we don't act from fear, we aren't nearly as likely to run out of resources as our inner lizards believe. Still, it's easy to see why evolution selected for brains that send continuous fear messages: Any animal will live longer on the open veldt if it's always obsessed with getting more resources and avoiding danger. That's the good news. The bad news is that our inner lizards continue delivering their ugly-twin messages even when we're not in any danger. A wild reptile may react to predators by running away in a panic, but once the predators are gone, the reptile doesn't sit around brooding about the dreadfulness of the experience. Its fight-or-flight reactions abate quickly, allowing its body and brain to rest until the next emergency requires quick action.

We humans, on the other hand, have the questionable intellectual advantage of being able to rev up full-on survival fear while driving our Hummers to our country homes in the Hamptons. Unlike other animals, we tell ourselves stories of danger that are sometimes vivid enough to create more fear than an actual disaster. Our TV news, dramas, even documentaries ("Stay tuned for *Shark Week!*") focus on terrible things that are happening or that will happen or that could happen around the planet.

Louise was one of many clients I've worked with who wake up every morning feeling terrified, then rush to turn on CNN or read the newspaper, searching for some awful story that will justify their panic. When I suggest that they stop watching or reading the news for one week, these folks react as though I've ripped away their one meager shelter in the hurricane of life.

"Oh, my God, I couldn't do that!" they gasp. "I have to be informed! It's the only way to stay safe in times like these!"

Actually, focusing on lack-and-attack fear fosters all the major diseases that tend to kill people in the First World: high blood pressure, heart disease, cancer, addiction, anything that feeds on degeneration and stress. Moreover, existing in a state of continuous panic turns you into a self-centered, obnoxious glutton, like Louise in her worst moments. It ruins your relationships, your body, your life—and it doesn't protect you from anything. In fact, it often creates what it fears. The billionaire magnate, obsessed with "lack" fears, ends up cheating on a stock trade, lying about it, and landing in jail—the only place she really will experience actual lack. The paranoid husband constantly accuses his wife of hating him, cheating on him, "attacking" his pride and honor. His behavior is so scary and upsetting to his wife that she leaves him, validating all his fears.

Sociologists call this "social contagion." When we're taken over by intense, high-adrenaline lizard fears about lack and attack, the people around us become anxious as well. They respond to our jitters by getting jittery, our defensiveness by becoming defensive. This is what causes people to trample each other in crowds, rushing blindly from some collective fear that may not be coherently recognized, let alone thought through. Panic spreads like shock waves, making it hard to be around a person who's fully lizard based without "catching" his fear.

On a more intimate level, we can turn lizard fears into conflicts that get blown out of proportion, becoming what I call a War of the Dinosaurs (the word *dinosaur* means "terrible lizard"). Psychologists call it projection and reaction formation: Each person responds to the other by projecting her own sense of fear and grasping, then reacting violently against signs of fear (which come across as aggression) in the other. This is what makes divorce turn ugly so often: When it comes to dividing resources, each ex-spouse becomes panicky about his or her own future, grasps at all the resources possible, and then sees the other as "attacking," trying to take all the goodies.

Think of fear-based people in your own life, and you can easily see how the grasping energy of the inner lizard repels good fortune and creates disaster. Your hideously controlling boss is so dictatorial that his employees really do want to rise up and depose him. Your defensive sister, who believes she never got enough help from you, is so angry about it that you don't ever feel much like helping her. The clingy friend who often shows up unannounced or refuses to leave, hoping to get every possible moment of your time? You avoid that person like the plague.

It's always fun to point out other people's lack-and-attack fears. I, personally, can break open quite the little piñata of knee-jerk judgements when someone else's inner lizard is causing bad behavior. Of course, my own fears seem far more impressive and serious to me. I've slid into them literally millions of times, mistaking them for reality with fervid enthusiasm. You probably do the same thing. Just knowing that part of your brain is designed to broadcast *The Lack-and-Attack Show* is the crucial first step in detaching yourself from your counterproductive reptile self. Then you can begin red-flagging lizard fears whenever they appear.

Know Your Enemy, Step 2: Your Lizard's Top Ten Tunes

Louise's reptilian brain had a typical set of lack-and-attack fears: "I'm going to end up a bag lady!!!!" "I need at least twenty million dollars to be safe!!!!"

"People are after my job!!!!" "Sycophants are trying to bleed me dry!!!!" We all have our favorite fears, refrains we sing to ourselves over and over and over and over, until we literally form synaptic "ruts" in our brains. To dissolve your identification with your inner lizard, it helps to take a peaceful moment and list its Top Ten Tunes. Here are some favorites I've heard from hundreds of clients.

Popular Reptile Refrains

"I'll never find love."

"Something may have gone right, but you know that other shoe is going to drop."

"You can't trust anyone in this rotten world."

"I have to keep secrets; people will use information to hurt me."

"Ultimately, everyone will betray me."

"The minute I get anything, someone will take it from me."

"Nice guys always end up getting screwed."

"Successful people have all the luck—I just get bad breaks."

Some of these statements may sound familiar to you. If not, I'm sure you can think up a few other catchy lines that echo through your head when life gets dark and scary. Finish the sentences below to get a sampling of your lizard's chart toppers.

My Inner Lizard's Top Ten Tunes

Oh, no! I don't have enough _____

If I don't watch out, someone will _____

People want to take my _____

I can't be perfectly happy until I get _____

Everybody pressures me to _____

You just can't trust _____

People will hurt me unless _____

If only I had _____

Someone's always out to _____

I must hang on to _____

The words you just wrote down, lyrics for your inner reptile's favorite lack-and-attack rap, probably feel very true to you—at least when you lose sight of your own North Star. "I know *other people's* lack-and-attack fears aren't absolute," you may be thinking, "but the ones I just listed? Those are *real*. Those are *solid*. Those are *irrefutable*."

One successful businesswoman put it this way: "But often they [the things on that list] are true! Especially in corporate life—many people are rightfully afraid of not having enough; they don't!" The noncorporate clients I work with (as well as those, like Alyssa, who have worked their way into white-collar jobs from less advantaged corners of society) would find this hilarious—the very fact that people are "in corporate life" means that they're far better off than, say, most of Africa.

If you're presently feeling fear and anger that I'm attacking your deeply held beliefs about scarcity, take a few slow breaths, remember that you're not in danger of starving or being eaten by a lion at this very moment, and fill out this little quiz.

Money Quiz for Lizards and Other Readers

1. Having "enough" money means I can afford . . .

   a. sufficient food and clothing to stay warm and well fed.

   b. my own apartment.

   c. two travel vacations a year.

   d. Jamaica.

2. I can stop worrying about running out of cash when I have . . .

   a. a mattress full of $1 bills.

   b. full health insurance.

   c. a wealthy spouse.

   d. hypnotic control of Bill Gates.

3. The only people who really don't have to think about going broke are . . .

   a. successful gamblers.

   b. people with steady jobs.

   c. white-collar executives.

   d. the dead.

4. My well-being would be threatened if I lost . . .

   a. my ability to work.

   b. my present job.

   c. my corner office.

   d. one of my oil wells.

Do you find it offensive that I would joke about issues like "having enough" and "being threatened"? If you do, and you have access to survival resources in your present environment—this instant of time, not tomorrow or ten minutes from now—your lizard is running your life. Logically, you can see that, to paraphrase Mark Twain, most of the terrible things that happened to you never happened. Continued insistence that they're *just about to happen* is the sign that your brain is rationalizing the fear your reptilian brain produces constantly, undeterred by rain or sleet or physical evidence. Learning to see your inner lizard as "not me" is often enough to step into the Stargazer's perspective. Start by using a strategy known to the mystics of many wisdom traditions: Gain power over the enemy by knowing its name.

Know Your Enemy, Step 3: The Name Game

In cultures that take Stargazing seriously, knowing the name of one's enemy, whether a person or a supernatural creature, is a huge advantage in battling it. For this reason, and because I am easily bored, I like to make my clients picture their reptile selves vividly—draw them, if possible—and give them names. Some actually buy small lizards made of plastic or jeweled gecko pins they can wear on their clothes.

My own inner lizard (for reasons I'll describe in a moment) is a small winged dragon named Mo, who sits on my shoulder weeping, wringing its claws, and telling me repeatedly that no one ever loved me and no one ever will. Also, I am in imminent danger of becoming a bag lady. When I notice that my Top ten Tunes o' Terror are blaring in my mind, I picture myself giving poor old Mo a grape. I pet it on the head. I say, "There, there, Mo. Thank you for sharing. Now go to sleep." Caring kindly for the reptile, rather than either believing it or struggling against it, is the way out of dread and into peace.

This silly visualization is actually a very serious, powerful exercise, rooted in sound psychological and neurological evidence. It may, in fact, physically change your brain. By calling on the nonreptilian part of your neural complex to watch the reptile, you subtract neural energy from survival fear and move it to a more highly evolved portion of the brain. Remember that study of monks who'd spent years watching their fear from a compassionate perspective and had thicker-than-typical neural matter in the part of the brain associated with happiness. The neuron pathways that carry lizard fears become weaker the more we observe them. Patients with "abnormal" brains, such as those with obsessive-compulsive disorder, have actually reconfigured their brains to "normal" by using self-observation techniques.

For example, Tibetan "loving-kindness" meditation is a form of dis-identifying with the inner lizard. So is Vipassana, or "insight" meditation. An enormous amount of research shows the beneficial effects of "mindfulness," which consists of simply focusing full awareness on the here and now rather than letting fantasy fears of the future run your brain. The great Zen master Suzuki Roshi used to ask his students, "What, *at this moment*, is lacking?" Considering this question yanks us out of lizard brain and into simple presence, where we can go about supplying the few needs that ever exist in the here and now.

Louise resisted naming her lizard for a long time, preferring to remain identified with it (she was terrified that if she let go of her fears, there would be nothing to stop them from coming true). She told me she'd relax when she had that twenty million dollars. Then she got a raise and a bonus in the same month and amassed just such a fortune. Louise felt great—for nearly a week! Then she was back to her old fearful self, up late at night wondering who was plotting against her, thinking that just a few more million would *really* let her rest easy . . .

At this point, just as I was preparing to fulfil another of her fears by firing her as a client, Louise finally got sick of being afraid. She arrived for our session with a small, jeweled facsimile of a frill-necked lizard, the kind that stands up and sprints on its hind legs when threatened.

"Meet Scarlett," Louise said. She'd named her inner lizard after Scarlett O'Hara, heroine of *Gone with the Wind*. Holding up Scarlett like a ventriloquist's dummy, Louise did a passable Vivien Leigh impression. "Oh, Lawd!" she said. "Ah'm down to mah last twenty million! Wherevah shall Ah get something to eat?" Suddenly, she was a different person from the anxious, covetous miser I'd come to know and not love very much. By naming her inner lizard and dissociating herself from it, she'd picked up a virtue that makes almost anyone fun to be around: She'd started laughing at herself.

Know Your Enemy, Step 4: Find the Ridiculous

A Catholic priest once told me that the only thing the Devil can't stand is being laughed at. I don't know whether this was his own opinion or Vatican doctrine, but I like it. I see evil as coming from human fear, not a horned demon, so to me, my priest friend's maxim suggests that learning to laugh at our fears is one of the best ways to conquer our own evil tendencies. This is ironic because most of the time, we unconsciously worship our fears, hold them deeply sacred. Your inner lizard's Top Ten Tunes may as well be the hymns of your unique personal religion, handed down from equally devoted forebears.

"I have money issues because of my dad," Louise told me. "He always said, 'There's not enough money, we're running out of money, the money's all gone.'"

"Uh-huh," I grunted. "So, which did your father die from, starvation or exposure?"

She frowned. "What do you mean? My dad died of cirrhosis. He drank."

"You're telling me he could always afford food, shelter, *and* booze?"

"Well, yes." Louise seemed annoyed.

"Miraculous," I said, "considering that he never had enough money."

Louise's face clouded with anger. I was attacking the most treasured doctrines she'd learned from her father's faith in his inner lizard. Then, just as she was about to give me the old smack-down, I saw the lights go on in Louise's mind. Recalling her father's lifelong fear of something that never actually happened to him, she began to laugh, the startled laugh of someone who has just courageously beaned a burglar with a frying pan, only to realize that the "intruder" was a guitar case.

I think this is what Reinhold Niebuhr meant when he said, "Laughter is the highest form of prayer." When we learn to watch our fears without believing them, we can burst out of a fearful universe into a totally safe one in an abrupt, irrevocable flash of insight—and for some reason, this often triggers gales of laughter. The Stargazer within you will find all of your lack-and-attack fears hilarious.

When I run intensive small-group seminars, Day One is inevitably filled with somber tension as the participants confide their deepest fears. By Day Three, the whole group will burst into spontaneous laughter when someone voices a fear—not a mocking laugh, but the Stargazer's recognition of a joyful truth where there was once an ugly lie. No one laughs harder at the reptile's fear than the person who used to be afraid. To my own amazement, I've seen the same phenomenon when working with people who really do face survival problems: people who are broke and unemployed, single mothers like Alyssa's mom, homeless heroin addicts. When even very convincing fear turns into laughter, a sense of contentment with the present and ideas for problem-solving emerge on their own to validate the new sense of security.

I experienced this myself during a publicity tour for a book I wrote about leaving my childhood religion. It is a considerable understatement to say that not everyone I know was pleased with that book. In fact, before it was even released to bookstores, an actual organization had been formed to discredit the book and its author, my own self. An e-mail chain had gone out among the members of the church, urging them to write the magazine where I was a columnist and convince my superiors to fire me. Thousands of defamatory claims, some true, some bizarrely false, began buzzing around the Internet and the news media.

Naturally, Mo (my inner reptile) found this briskly stimulating. The Top Ten Tunes in my internal repertoire—already so convincing to me— were reinforced by dozens of threats from other people, some I knew very well, others I'd never met. These folks vividly described the damage they intended to wreak on my career, my reputation, my life in general. They would send me to prison for many, many years, they said. They would see to it that I was physically attacked, financially ruined, separated from my children. I'd end up in a slough of infamy so deep that I'd never draw a peaceful breath for the rest of my life.

One day during this exciting time, I was cleaning my office, calming myself by putting disordered things in order, while my beagle, Cookie, kept me company. Among the objects I dusted and repositioned was a bookend in the shape of a winged dragon, about ten inches tall (it's sitting beside me now as I write). I set the bookend on a coffee table near the spot where Cookie was taking one of his fourteen or twenty daily naps. After a while, Cookie woke up, yawned, stood—and found himself eye to eye with the bookend dragon.

"*Oh, my God in heaven!*" Cookie shrieked (no other breed of dog can shriek like a beagle). "*Help! Help! Look out, everyone!*" The hair on Cookie's back bristled like a scrub brush as he leapt backward, baring his teeth, trembling violently. "*Oh, save me, Sweet Jesus!*" he bellowed. "*It's going to kill us all!*"

Probably because I was feeling ever so slightly on edge to begin with, I found this hysterically funny. For one thing, Cookie is Jewish. For another, as he fled at top speed, checking behind him every two steps to make sure the dragon wasn't upon him, I saw in my terrified dog the embodiment of my own fearful self.

I laughed so hard I had to lie down on the floor. All the threats I'd heard from others—that I'd be captive, penniless, alone—shrank to wisps of unreality even less threatening than that ten-inch-tall bookend. I could see that there was nothing in that moment to fear except my own internal repetition of frightening concepts. It was useless to even bother thinking those thoughts until an actual threat was present, at which time I didn't need to fear reality, only deal with it.

So that is what I did, hiring lawyers when that seemed a useful action, shrugging when people attacked my character (they have as much right to their version of reality as I do to mine). Long before the dust settled, when I was still receiving threats, I knew that any time I stepped away from my inner lizard, I would find my own fears ridiculous. To the part of my mind that isn't a terrified reptile, fear in the absence of an actual physical threat (such as, say, a grizzly bear) is always ridiculous because it's not action-able—there's nothing I can do about an imagined danger except develop ulcers and high blood pressure. Dealing with present dangers from a fear-less place and letting go of all fears that can't be addressed because they exist only in your fantasies is the only way to thrive.

Know Your Enemy, Step 5: The "Shackles" Test

I would have been much more upset when that book came out if I hadn't already spent years weighing my decision to write it. I'd decided that the reason I shouldn't write it (basically, to avoid other people's wrath) felt far less like my best destiny than the reasons I should (to give a voice to other people who had felt trapped by religious fundamentalism, particularly as children, and offer them my present belief that God is love). No matter how many ways I looked at it, no matter how many times I decided against it, writing the book always felt more like my best destiny than not writing it.

Most people I coach tell me they feel stuck, uncertain, or blocked. "I can't find myself," they tell me, or "Maybe I have no purpose." What this really means is that what they sense about their destinies is triggering their reptile fears. When our sense of destiny moves us toward actions that spark lack-and-attack fears—especially when they violate the norms of the people who socialized us—our inner lizards can stop us dead in our tracks. Here are some examples I've taken from actual clients. They're specific to real situations, so you may have similar fears for different reasons. Just contemplate these real-life examples to see how rationalization may differ from hard, cold reality.

Case Studies from Real-Life Clients

The Mind's Rationalizations	The Plain Old Lizard Fear
I'm so torn—I just don't know whether or not I want to stay in this marriage.	I want a divorce, but I'm afraid people will judge me because my marriage failed.
I'm so pissed off at my boss, my coworkers, and my customers—they'd better make it worth my while to do this damn job.	I went into a career I hate because I was totally focused on money, and now I'm miserable but afraid to quit.
I really stood up for myself today—the bagger at the supermarket put my eggs on the bottom, so I had him fired. Hah!	I feel small and powerless in most of my life, so I make myself feel powerful by attacking people who are defenseless.
I've wanted for so long to live my dreams, but no one will let me. I have to take care of everybody else's needs, not my own.	I want to succeed at something I love, but the thought of having to compete—and possibly fail—is so terrifying I never start.
Tiffany-Lynne is so sensitive, I just don't know if she's ready to fend for herself. I mean, she could end up a bag lady.	My adult daughter is freeloading and taking advantage of me, but if I told her to move out, she'd yell at me, and that scares me.

The problem with our mental rationalizations of lizard fears is that they're so convincing. They're often the same beliefs we've heard voiced by our parents, siblings, spouses, social groups, and television news pundits. We become so hypnotized by our fantasy fears we can't see that what's blocking us is nothing noble, nothing complex, nothing impenetrably difficult. It's just boring lack-and-attack fear packaged to satisfy the ego.

So how do you recognize the right thing to do when everything feels bad? What if the present situation is wretched, but the alternative is terrifying? There's one simple way to tell the difference between a wise course of action (even if it's scary) and a lizard response (even if it sounds comforting). I call this the "shackles on, shackles off" test.

The Buddha often said that wherever you find water, you can tell if it's the ocean because the ocean always tastes of salt. By the same token, anywhere you find enlightenment—whatever improbable or unfamiliar shape it may have assumed—you can tell it's enlightenment because enlightenment always tastes of freedom. Not comfort. Not ease. Freedom.

In other words, the way you can tell you're following fear away from your North Star is that while this course may feel safe, it will also feel imprisoning. The way you can tell that something lies true north, even though inner-lizard fear says to run from it, is that it feels liberating. If you pay even basic attention to your own reactions, you can identify what I call a "shackles on" sensation and distinguish it from a "shackles off" sensation. This difference will be perceptible to you whether or not you are afraid to take a certain course of action.

Many Westerners are leery of this claim because of a basic philosophical position that differs from Eastern thinking. Most Asian cultures see human beings as innately good, born perfect but then pulled off course by false beliefs, unfounded fears, and other delusions. The Judeo-Christian tradition that undergirds Western philosophy sees humans as innately imperfect, born with all sorts of problems (original sin, carnal nature, ignorance of God's laws) that must be rectified and controlled if we are to become worthy. From a Western perspective, setting the original self free is shocking and dangerous: "Why, if we just act from a place of freedom, we'll all be pillaging and looting by nightfall." In Asian psychology, pillaging and looting (etc., etc.) come from a place of delusion, from imagining ourselves as separate from others, so that our welfare and theirs are disconnected.

Because you're probably a Western reader, I'm going to ask you to put up those mental brackets and consider what I've observed after working with thousands of people. The Stargazer part of us is the only part that can feel true freedom. But it also perceives itself as connected to all that is. This means that like all great wisdom teachers, your deepest self knows that you can't do damage to any other being—humans, animals, plants, the earth itself—without hurting yourself and feeling a loss of freedom. When I've worked with criminals, I've been amazed and gratified to discover that the thought of committing a crime makes them feel "shackles on," even if they get away with it. The thought of living without crime is always "shackles off." Perhaps this isn't true for genuine sociopaths, but unless you're one of those, freedom and ethical behavior seem to ride the same wave.

To identify your personal "shackles on" feeling, bring up a thought of something or someone that you know is wrong for you. It could be a subject you hated in school, a job that ruined your physical and mental health, a smarmy neighbor. Name this person or thing in the space below. Then, let the thought of it fill your mind. Notice how your body reacts. I like to think of this as reading entrails—not the guts of a pigeon or a goat, which used to be studied by shamans and priests, but your own living guts, which are far easier to interpret. Heading away from your North Star will always create muscle contraction somewhere in your body. This is the sense of "shackles on."

One person, place, or thing that doesn't serve my destiny is _____

_____

When I let this person, place, or thing fill my conscious mind, my body and mood react in the following ways: _____

_____

THIS PHYSICAL REACTION IS YOUR "SHACKLES ON"
FEELING. REMEMBER IT.

Now, think of a person, place, or thing that has proven to be genuinely good for you—something or someone that reliably leaves you feeling happy, capable, and on purpose. Think about this thing without worrying whether any frightening or joy-diminishing thing may be associated with it. When a scary thought does come up ("Well, I love my mom, but she'll die some-day." "That red sports car was so much fun to drive, but of course, it's not the safest thing on the road."), know that these come from your inner lizard as it spits its toxic paranoia into your *soupe de joie*. Scoot your fear aside until your wonderful memory occupies your full consciousness. Then fill out this form.

One person, place, or thing that does serve my destiny is _____

_____

When I let this person, place, or thing fill my conscious mind, my body and mood react in the following ways: _____

_____

_____

THIS PHYSICAL REACTION IS YOUR "SHACKLES OFF"
FEELING. REMEMBER IT.

Get your lizard to back off, and you'll see that life can be this simple: If you do nothing more than choose whatever feels most "shackles off" to you, moment by moment, you will fulfil your best destiny. If you choose to obey lizard fear, even when it's accompanied by a sense of "shackles on," you won't. Don't wait for your lizard fears to go away; they never will, as long as you have a brain. *You will never realize your best destiny through the avoidance of fear. Rather, you will realize it through the exercise of courage, which means taking whatever action is most liberating to the soul, even when you are afraid.*

Know Your Enemy, Step 6: Steering into Peace

In the spaces below, write down some notes on recent choices you've made. You'll find that it's easy to see whether those choices increased your sense of freedom or made you feel more trapped.

Shackles On, Shackles Off

1. Think of something you recently did for someone you love. What was it? _____

_____

_____

Recall doing that thing and notice how your body reacts. Do you feel more "shackles on" or more "shackles off"?

SHACKLES ON   SHACKLES OFF

2. Consider the clothes you are wearing right now (if any). Briefly describe them: ___

_____

_____

Remember choosing those clothes when you put them on. Do you feel more "shackles on" or more "shackles off"?

SHACKLES ON   SHACKLES OFF

3. Choose one thing on your list of "things to do" this very day. Write it here: _____

_____

_____

When you contemplate doing this thing, is your body's reaction more "shackles on" or more "shackles off"?

SHACKLES ON   SHACKLES OFF

4. What's the last task you performed that you would call work? It might be housework, your job, sending out résumés—anything that counts as work for you. ____

_____

_____

Recall performing the task. Did you feel more "shackles on" or more "shackles off"?

SHACKLES ON   SHACKLES OFF

5. Think of a person you interact with every day: _____

_____

Picture interacting with that person again. Notice how your body reacts. "Shackles on" or "shackles off"?

SHACKLES ON   **SHACKLES OFF**

You see where this is going, right? Of course, not every choice is one hundred per cent "shackles on" or "shackles off." One of my favorite therapists asks her patients to imagine two alternatives on a set of old-fashioned scales. You're not looking for absolutes; rather, you're noticing which way the scale tips.

If you find you're confused about which way feels freer—if the scales are dead even—you need to break each part of your decision into smaller components and see which components feel "shackles on" and which are "shackles off." For example, in my case, caring for my kids felt muddy and semi-confining when they were toddlers. When I broke down the components of child care, however, I found that the kids themselves rated a big old "shackles off!" while trying to do things I saw as "motherly" (baking, playing peek-a-boo, singing nursery rhymes) was hugely "shackles on." I stopped any attempt to cook by purchasing healthy food that was already prepared (did you know grocery stores sell premixed salads and organic turkey breast?) and began talking to my kids about things that interest me, such as zoology and physics. My kids, who, after all, have genetic reasons to share my proclivities, turned out to love this as much as I did.

I suggest that you make lists of everything in your life—objects you've purchased, invitations you've accepted, people you've blackmailed—and check your shackle responses for each and every one. See whether all or some of your reasons for having this in your life are motivated by your inner lizard (which will always feel like "shackles on").

If you find that you make a lot of heavily shackled choices and think these have been forced on you because you lack wealth or power, think again. I've worked with many wealthy, powerful people who are bound hand and foot by their inner lizards. All their choices come from fear and avoidance rather than excitement and joy. They make "shackles on" choices grounded in their dread of public opinion, of losing their hard-won status, of being exploited, of failing. I've also worked with people who began making "shackles off" choices and became more peaceful immediately, even though an outside observer may have thought these people had no options. *Freedom is available at any time, to anyone—and so is captivity.*

If you circled "shackles off" on every one of the items above, you have an unusually strong ability to steer by starlight. You've probably been through a few dark, scary situations in the past and learned that moving away from fear is not nearly as realistic or productive as moving toward freedom. If you got "shackles on" responses for *every* item, you may be as tense and miserable as Louise was when I first met her. In any case, fill in the following blanks to complete this exercise.

Preliminary Unshackling Practice

Choose one thing in your life that you are doing because you feel shackled and write it here: _____

_____

Now, go to the magical "end state" you created in the previous chapter. Picture a place where there is nothing to fear and all your dreams have come true.

Once grounded in this absolutely safe imaginary place, think of an alternative course of action you might take (instead of the activity you just wrote down) that would feel like "shackles off." *You don't have to do this new thing yet, just think about it.* Make a note of it for later: _____

_____

When Louise began unshackling herself, her whole schedule was established by Scarlett O'Hara, the red-frilled lizard. Obeying Scarlett, Louise stayed at the office until late at night, never relaxed, and sacrificed bonding with loved ones, her leisure-time activities, and her physical health. After deciding to follow liberation instead of fear, Louise began to make some scary—but freeing—decisions. Specifically, she started working less and living more.

Of course, this process was very much two steps forward, one step back. The brain ruts Louise had created by obeying her fear often got the better of her. But she noticed over time that fear-based action never improved her situation either psychologically or financially, while detaching from her inner lizard and acting out of peace improved her life at every level. The more practice she had going to a place of calm, clear lizard observation, the sillier she found Scarlett O'Hara, and the faster she regained her equilibrium after a scare.

Initially, Louise thought this whole process would lead to financial disaster. It didn't. Her career continued without much change, regardless of breaking her inner lizard's list of rules. In addition, Louise encountered so many fine new things on her path to freedom that work began to take a back seat in her mind much of the time. She took up competitive rowing, which she loved. She got a dog, which she loved even more. Then she met a man whom she loved more still. They had a baby, and she found a whole new world of love. By choosing "shackles off" more times than she chose "shackles on," Louise transformed herself from a lizard with a lot of money to a wizard who was genuinely rich.

Of course, the lizard fears never went away. They will always be part of Louise's brain. Every now and then, when Louise takes a day off or delegates a project she might once have done herself, Scarlett O'Hara flaps her neck ruffle, stands up on her hind legs, and begins cawing the same old survival fears: *"Stay at the office, you idiot! Do you want to lose your job? I hope you're training your replacement, because you're going to be a bag lady! A bag lady, I tell you!!!"*

"Maybe she's right," said Louise the last time we talked. "Maybe if I'd kept making all my choices from fear, I'd have done a little better at work. Maybe I'd have made partner five years earlier. Maybe I'd have more money in the bank right now. But then again," she smiled, "why would I want to live in poverty?"

CHAPTER 3

Digging out of
the Dungeon

Gavin was what psychologists call a "hot reactor." He was born to a single, drug-addicted mother, taken from her at the age of five, and then shuttled between foster homes until he finished high school. There were two ways to go from this childhood: rebellion and anger or abnormally intense efforts to fit in. To his everlasting credit, Gavin chose Door Number Two. He was a polite, thoughtful, selfless mirror for everyone around him. But he had no idea who he really was or what he really thought.

Gavin was in his early thirties when I met him. He was in therapy, making progress on healing from his childhood, but hadn't found a peer group that felt safe and supportive. I asked him to join a small-group workshop because he was so responsive to social context that I knew that even a few hours speaking openly about his life to a critical mass of sympathetic others could install some new, fine software on the hard drive of his social self.

Sure enough, Gavin changed dramatically during the three-day workshop.

At he outset, he seemed timid, quiet, and unemotional. But he was also very willing to throw himself into every challenge, and watching him do so was like seeing a flower blooming on a time-lapse film. It's hard to believe how quickly people can gain new perspectives from focused group work, and Gavin's was one of the most dramatic responses I've ever seen. After 3 long days of intense work, the timid drone Gavin was gone, replaced by a relaxed, responsive man with big dreams and a knack for telling hilarious stories.

The metamorphosis was so dramatic that one of the other participants, a professor of English literature, gave Gavin a nickname. "You're the opposite of what you were three days ago," she said. "You were Gavin the Drab; now you're Gavin the Bard." She had to explain to the rest of us that "bard" is "drab" spelled backward, but once we got it, we all agreed that it was a most excellent title.

A few months later, Gavin called to ask if he could see me for one private session. I was excited to talk to him, eager to hear whether he'd been able to sustain his new perspective after his big weekend. Unfortunately, the guy who showed up wasn't Gavin the Bard, but Gavin the Drab—and he was hurting, big time. Though he'd seen a glimpse of what was possible for him, he'd gone directly from the workshop back into a highly dysfunctional environment. His critical alcoholic wife and soulless job quickly eclipsed even the memory of his own dreams. Gavin the Bard had visited the observatory in the highest turret of the castle, looked out at his own North Star, slain his resident inner dragon—and then been chained up in the dungeon, where he became Gavin the Drab once more.

Dreadful Daily Dungeons

Transporting yourself forward in time and learning to cope with your inner lizard are essential for getting in touch with your Stargazer self, but they aren't enough to take you all the way to your best destiny. Some people feel even more directionless, stuck, trapped, or paralyzed after they've glimpsed their

North Stars than they did before seeing the sky. If you're incarcerated in a life like Gavin's, steering by the stars for a few brief moments may only highlight the agony of being stuck in a life that feels like a deep underground dungeon.

For example, maybe you've just met a person who adores you and feels like your soul mate—but you're still married to a person who scares you and feels like your cell mate. Maybe you've realized you want to fly jets but are still paying off your dental school loans by drilling teeth 10 hours a day. Maybe you're trapped by financial dependency, the needs of your children, the expectations of your fans. Situations like these can make "steering by starlight" sound like cruel mockery. To do it, you'd have to see through dungeon walls, and then you'd have to dig your way out.

Fortunately, that's exactly what you're about to learn how to do.

Dying to Leave the Dungeon

"Sometimes," said Gavin in his zombie voice, "I just think I should check out, you know? I have these pills my psychiatrist gave me. They're supposed to help me sleep . . . "

I knew what he meant. I've been there, so it doesn't scare me, but it's always delicate territory. "To sleep, perchance to dream?" I said. "Ah, there's the rub. Gavin, you're a good Catholic boy. Suppose you eat that bottle of pills, and it turns out there really is life after death?"

Gavin shrugged one shoulder. "Hell couldn't feel worse than the life I'm living now."

"True. But if you stay on this side of the grave, I'm sure we can get you out."

"Sometimes I don't think there's any way out but dying."

"Oh," I said, as kindly as I could, "there isn't."

Gavin looked up. "But you said . . . "

"You'll definitely have to commit suicide to be free," I told him. "In fact, ideally, you'll do it all the time. Not physically. Mentally."

"You want me to kill my mind?"

"Not all of it. Just the dungeon."

I'm paraphrasing psychologist Steven Hayes, Ph.D., author of the innovative book Acceptance and Commitment Therapy. "Human vitality is most likely," writes Dr. Hayes, "when the person voluntarily and repeatedly engages in a kind of conceptual suicide, in which the boundaries of the conceptualized self are torn down." The "boundaries of the conceptualized self" are the dungeon walls that keep Gavin—and the rest of us—from steering by starlight. We believe, in all good faith, that *situations* keep us from living our best destinies; we're imprisoned in obligations, jobs, relationships, yada, yada, yada. But actually, we're never trapped by situations. We're trapped by concepts.

My favorite cartoon shows two haggard captives staring through the bars of a prison window. The odd thing is that there are no walls on the prison; the two men are simply standing in the open, holding bars to their own faces with their own hands. This is a brilliant illustration of what most of us are doing when we say—when we deeply believe—that we are "trapped."

As a prisoner in Auschwitz, Viktor Frankl decided "there are two ways to go to the gas chamber: free or not free." The Nazis who obeyed their military superiors and did monstrous things truly believed they had no choice; they possessed physical freedom but no *perceived* freedom to choose their own actions. They were so sure they "had to" obey orders that it amazed them when the rest of the world thought they'd had a choice to disobey. On the other hand, Frankl—from whom all physical freedom had literally been taken—realized that he was free to choose the meaning he would give to his life experience and his dreadful situation.

Compared with an Auschwitz prisoner, Gavin's sense of being "trapped" was patently ridiculous. True, he'd had an awful childhood, but as an adult he faced no physical obstacles to keep him from quitting his job, ending his marriage, or creating a life that would nourish his soul. Yet he was gripping imprisoning beliefs in both hands, pressing them like bars against his face, then imagining walls of thick mortar and impenetrable stone all around him. His therapy, though far better than nothing, had devolved into a repetition of facts about his childhood pain that was actually reinforcing his sense of captivity. It was time for him to stop telling his old stories and start writing a new one.

Multi-Story Prisons

One reason Gavin felt so stuck was his talent as a bard—in other words, a persuasive storyteller. The bricks and bars of his dungeon were made of tales he told himself, stories he believed without question. There was the story about how good guys don't leave their wives (even wives who pickle their livers in gin, sleep with other men, and steal money). There was the old chestnut about never breaking your parents' rules, even when those rules cause untold suffering. There was the story that said "you've invested a lot of time in this job you hate; you can't quit now."

If you feel stuck in your present life, if you feel no enthusiasm for anything, if you think you have no purpose or that you lost that purpose somewhere along the way, I guarantee you are living in a dungeon made of stories—and that none of those limiting stories are true. There is no such thing as a true story that keeps you from your best destiny. All thoughts that separate you from genuine happiness are lies. Conversely, no matter what kind of dungeon your life seems to be, you can dig your way out by seeing through your own false beliefs.

Seeing the inaccuracy of your own limiting ideas and thoughts is the only way to genuine freedom. If your entire life situation were to change at this moment but your false beliefs remained embedded in you, you'd very quickly find yourself right back in the same sort of trapped, optionless hell you left behind. Early in my coaching career, I repeatedly made the mistake of helping people change their circumstances without examining their imprisoning beliefs. Almost instantaneously, they'd find an exact replica of that dreadful mate or abusive boss and experience the same kind of wretched failure they'd experienced before. Nowadays, I focus almost exclusively on helping clients see through the dungeon walls of their false beliefs. As their illusions drop away, the clarity of their Stargazer selves begins to guide them toward new, unprecedented choices—choices that create an outer life as genuine and vibrant as their newly liberated inner life.

So, how do you dig through these dungeon walls? While still captive in your life's dungeons, you must view your life through a Stargazer's eyes. Falsehoods, even those that seem absolutely true to you, are always insubstantial to your Stargazer self—and it's always communicating with you, telling you what is true. It does this by making you feel shackled every time you believe a lie. Aligning yourself with your Stargazer is so simple that your dog, your cat, and even your goldfish sustain it as a matter of course. But to humans, with our "higher" intelligence, it sounds so paradoxical that most of us never even imagine it, let alone try it. What is the secret to this simple, mysterious practice? *You must stop believing anything made of language.*

Dirty, Dirty Words

Dr. Steven Hayes, who pioneered a new kind of clinical approach to psychological healing, divides all suffering into two categories: clean and dirty. "Clean pain" is the unpleasantness you feel when something bad happens to you: You catch the flu, lose a relationship, get in a car accident. *"Dirty pain" is any suffering that comes not from these events themselves but from your thoughts about the events.*

"Oh, my God," you think as your fever rises, "what if this is bird flu and I die horribly?" Watching your loved one hit the high road, you think, "I can't live now that Harold is gone; without him, I'm nothing." Rattled by the impact of the fender bender, you brood, "That son of a bitch in the other car was *trying* to hit me. I need revenge!" The fear, desolation, and rage that emanate from these thoughts are different from—and much worse than—the "clean pain" arising from the fever, the unanticipated solitude, the rude bump of the car fenders.

If you pay just a little attention, you'll see that the vast majority of the pain in your life is really dirty pain. I, personally, am a dirty-pain champion. For example, I believe that people will attack me if I do not single-handedly drag them into a lifetime of magnificent success. (Ahoy, fellow life coaches! Greetings to all who share my disease!) Recently, I apologized to a former client for failing to bring about higher levels of success in his life. I'd encouraged him to write a book—which he did, beautifully. But all the publishers he'd queried had rejected it. As someone who should know at least a little about the publishing industry, I'd really thought the book would sell. When it didn't, my guilt was as sharp as my client's disappointment.

"I hope you can forgive me," I said.

"What are you talking about?" he said. "Why would I have to forgive you? Did you do something wrong?" He was genuinely puzzled.

For over a year, I'd winced every time I thought about this person, imagined his anger and disappointment toward me; brooded over what I could have done differently; and had imaginary conversations in which I tried to explain that even though I loved his book, I couldn't make publishers' decisions for them. The entire time, he'd been thinking of me warmly, grateful for my input and encouragement, disappointed not in me but in himself. All that pain I'd suffered was dirty. Every bit of it.

From where I sit, virtually all human suffering is caused by dirty mindstuff, not clean experience. I've often noticed that the people I've met in the Third World, who by rights should be in much more distress than comparatively well-off Westerners, actually seem to worry less and let go of unrealistic fears more easily. My impression is that when we're not facing the real threats we evolved to handle (starvation, predators, death by exposure), our brains are free to concoct all sorts of potential suffering.

Think about it: If you were walking in the woods, worried sick about your retirement savings, and a bear jumped out at you, your mind would be entirely occupied with action, and there would be little time for dirty pain. If the story of pending destitution remained the focus of your attention, rather than the bear, you might just stand there calculating interest rates rather than taking evasive action. Very soon, you'd have some serious clean pain to think about (on the upside, your retirement worries would be over). This is an extreme example but not as outlandish as it might sound. Many of my clients have spent so much time focusing on dirty-pain stories that they failed to notice relationships falling apart, ill health creeping in, or joylessness overwhelming their real lives. We do violence to our destinies whenever we trust our stories over our experience.

Killing Your Destiny to Fulfill Your Stories

Maybe you've heard the joke about the adulterer who, when his wife walks in on him having sex with his mistress, leaps up shouting, "Who are you gonna believe—me or your lying eyes?" This is funny (sort of) because people actually do behave this way in real life. Cheaters really do invent bizarre stories, and the cheated often accept these stories as truth, even when all evidence points to the contrary. As I write these words, a congressman who propositioned an undercover officer (and who initially pled guilty to his illegal actions) is explaining, via TV, why we should all believe he didn't do the things the officer—and formerly the congressman himself— said he did. How true it is that denial ain't just a river in Egypt.

If you're a normal person, your suffering—the suffering that drives you, limits you, shapes your world—is probably dominated by dirty pain. Like me, you often choose to believe mere words even when the evidence of all your senses discredits them. This would be merely curious if its effects weren't so potentially devastating. In fact, dirty pain is one of the few things in the world more agonizing than physical death.

Consider Gavin the Drab, sitting there in my office. He was physically healthy, intelligent, resourceful, financially solvent, in full possession of all his faculties. Yet he was suffering so deeply that his pain was overwhelming his will to live. Watching him was like watching an animal that has been beaten half to death. It was especially excruciating to see when I knew Gavin's real self: the caring, funny, bright, and lovable guy who'd been lost somewhere in all those foster homes. I understood completely why Gavin's life had led him to the conclusion that he would never be happy. But that didn't make it true. He was free to make the changes that would take him toward his North Star, but he was miserable because his thinking had trapped him in a torture chamber of beliefs.

No other species of animal would do this, because no other animal believes words over experience. For example, chimpanzees can learn many words in American Sign Language, but even these clever beasts don't create thought-structures elaborate enough to destroy their awareness of their actual situation. If you signed to a chimp, "Washo, your hedge funds took a dive; you're bankrupt" or "Everyone saw you mating with Tum-Tum, and the tabloids are calling you a slut," Washo would not throw herself on the electric fence. She'd probably just sign, "Banana, please." If you gave her a banana, the real, present-moment pleasure of eating it would be far more powerful than dark thoughts about the upcoming suffering arising from her empty bank account and ruined reputation.

When I mentioned this to Gavin the Drab, he answered, "What's your point? That just shows that chimpanzees are total morons."

Gavin shared the common (and insane) human belief that it's much more "intelligent" to stay trapped in our self-invented dungeons than to walk away from the causes of our suffering and toward what brings us joy. The belief that dirty pain is intelligent is itself the fundamental lie we keep mashed against our poor sad faces. We can free ourselves from this the instant we choose to believe in our felt experiences over our self-created stories. To the extent that you feel stuck, you are erasing your destiny to fulfill your stories. Continue far enough in that direction, and you'll become like Gavin the Drab, a dead man walking. It's time you began erasing your stories to fulfill your destiny.

Dungeon Digout, Step 1: Your "To Do" List

To start digging out of the dungeon, make a list of 10 things you have to do this week. If you have such a list written down somewhere else, go get it. If the list exists only in your mind, write it down here. This list can include anything that occurs to you, from cleaning the kitchen to running for president.

Some Things I Have to Do within the Next Week

1. _____
2. _____
3. _____
4. _____
5. _____
6. _____
7. _____
8. _____
9. _____
10. _____

Dungeon Digout, Step 2: Spot Your Shackles

Now, look over this list and recall the "shackles on, shackles off" sensations you learned to notice in the previous chapter. As you imagine doing the tasks you've listed, notice whether your body has a "shackles on" reaction to any one of them (for Gavin, everything on the list was "shackles on").

Dungeon Digout, Step 3: Ask Yourself Why

If you got any "shackles on" reactions, focus on the most painful item and answer this question: Why are you planning to do this thing that makes you feel trapped and chained? Why in the world would you undertake such an unpleasant task?

Most people look at me incredulously when I ask them this question. To them, the answer is obvious: They *have to* do whatever it is they hate, because . . . and then they make a statement that they believe to be absolutely true but that has no reality other than the meaning they associate with it in their verbal minds: "I can't disappoint my mother!" "The Bible says I should!" "Brad will kill me if I let him down!"

It may well be true that the people telling such stories aren't sure what other alternatives exist or that other options might be immoral or repugnant to them. But saying, "That's morally repugnant to me" creates a very different mind-set than saying, "I can't." One is a statement of power and choice, the other of helplessness. When the mind labels itself helpless, it stops seeking options. To liberate our minds enough to begin seeing alternatives, we must realize, prosaic as it seems, that we are *physically capable* of not doing almost everything we think we have to do.

For example, Gavin's "To Do" list included the item: "I have to go to work." When I asked him why, he hauled out the tired old lie I've heard from hundreds of other dungeon dwellers: "Because it's my job."

This ridiculous story is true only if you share the conviction that Gavin had no other possible ways of making money or that his God-given mission in life was to sit in some horrid little cubicle, hating himself and his life. Are you shocked or offended that I called his story "ridiculous"? Then you are almost certainly captive in a belief that's similar to his—I'd expect that, since this is one of the most devoutly held doctrines of our culture. The reality (as I learned working on a longitudinal study of career patterns at Harvard Business School) is that people who think they're "stuck" in their jobs get back on their feet with amazing speed when they're fired or their jobs are outsourced. In fact, we live in a time when being flexible, being creative, and embracing change is a far better mind-set from which to build a career than attachment to one job.

I've had thousands of hours of practice helping people see through the popular fib "I have to keep my job," so to me, seeing through Gavin's version of the story was easy. But since it was part of the way he thought, Gavin hadn't even scrutinized this belief, let alone discredited it. His next step was to turn his mind on itself by really, truly examining the belief that drove him to hard labor in the dungeon of his life.

Dungeon Digout, Step 4: Figure Out Where Your Imprisoning Story Is False

It's easy to see through erroneous beliefs if they're very different from your own set of biases. Years ago, traveling in Bali, I met a man who felt horrific guilt because he had sneaked into the tooth-filing ceremony of the woman he loved, even though a man of his caste was forbidden to attend. I just sat there blinking, wondering what a tooth-filing ceremony was (it involves the painless filing of the exterior enamel on certain teeth and is considered a key rite of passage for a Balinese woman) and why on earth anyone should feel bad about sneaking into one. To me, the guy sounded like a hero.

My cultural stories were so different from my Balinese friend's that nothing in his storytelling mind dovetailed with anything in mine, and his beliefs appeared random and strange to me. But when we chatted about my life, he felt exactly the same way about my belief that I "had to" finish graduate school. We all tend to agree with the dominant lies of our own cultures. Other cultures? Well, they're clearly ridiculous. But the stories told by our own people, our own parents, our own social systems—those are The Absolute Truth.

So in this step, I want you to notice how your *body* and *mood* react to the stories that drive your "shackled" actions. I want you to consider that even your most venerated reasons for suffering may be no more substantial than a strange story about tooth-filing ceremonies and subordinate social castes. Below, I've listed a few casual but extremely confining assumptions—mind stories—that are so common in our culture you may hear them go by a thousand times a day without ever questioning their veracity. But all of them are human creations, and all of them will be false *in any circumstances where they cause suffering.*

Common Shackling Beliefs

I have to do things that make me feel trapped and lifeless, because . . .

That's just what a good person does.

Parents should always put children first, self second.

It's bad to be a quitter.

I must protect my reputation.

Family traditions must be upheld, even if they're wrong.

I can't think of anything else to do.

Everyone would be mad at me if I broke the rules.

I have to please my customers.

It would kill my parents if I didn't fulfill their expectations.

No one would love me if I lived in a way that made me happy.

I couldn't bear to have less success than my rivals.

Practice this step by thinking through ways that each of the statements above might be false. For example, the rule "Parents should always put their children first" is the worst instruction you could follow on a depressurizing airplane (a breathing parent can help an unconscious child; a breathing child can't necessarily help an unconscious parent). But the story that says "children first, parents later" is so deeply trained into us that every time we get on a plane, we have to be specifically instructed to put on our own oxygen masks first, our children's second.

A modern master at seeing through false beliefs is author and teacher Byron Katie. She was once a lot like Gavin the Drab: a miserable middle-aged American living in a mental torture chamber that made death sound like a vacation. But when she was 43 years old, something very unusual happened to Katie. One morning, she woke up unable to believe her own thoughts. Any of them. This strange occurrence was never explained, although other venerated teachers, such as Eckhart Tolle, have gone through similar transformations. (I could hazard a wild guess by saying that the observing part of Katie's brain "hijacked" the storytelling part that was causing so much pain, much as the muscle-activation brain regions hijack the neocortex when danger looms. But since no one studied Byron Katie's brain before and then after this event, we'll probably never know what caused it.)

Katie's mind still told the stories that had driven her to the brink of despair, stories like "My mother didn't love me" and "I have no purpose." She noticed that her body reacted to these thoughts by contracting and recoiling. She also noticed that none of her stories were Truth: They were all simply conglomerations of words. And this realization turned her thoughts from an inescapable torture chamber into one long, hilarious comedy routine. Katie wasn't just laughing at her reflexive reptile fears; she was laughing at her whole storytelling mind. She could see that for 43 years, she'd been a walking cartoon, a prisoner crushing bars against her own face and fantasizing dungeon walls where there was nothing real at all.

Katie's ability to disbelieve her thoughts made her world famous, though as far as I know, she has never bothered with publicity. She just spends all her time helping people see through the innocent lies in their minds. The reason people need this help is that it feels so alien to beginners—by definition, it's hard to spot the lie in something you believe. The key is to *trust your nonverbal, felt experience. If a thought causes suffering, it isn't true.*

I strongly recommend Byron Katie's work for anyone trying to escape a life that feels like a dungeon. She's brilliant at identifying ways that true-sounding lies may be false. This isn't so easy for people who haven't experienced a mysterious transformation, so when I work with clients, I give them some prompts to help them identify flaws in the logic of their own tortured minds. It's fascinating to watch people do the exercise below, because they are literally creating new synapse patterns in their brains, and you can almost see the machinery whirring. Often, when I ask them to identify logical reasons why their painful thoughts aren't necessarily always true, people go into lengthy periods of rapid eye movement, as though their heads are computers desperately searching for unfamiliar information in obscure corners of their hard drives.

Right now, take the story that's driving your "shackles on" activity and see if the following prompters can help you see where it may be false. *The point of this exercise is not to come up with "the right answer." It is to force your brain into new patterns of thinking, so that the biases you've been practicing for years begin to lose their absolute power.* It doesn't matter if your responses seem outlandish, improbable, or strange, so long as they're *possible*. Liberation is the ability to see multiple options. No matter how silly a circumstance may sound, if it gives you the ability to widen your perspective, it helps set you free.

The process of weakening a false thought is a little like losing a baby tooth; at first, you may only feel a tiny bit of "give," a slight wiggle away from rigid belief and constant emotional pain. But as the mind turns its energy to *disproving* a painful thought, rather than proving it over and over again, the wiggling becomes more pronounced. You feel freer and freer, until one day you forget you ever believed something that is now obviously untrue. So, write down a thought that causes you suffering and consider the prompts below.

Prompts That Can Help You See through Your Thoughts (To Be Used Alone or in Conjunction with the Work of Byron Katie)

Write a painful thought that often troubles you (e.g., "Nobody loves me," "I'm not good enough," "I shouldn't have sneaked into that tooth-filing ceremony").

My Painful Thought: _____

_____

_____

Now investigate your thought in light of the following questions.

• *Is your imprisoning thought* always *true, or are there times when it could be false?* (For instance, "Parents should put children first" is false in a depressurizing airplane, since a parent with oxygen can help a child put on a mask, but not vice versa. A parent might also go first when entering a dangerous location or trying something very difficult in order to teach the child. Now think of some on your own.)

• *Can you think of a* hypothetical *situation, no matter how silly, in which the thought you wrote down above might be obviously untrue?* (For example, "I must always keep my promises" might turn out to be untrue if a murdering sociopath tricked you into promising you'd help him with a little project that turned out to involve homicide. If you were born into a family with a blood feud and promised your mom you'd always do what she told you, breaking the promise by mending fences and ending bloodshed might be a noble thing.)

• *Can you think of any time you acted as if the thought above weren't true and yet the world didn't end?* ("I can't bear to fail," you may say—but the fact is, you've failed in the past, and you bore it. "I can't disappoint Dad," you fret, but you absolutely can disappoint Dad and probably have in the past, without destroying the universe.)

• *Can you think of times you acted as though the thought you wrote down above were true and things still turned out badly?* ("I have to do my best or I'll hate myself," you may say. Well, have you ever done your best and still hated yourself? Hmm. Interesting.)

• *Can you think of a historical figure who "broke the rules" defined by your painful thought and achieved a positive result?* ("I can't just go off and do whatever feels right to me!" you exclaim. Yet that's a pretty good description of the lives lived by folks like Jesus, the Buddha, all great civil rights activists, most great artists, the framers of the American Constitution . . .)

• *Would you force this thought on any other person you cared for?* ("I have to stay with my abusive spouse so that my children will be happy," said one of my clients. When her young-adult daughter's husband became violent, my client was horrified—even though that was precisely what she'd modeled for her daughter. It never works to inflict on yourself anything you wouldn't force on someone you love.)

Dungeon Digout, Step 5: Act as You Would If You Had No Language

The final step in leaving the dungeon of false thoughts is to see what action would arise spontaneously *if you had no words in your mind.* A few pages ago, I mentioned that most animals, not having language, don't allow abstract ideas to overwhelm their experience of reality. This is a fundamental basis underlying Acceptance and Commitment Therapy (or ACT), of which Dr. Steven Hayes is a well-known theorist. Dr. Hayes and other ACT theorists call the mind "the word machine." It pumps out language all day, every day, the way your heart pumps blood. It's like the crawl of words at the bottom of your TV screen on an all-day news channel. These words may be composed by your inner lizard, your grandmother, your minister, or your higher self. Before you learn to pay attention to them, you don't have much control over the content—which is unfortunate, because the content has a good deal of control over you.

Meditators, patients in ACT therapy, Byron Katie, and other people who feel unusually free may have as many words pouring from their minds as the rest of us. But what differentiates them from the rest of us is that these people have come to realize that their thought-streams consist mostly of nonsense. People like Gavin the Drab, on the other hand, take their thoughts very seriously, believing mind stories no matter how erroneous or even absurd they are. The reason Gavin suddenly went from depression to elation during a 3-day seminar was simply that he was focusing on a different stream of words and allowing himself to believe *them.* Which words were The Truth? None of them. Words are never The Truth. They are arbitrary combinations of sounds that we happen to associate with ideas. Getting attached to *any* concept, any verbal thought, ultimately traps us.

This might seem heretical if you were raised with the belief that you are basically flawed, perhaps even wicked, and that you must learn laws and precepts in order to bring your bad self in line with decent, moral behavior. We have arrived once again at a basic value difference between Eastern and Western thought: Eastern philosophy sees essential human nature as good; Western thought generally sees the "natural" untutored self as either bad or, at the very least, appallingly uninformed.

I can't prove either contention, but I can tell you that I've talked to many, many people about the destructive things they've done, and *invariably,* they did these things because they believed frightening thoughts like "I have no choice," "I *have to* do this," "It's the only way I can survive." Without those thoughts, they become more relaxed, compassionate, and loving. With this as with any other concept, try it before you pass judgment. See if you, yourself, are more likely to act destructively when you are free from frightening thoughts.

There are many techniques for digging out of the dungeons built by the mind. Prayer, meditation, fasting, taking hallucinogens, undergoing confusing rituals, using yoga poses to relax the muscles you contract when you believe your own lies—pick your trick, they can all work. Ultimately, they get you to the same all-important point—the point where you're free to act as you would act without being trapped in any concepts whatsoever.

When Gavin asked himself what he'd do if he could perceive only a simple, clear experience of present-moment reality, his path was clear. He'd divorce his wife, who reminds him so much of the mother he lost at 5, and grieve the loss of both women. Then, aided by therapy, he'd move on to healthier relationships. He'd change jobs as kindly and lovingly as he could. Leaving Cubicleville behind forever, he would put every ounce of effort into earning a living doing something that actually felt like, well, living.

When he'd first seen this path, at the seminar he'd attended, Gavin had been so enchanted by the view from the observatory, so high on the adrenaline of laughing at his inner lizard, that he hadn't really believed he'd need to *dig* himself out of his life. He thought he could leap directly from underground captivity to the position of the Stargazer. I'm so impressed by thoughts like these. I'm mesmerized by the smashing sound they make when they come back to earth. And I love working with people whose disillusionment has made them really serious about digging out of the dungeon.

That's what we did during Gavin's follow-up session. Methodically, one belief at a time, we began shoveling away the beliefs that held him captive. "A good man never leaves his wife, no matter how drunk and promiscuous she may be." "A good son does whatever his parents think is impressive." "A man who quits his job at 45 is a loser." It was like watching the Count of Monte Cristo begin tunneling his way through solid rock. After an hour, we'd barely scratched the surface, but at least I could see that Gavin knew the process. I had to trust him to keep it going. I knew that if he did, something wonderful would happen. Once he was free from *all* thought stories, Gavin's Stargazer self would begin playing out his best destiny, all by itself.

Letting Your Destiny Emerge

I designed my backyard to look like a little desert oasis. It has a small pool shaped like a natural pond, lots of desert shrubs, and two small statues: one of St. Francis of Assisi and one of Siddhartha Gautama, aka the Buddha. I chose those statues because I want animals to feel welcome in my yard. These two saints were famous for loving all sentient beings, including animals, and legend has it that animals—even wild animals—loved them back.

So I was a little chagrined when my dog, the portly and venerable Cookie, reacted to my animal-friendly statuary the same way he'd reacted to my winged-dragon bookend. The first time he noticed them, Cookie's beagle-shriek rang out through the house. *"Oh, no!"* he bellowed, looking out the window at the two figures. *"There are tiny frozen humans in our yard! I'll hold them off as long as I can—you go protect the children!"*

After enduring about 5 minutes of howling, I coaxed the terrified Cookie into the yard and showed him that the statues were innocuous and inanimate. Even so, he growled and bristled at them for a good half hour.

Later that day, when I'd forgotten all about it, I looked out the window to see Cookie slowly approaching the statues, sniffing them all over, then carefully and ceremoniously urinating on each one.

I was shocked. "Cookie!" I yelled—and then stopped abruptly.

It was so clear what had happened: An unexamined part of my belief system had risen up in horror at the "sacrilege" of peeing on St. Francis and the Buddha. But within half a second, I'd seen at least three reasons my perspective on this point was silly and false: (1) In Cookie's world, peeing on something isn't disrespectful; in fact, it is a dog's way of saying, "I accept this thing as part of my home. I love it and will defend it; thus I anoint it." (2) Cookie is certainly no less God's creation than were the people represented by those statues; in fact, to me, Cookie is just another aspect of the divine, God dressed in a scrofulous, smelly little fur suit. (3) If there were two people in all of human history who wouldn't mind a dog peeing on their statues, it would be the saint and the Buddha, my boys Frank and Sid. That's exactly why I put them there.

All of this occurred to me in less than a heartbeat, and it made me laugh at myself for a long time. After you've been digging out of your thought-dungeon for a while, almost everything you think starts to affect you this way. Over and over again, you find yourself locked in an inescapable dungeon, then quickly realize that the dungeon doesn't even exist. Then you can drop the window bars from your face, laughing every time at that same cartoon, each time seeing it a new way.

Freedom of Speech, Freedom from Speech

I have a huge advantage over most people when it comes to understanding that a human life can be virtually free from the terrible confinement of the mind, free from the dirty pain arising out of errant, unexamined thought. For 19 years, I've been living with and learning from a Zen master in the form of my son, Adam.

Many people with Down syndrome have excellent language skills, but Adam isn't one of them. He has never been without multiple speech therapists or daily exercises to develop his articulation muscles. But his brain apparently doesn't contain the ability to structure and express language.

Children raised around many adults who speak different languages often create their own dialect, called a "pidgin" language, based on a blend of all the Babel-tongues spoken in their vicinity. I ran across this in Singapore, a tiny country filled with immigrants from all over Asia. Singaporean children use a huge variety of words from Tamil, English, Dutch, Malaysian, and many dialects of Chinese. But no matter how much they toss unrelated languages together, they always use the same basic structures and parts of speech used in other languages. Verbs, pronouns, and adjectives will follow a consistent pattern, and all the children will use the same pidgin terms.

Anthropologists and linguistic epistemologists have used this phenomenon to show that the structure of language is hardwired into every typical human brain. But not into Adam's. He has given me permission to quote here from a card he recently created for his sisters, Katie and Lizzy. Here's what he wrote, ex tempore, in his careful hand.

> Happy Katie and Lizzy to a you do good time use Katie and Lizzy. But I can with me going day use see so a game is play a fun too if you like's Katie and Lizzy good you Love' Adam Beck

Clearly, this kid is another James Joyce. I look forward to the publication of Adam's first novel. And I can assure you that it will make no sense whatsoever. The tree of etymology that sprouts in the typical human's neocortex just doesn't exist in Adam's. I used to think this was a tragedy. Then, for some years, I thought it was a trial. Now I believe it is an incalculably valuable gift.

Because Adam has little language, he never builds dungeon walls of words or concepts. He never believes he's "trapped" by rules or conventions. Yet his social and emotional intelligence is enormous. I don't mean this in a patronizing, smarmy way: "Yes, my son has the analytical powers of a fur-bearing animal, but he just hugs and hugs everyone he sees." Adam doesn't hug people unless it's absolutely appropriate. He's kind, thoughtful, gracious. If someone treats him badly, he walks away, instantly shrugging off negative energy. He never makes himself crazy by pretending a "shackles on" experience feels good. He never blames himself for things that aren't his fault. He says yes or no from his heart, without guilt, anxiety, or fear of losing favor in someone else's eyes. His actions arise from clear acceptance of what he truly feels, without the dirty pain that is produced by complex stories made of abstract ideas.

When Adam was 15, he took the time to teach one of us "normal" folks a little of his natural wisdom. That year, he received a new watch for Christmas, and he was very proud of it. The first day back at school after the holiday, a classmate borrowed Adam's watch, dropped it, and broke it. The teacher (who told me about this later) was horrified.

"Jared!" she exclaimed to the watch-breaker. "You should have been more careful! That was Adam's watch!"

All day, the teacher felt horrible about her part in the watch-breaking incident. Her mind spun out long stories about how irresponsible she'd been to let Jared borrow the watch, how she should have known better, how Adam was suffering, and how angry his mother (I) would be. She dealt with her own guilt and shame by repeatedly scolding Jared for the entire day. The next day, she raised the subject again. Later, while the class was working quietly on a project, Adam approached her desk.

"Ms. Morrison," he observed politely, "it was my watch."

"I know, honey," Ms. Morrison groaned, feeling just awful. "I shouldn't have let you lend it to Jared."

"No," said Adam, frowning with frustration. "It was *my* watch."

"And it was awful that he broke it. I'm so sorry.'"

Adam began to laugh. Then, for several seconds, he thought very hard, the way he does when he absolutely has to make himself understood, the way I used to think in Chinese class when I had to describe a complicated situation in Mandarin.

"Ms. Morrison," he said very slowly, "it . . . was . . . *my* . . . watch. Not . . . yours." He looked at her intently to see if she'd get it. And then, for Ms. Morrison, the light dawned.

"Oh," she said. "You mean, I should let it go?"

Adam burst out laughing again, heaved a huge sigh of relief, and went happily back to his seat.

Thus does my son, the Stargazer, liberate the unfortunate dungeon prisoners with whom he shares his destiny.

The BARD Method

The process Adam knows instinctively is something most of us have to learn deliberately. It's awkward at first but can become as smooth and automatic as tying your shoes. The process, in simple steps (simple but not easy, as promised), looks like this.

Summary of Method to Eliminate "Dirty Pain"

1. *Believe (but notice what you believe)*

   Become aware of unhappiness in any form. Rather than avoiding it, notice it and allow it to come into consciousness so that you can address it.

2. *Articulate (spot the thoughts behind the pain)*

   Pay attention to the thoughts that fuel that unhappiness—anything you say in your mind that stimulates feelings of helplessness, despair, futile rage, or abstract terror with no action implications. Articulate these thoughts if they're vague.

3. *Recognize (why the thought is not absolutely true)*

   Examine the belief to see if there are any flaws in its logic, using these prompts if necessary.

   a. *Is your imprisoning thought always true, or are there times when it could be false?*

   b. *Can you think of a hypothetical situation, no matter how silly, in which the thought might be obviously untrue?*

   c. *Can you think of any time you acted as if the thought weren't true and yet the world didn't end?*

   d. *Can you think of times you acted as though the thought above were true and things still turned out badly?*

   e. *Can you think of a historical figure who "broke the rules" defined by your painful thought and achieved a positive result?*

   f. *Would you force this thought on any other person you cared for?*

4. *Detach (from the thought by recognizing possible alternatives)*

   Allow the thought to "wiggle" like a loose tooth as your brain follows the unfamiliar neuron tracks created by logically *dis*proving it. Repeat the process until the thought disappears—in other words, when the suffering it causes is no longer present (often, you won't even notice this happening).

I use the acronym BARD to remind people of this process: Believe, Articulate, Recognize, and Detach. The reason to remember the acronym is that when you're overwhelmed by dirty pain, you may become muddle-headed, convinced by your own untested ideas, unable to remember how to use your verbal mind to disassemble its own creations. The BARD method is something you can turn to when you wake in the middle of the night, terrified of things that may or may not happen. It's something to turn to when you've been dumped by your beloved, fired from your job, trapped in a situation you wish you had avoided.

When Gavin came back for his one-on-one session, we ran through the BARD process over and over again. We looked for areas of Gavin's life that were plagued by unhappiness and found the thoughts that were inducing him to keep those situations in place or to stay in them when he was physically capable of leaving. Gavin articulated many true-seeming false thoughts that had arisen in his mind during his chaotic early life (so many parents, so little consistency). We covered beliefs like "Good boys never complain." "I shouldn't expect people to value me." "I'm not as good as people who grew up with their real parents." "I have to accept whatever my wife does, because it's a miracle anyone even married me."

We could have spent hundreds of hours more dissecting all the painful life events that put these thoughts in Gavin's mind. But they were like shrapnel in a wound: Getting rid of them was more important than discussing exactly how they got there. So we just kept subjecting each belief to the basic scientific process—note the hypothesis, look for an antithesis, create a better hypothesis. Simple, right? *But not easy.* So difficult and counterintuitive, in fact, that only suffering convinces most people to learn it. During his workshop experience, Gavin had assumed his excitement and optimism would make such painstaking self-examination unnecessary. Now he learned to disassemble the dungeon in his brain one brick at a time. After several repetitions of the BARD process, I knew he could continue on his own whenever he found himself in pain.

"So," I told him as I hugged him good-bye, "be Gavin the Bard, not Gavin the Drab. You built the dungeon, you can dissolve it."

"What dungeon?" he said, grinning uncertainly. "There is no dungeon." He held his hands up to his face as if they held window bars. His voice wavered, like a surgery patient standing up for the first time, but I could hear an underlying conviction I hadn't heard before.

"By George," I said, "I think you've got it."

Five years later, I was in Los Angeles on a book tour, waiting in the lobby of a radio station where I was scheduled to record an interview. I'd never met the interviewer before and wasn't sure what he would look like, so when a handsome guy in a turtleneck walked into the lobby and stood looking at me, I assumed he must be my host.

"Am I here to talk to you?" I said.

"I don't think so," he said. "But I'm here partly because of you."

I had no idea what he was talking about. The guy just stood there, looking at me, until I started to feel a little nervous. Then he lifted his hands to his face, gripping imaginary bars.

"Gavin?" I gasped. He looked completely different: bearded, relaxed, 30 pounds leaner, radiating confidence and contentment. And, in fact, he *was* completely different. Since the last time we'd met, he had ended his marriage (the shock of losing her favorite codependent had driven his wife into rehab and helped her get her own life together). He'd also quit his job at the software firm and become a successful music producer.

Gavin the Drab was gone. That poor guy had committed suicide—again and again and again. The man I met in the radio station was purely Gavin the Bard. He was steering his life not by obeying concepts, not even by telling new stories. He was accomplishing this by *un*telling every tale he'd ever believed, dissolving the dirt and mortar that had once seemed an impenetrable barrier to his right life. The Gavin who'd survived and emerged from the rubble had no idea what would happen to him next, but he didn't mind that at all. He'd learned that his real story—the story of his best destiny— was already written in the stars.

CHAPTER 4

The Ring
of Fire

Realizing that ultimately most of the pain we experience is of our own devising, that we believe our way into self-created dungeons and can disbelieve our way out, was a turning point for me as a person and as a coach. Where I used to spend lots of time discussing stories about how emotional injuries occurred (childhood trauma, parental mistakes, freak accidents at Christian amusement parks), I now focus almost entirely on the injuries themselves (the present beliefs that create and sustain ongoing fear, captivity, and sadness).

Looking directly at belief systems and dissolving the cause of suffering make it relatively unimportant to talk about how the wound occurred—surprisingly so for anyone versed in typical forms of therapy. Many of my clients have spent years discussing their childhoods with counselors without ever fully freeing themselves from the emotional wounds of their childhoods. Over and over, I've been amazed how fast a little dungeon-digging can liberate these people when a lot of storytelling can't.

This approach also highlights something I hadn't fully realized before: Adopting the perspective of the Stargazer not only leads us toward our future best destinies but actually transmutes past unhappiness into treasure. This is because, in emotional terms, everything is made from its opposite. The raw material for joy is sorrow; the raw material for compassion is anger; the raw material for fearlessness is fear. This means that the very people who hurt you worst may turn out to have enriched you most. "Forgiveness" isn't even an issue from the position of the Stargazer. Why would anyone bother to "forgive" someone who'd made them rich?

Of course, the alchemy that transmutes bad experiences to good ones, emotional lead to gold, doesn't happen by default. It requires a particular kind of magic, similar to dungeon-digging but more dramatic. This process is even more counterintuitive than disproving all your own concepts, because it happens only in a psychological place most of us spend our whole lives avoiding. I call this place "the ring of fire," and this chapter will help you turn it into the path to your best destiny.

Your Three-Ring Life

Picture your life, your consciousness, your reality as a series of concentric spheres like the ones in the illustration below. As you can see, this sphere has three layers, of which we shall now take a brief guided tour.

Shallows

Ring of Fire

Core of Peace
(Stargazer)

One Metaphor for Your Psyche

The Shallows (Material Reality)

The exterior shell of your life is what I call the "shallows." You might also call it the world of form, of physical objects and the thoughts that cluster around them.

When your consciousness is fully attached to this realm, you are a material girl or boy. You're mentally trapped in your concept of yourself as isolated, limited, and separate from all other things. Your socialized beliefs and your lizard fears direct your actions, which consist of running from things you dread and grasping at things you desire. Maddeningly, no matter what you do, danger is never fully averted and desire is never permanently fulfilled. To quote Samuel Beckett, you are "born astride of a grave, and a difficult labor."

If you want to know what the generalized human outer limit looks like, take a gander at advertising, especially American advertising. It's a dazzling display of outer-limit rewards: wealth, status, sex, fame, power, approval. Asian folklore includes a type of demon called a "hungry ghost," which has an endless, ravenous stomach and a tiny pinhole mouth. Because hungry ghosts can't eat enough to satiate themselves, they're perpetually desperate, devouring, grabby, needy. Someone once asked the Vietnamese monk Thich Nhat Hahn, "What does the realm of the hungry ghosts look like?" He answered with one word: "America."

Mind you, I'm not knocking the prosperity and ease of the wealthiest culture in human history. I'm eternally grateful that I was born into it. The problem isn't that some people have a lot of stuff—that's wonderful, especially if we learn how to share it—but rather that no matter how much we have, in the shallows, nothing is ever enough. Fortunately, there's more to us than our outer-limit lives. If you've done any of the exercises in the previous chapters, you know what I'm talking about.

The Core of Peace (The Stargazer)

At our very cores, unperturbed by the disturbances of the shallows, lies the Stargazer self. No untruth can exist at this level of awareness: no apparent separation from the fabric of the universe, no pain, no fear, no death. The real reason we feel so starved in the shallows is that we aren't made to be satisfied with material possessions or with concepts of ourselves as famous, noble, smart, handsome, righteous, influential, blah blah blah. What we really want is the peace of the Stargazer. The irony is that this is already present in every single one of us, though it's obscured by the dense matter of our lives at their shallowest. Clinging to the shallowest sphere of existence, losing touch with our cores, is the primary cause of all our unhappiness. So why does almost everyone spend enormous energy doing it?

To avoid the ring of fire, that's why.

The Ring of Fire

In the previous chapter, we saw Gavin the Bard begin digging himself out of his mental prison with great facility. That guy could dissolve a limiting belief in a trice, whatever a trice is, but not just because he was metaphysically talented. Gavin's dungeon walls, his beliefs and his ego defenses, were already comparatively weak by the time I met him. Gavin had spent so much time in the place I call the ring of fire (apologies to Johnny Cash) that his thought structure was practically burned to a crisp.

The ring of fire is the emotional process we must go through in order to reach the core of peace. There are only two ways to accomplish this. We can *disbelieve* any false ideas that are causing unnecessary pain. And we must *grieve* any unavoidable pain—loss of health or a loved one, for example.

Whenever outer-limit rewards escape us—when our hearts are broken, our trust betrayed, our health compromised, or our dreams dashed—this process of grieve-or-disbelieve is triggered, and our attachment to the shallow material shell of life weakens. The gravitational pull of the Stargazer self draws us inward, trying to get us to the place where our hearts can heal once and for all and our real dreams come true. *This is a totally benevolent process.* But the Stargazer reality is so intense, its light so bright, that nothing impermanent or false can survive it. Everything that we think defines us and makes us important may burn up as we get closer to our cores.

If we stay in it, the ring of fire eventually vaporizes every dysfunctional concept learned by our social selves and every self-protective superstition manufactured by our inner lizards. It disintegrates ideas just like dungeon-digging but much more quickly and dramatically. The deeper you go, the more components of your ego start to burn, immolated by flames hot enough to vaporize solid rock. Sound like fun? Oh, it isn't. But when you get the opportunity, I'd advise you to do it anyway. In fact, the rest of this chapter will challenge you to walk straight into the ring of fire, wherever your own life grants you access to it.

Why You Should Walk into the Ring of Fire

At the same time I was working with Gavin, I had another client I'll call Clarice, who was one of the most successful businesswomen of her genera-tion. Clarice had never caught a bad break in her whole life. She was born beautiful, intelligent, and wealthy. She had an idyllic childhood, with ponies and adoring nannies and all that. She married well, had two gor-geous children, and built a business empire that raked in revenues higher than the annual budgets of some major Third World cities.

Then, just when everything was going so well, something totally unex-pected happened to Clarice: She got old. Having suffered so few losses in her life, she was absolutely unprepared for this. She wasn't good at dying; no part of her outer-limit ego had ever died. She'd been able to spend decades in the purely material realm of life with virtually no suffering and no significant disappointments.

Don't you wish you could do that? Don't we all? Well, I used to, but not anymore. Not after working with Clarice.

The last years of that woman's life were one long, violent inner-reptile war against the inevitable. Clarice got so much plastic surgery her head looked like it'd been assembled by a committee—because it had. I strongly suspect she also paid to have the head frozen after her demise, to be reattached to some young, nubile body once medical science had figured out how this could be done. The older she got, the more outrageously Clarice finagled to increase her fortune, her public profile, her political influence. She looked and acted like a bizarrely extreme caricature of a bitter old woman. Interacting with her was like putting your face in a meat grinder; she cursed at her servants, alienated her friends, reduced her daughter to an ashen, weeping shadow. I continued working with her out of the same fascination that made me a fan of Mafia movies. And what stunned me even more than Clarice's reaction to her upcoming death was her description of her inner life.

"I never quite made it," she often said, in a voice shaking with age and rage. "If I'd had just a few more years, I could've really achieved something. I would've shown everybody."

The irony of it just blew me away. Here was a person with all the evidence one could imagine to prove that success in the shallows doesn't equal happiness. Yet she never gave up her false belief that one more conquest, one more acquisition, one more pot of money was what she needed to finally be content. Clarice spent her entire life chasing a bus she'd already caught, and she died—horribly, I was told, fighting like mad, gasping for air—still imprisoned in the illusion that she hadn't run quite fast or far enough.

Becoming Willing to Burn

The definition of success for the shallows-oriented ego is to do what Clarice did: get as much stuff as possible and hang on to it as long as possible. By contrast, the definition of success for the Stargazer self is letting go of absolutely everything, including our own existence. The Stargazer knows that if we let ourselves die before we die, we discover that death is nothing to fear; when we're willing to be nothing, we become everything. But our outer-limit selves can't see this. When we experience the death of a hope, a dream, a relationship, we initially understand it from a naïve, outer-limit viewpoint. All we can see is terrible loss.

The emotions that follow loss are familiar to most people, thanks to the famous work of Elisabeth Kübler-Ross, M.D. After studying many terminally ill patients, Dr. Kübler-Ross described the well-known "grieving process," which includes denial, bargaining, anger, sadness, and acceptance. Sometimes we feel each of these in tidy sequence, but more typically they come at us in a chaotic jumble, repeating and shifting randomly, after any sort of shock or disappointment. We burn, burn, burn until our attachment to whatever we have lost is completely incinerated. The grieving process is not warm and fuzzy (unless you define "warm" as "hot enough to make your head explode like a jawbreaker in a microwave"), but it is a powerful and wonderful magic.

I'm always surprised when I'm working with a group and one person enters the ring of fire and others are upset by this. "Do something!" they tell me. "Bob's *crying*, for God's sake!" One client stinted her own tears long enough to shout at me, "Why won't you just say something nice to stop me from feeling this way? Why won't you distract me with small talk? *Give me what I need!*"

To me, this sounds as weird as trying to help a laboring woman by pushing her baby back into the womb. When something "terrible" is happening to us (from a "shallows" perspective), something wonderful is always being born (from the Stargazer's perspective). You see, once we're in the ring of fire, we don't have to painstakingly dig out of our mental dungeons. The fire of grieving does that job for us, melting solid rock into flowing volcanic lava. While this is not exactly a picnic, it is a consummation devoutly to be wished. Because when our attachment to our old false concepts is fully burned up, when we utterly and truly let go of the way we once thought things should be, the magic happens. The alchemy of the Stargazer transmutes psychological lead into gold. Pain becomes joy. Fear becomes peace. Anger becomes absolute compassion. There's nothing more awful than the ring of fire, but there is nothing, nothing, *nothing* as sweet as what it can yield: reunion with the Stargazer.

If your life is going well right now, hang on to your shallows-based pleasures and advantages as long as you can. Dig out your mental dungeon bricks one by one when you're in the mood, perhaps at church on Sunday or during boring meetings with your parole officer. Take your time. But when misfortune enters your life—or if you happen to be reading this book at a time when you're also experiencing loss and suffering—congratulate yourself. Then, *lean into it.*

Leaning into the Fire

Our culture encourages us to avoid the agony of loss and defeat at all costs. But every body of ancient wisdom includes archetypal tales about heroes who knowingly and consciously walked *into* the ring of fire. Beowulf let himself be lashed to a tree for 9 days and nights. Ulysses left Calypso and went back out on the dangerous sea. Moses chose to wander with his enslaved people rather than please his royal adopted father. Jesus rode into Jerusalem with a price on his head. Siddhartha cut off his hair, doffed his princely robes, and walked into the jungle. Archetypal heroes are always snatching defeat from the jaws of victory. When the going gets tough, the tough get going—but the enlightened? They surrender.

Surrendering is so contrary to my socialization, so appalling to my inner lizard, that I find it totally unacceptable. Never, ever have I wanted to suffer. Fortunately, there have been times when I had no choice (that's what being alive'll get you). I've been much luckier than my old buddy Clarice because on several occasions, fate has conveniently stripped from me the shallow ego identities I'd mistaken for myself.

For instance, as a teenager I was deeply identified with being a marathon-distance runner. Obsessed with fitness, I felt peaceful only when I was jogging. Then I developed a chronic pain condition that not only stopped me from running but also left me crippled, often unable to walk, for more than a decade. At the time, I was working at the only actual job I've ever loved: teaching studio art as a fellow at Harvard. I'd been drawing 10 or 12 hours a day since I was a year old, and creating art was a fundamental part of my self-concept. But soon the disease that had ended my running career affected my hands, and I lost the ability to draw or paint.

Since my body wasn't doing so well, I next hitched my hope for success on my mind, working toward a Ph.D. I also started a family, fully intending to have "perfect" kids. Then, whaddaya know, my second child turned out to be mentally retarded. Suddenly, Harvard-style beliefs like "To be perfect, you must be smart" and "Achievement is necessary for happiness" made my baby's life look unbearably tragic. The pain from my thoughts about his future was worse than anything I'd ever felt for myself.

With Adam on board, I felt alienated at Harvard, where the folks were definitely not down with Down syndrome. So I moved back to my intensely religious childhood community, assuming that where "smart" hadn't worked out for me, "spiritual" would. But hold on a minute—after a few years of being devoutly religious, I realized that I felt *less* connected to God, not more. I found this unbearable, so I became an apostate, a sin worse than murder to pretty much everyone I'd ever loved. Into the ring of fire went almost all my childhood and adolescent relationships, my community, my reputation as a good and righteous person.

Every one of these experiences felt like being burned alive. Of course, looking backward (remember Chapter 1?), it's obvious they were all priceless gifts. They quickly burned away my mental prison walls, while giving me the raw material for so much happiness that *people now pay me money to give them advice*, a fact that will never cease to amaze my children, friends, and dogs.

Yes, the ring of fire has proven to be a cash cow for me, and if you're in pain right now, you too are walking in the magic zone of transmutation. Your suffering, no matter how dreadful, is also useful and purposeful. It's the Stargazer pulling your life back toward true north, toward your destiny. Fight this as long as you can. Then, when you're ready, stop fighting.

How to Surrender to the Stargazer

For years, I read books—recovery manuals, self-help systems, spiritual tomes—that encouraged me to "surrender." But they never said *how*. It's not as if I didn't try. When I was in emotional pain, burning alive in grief or despair or anger, I'd try to surrender in every way I could imagine. "I surrender, already!" I would shout to the empty air. "Look, here's my white flag! Uncle, uncle! I give up! You got me! I'm done! My goose is cooked! You win!"

This never brought relief, only frustration. I believed that history's many "surrender" advocates were on to something because they all agreed with one another, but I couldn't figure out how to operationalize their advice.

Twice during those long years of depression and angst, I stumbled over the right technique for surrender. The first time was just before Adam was born, when I was too sick and sad and exhausted to keep going. The second time, I was also sick and sad and exhausted, but this time I was also under general anesthesia, which I'm sure helped a lot. Both times, I felt a certain kind of emotional *collapse*, but not something I could replicate, any more than I could replicate an earthquake. The moment after the collapse, I became aware of a presence so absolutely loving, so infinitely joyful, that every pain I'd ever suffered seemed about as upsetting as a fluffy bunny in a summer field.

These experiences were not visual, but they had visual components: In one case, I saw an actual being made of light; in the other, just a pure shining sphere. These words and their associations are so inadequate to describe the experience that using them feels almost blasphemous, but they're as close as I can come. For reasons I can't possibly convey in language, they were so overwhelmingly beautiful that I spent years trying to make them happen again. Long after I had the "white light experience" during surgery, when another doctor told me I needed a different operation, I was ecstatic. I danced around joyfully until I realized that not every medical procedure involves a visit from a brilliant, comforting sphere of light. Sure enough, during that second surgery, it didn't show up. Even medication couldn't help me surrender volitionally. I didn't begin learning how to do that until years and years later, when I had my brain mapped.

Reading the Old Map

"Brain mapping" is one of the most exciting developments in modern psychology. It uses computer technology to pick up and record the electrical signals produced by the human brain at work. To create a brain map, researchers attach electrodes to specific positions on your head, then connect the electrodes to a computer. Different frequencies of electricity, at different places in the brain, create observable movements of the computer cursor and also correlate to different states in your felt experience.

When I heard about this, I hastened to plunk down a handsome chunk of change and have some brain cartographers map out my own gray matter. Once I was hooked up to the computer, the researchers told me I suffered from very high anxiety (imagine that!) and that this anxiety was hardwired into my brain. However, I could change my neurological patterns now that I had the computer giving me feedback. My task was to sit there staring at the screen and pushing down a cursor that showed my level of beta waves, which are associated with fear and worry. And how was I supposed to do that?

"We can't tell you that," said the researchers. "It's like riding a bicycle. You just keep trying to get the cursor to go down until something works. Then you lock onto it. Your brain will know how to do it forever after."

They said this would take about 40 hours of computer feedback. I thought I could beat that time. After all, I'd spent years practicing anything that promised to help me calm down. I'd done yoga, vipassana meditation, Zen meditation, walking meditation, written and spoken prayer, devotional reading, tranquilizers, stronger tranquilizers, resolute Enya appreciation, high doses of ice cream, and, of course, therapy. I thought I'd done a pretty darn good job of lowering my anxiety levels already.

So, when the brain-mapping researchers left me alone with my electrodes, I fully planned to come on like a ringer. I went into the calm, observant state I'd learned to adopt in meditation. But to my consternation, my "anxiety" waves didn't go down. Another electrical signal (my theta waves) went up, indicating that I'd relaxed, but my anxiety was still high. Okay, I thought, that makes a certain kind of sense. In meditation, I'd learned to watch my emotions without trying to change them. Meditation hadn't stopped me from feeling anxiety; it had just taught me not to care as much when I was anxious. Well and good, but I wanted to make that cursor go down, and I still had no idea how.

I began to think random thoughts, recall all sorts of memories, just to see what happened on the screen. After a few minutes, I noticed a pattern—and it was the last thing in the world I would have expected. My anxiety levels dropped when I remembered situations where I'd spoken in public to huge audiences or been in serious physical danger. This seemed so strange that I double-checked, then triple-checked, then quadruple-checked. Sure enough, the more high-risk the situation I imagined, the less anxiety my brain produced.

Now that I was alert to it, I realized that I could feel the calm associated with these intense, high-pressure situations. I even had a name for it: I called it the "Place beyond Fear." It wasn't a place where I felt naturally safe but where fear was so intense that to function at all, I had to deliberately push it aside. Brain mapping is still too new for me to know if I'd stumbled upon a common phenomenon. But scholars like Mihaly Csikszentmihalyi, Gregory Berns, and Ellen Langer, who study human happiness, concur that we are most centered and blissful "in the zone," when we're intensely focused on something that is almost too hard or scary to do—hence the human proclivity for rock climbing, skydiving, white-water rafting, and shopping sales on the day after Christmas.

The Place beyond Fear

I'd learned to go to the Place beyond Fear precisely because I'm so naturally anxious. The first time I spoke in public, at a high school debate tournament, I actually fainted dead away. In order to get up and speak again in the next round, I had to push my phobias into the background and just get the job done. The same need arose later in my life when I was, say, skiing on the edge of an icy cliff in a heavy snowstorm with zero visibility or appearing on live TV with an audience of millions.

So there I sat in the brain-mapping clinic, with my pin-cushion head, recalling the most high-risk situations I'd ever faced, watching my anxiety waves drop to near zero. After half an hour, I was able to articulate how I managed the magical trick of entering the Place beyond Fear. It was the thing I'd missed while trying to "surrender" during various searing excursions into the ring of fire. To minimize the agony of loss and reach my peaceful, directed Stargazer self immediately, I had to do just two things: dive into the ring of fire and then renounce time.

That's what we'll discuss doing in the rest of this chapter. First, I'll describe the two ubiquitous "failure modes" that keep most of us stuck in the ring of fire much of the time. Then we'll talk about reversing those failure modes, a process that steers you *into* the ring of fire. Once you're there, you'll find yourself highly motivated to step out of time. At that point, the Stargazer appears.

Fondling and Fleeing: How to Get Stuck in the Ring of Fire

We get stuck in the ring of fire whenever our thoughts about events that happened in the past or events that may happen in the future dominate our experience. Getting stuck in the past is a failure mode I call "story fondling." Its mirror twin is getting stuck in the future, which I call "fire fleeing." Almost all of us use both failure modes, though we tend to prefer one or the other most of the time. See if the descriptions below sound familiar.

Focusing Only on the Past: Story Fondling

I had a friend I'll call Dinah who struggled on the edge of poverty for years. One day, we were talking on the phone when Dinah told me sadly, "You know, it's been over twenty years since I've been on an airplane." That very hour, I cashed in some frequent flyer points and got Dinah a round-trip ticket to Phoenix. We spent two happy days shopping, eating, laughing, and sightseeing; then she flew home. The next week, I called to see how Dinah was doing. I mentioned I was traveling that week.

"You know," said Dinah sadly, "it's been over twenty years since I've been on an airplane."

This gave me pause. I said, "Er . . . what about last week?"

"What about last week?" Dinah said. Then she remembered. "Oh, oh, of course, that's right," she said. "I went to Phoeni—but you know," she said, and her voice went back to precisely the same sorrowful cadence, "aside from that, it's been over twenty years since I've been on an airplane."

Dinah wasn't just retelling the story of her woefully ground-bound existence, she was *fondling* it, the way you'd pet the head of your favorite pug. The story, including the dejection it produced, was actually a kind of comfort zone for Dinah. She knew how to be poor and sad; she used her unhappiness to solicit pity from herself and others, and it generally worked to get her through life. Sadness about the past was her *currency*, the stuff she used to buy things. So she counted the days, months, and years of her sadness the way a miser counts money. This left her so attached to sadness that no happy version of her life, no joyful here-and-now, could even come up on her radar screen.

You undoubtedly have story fondlers in your life. Take a quick look in your mental Rolodex. Maybe it's the coworker who constantly drops by your desk to tell you about the injustice she suffered in her last relationship. Or the brother who never stops talking about the terrible things done to him by a crazy boss. Maybe the story fondler in your life—'fess up, now—is you. Most of us have done our share of ruminating about painful episodes in our childhoods, relationships, careers, and so on.

The next time you notice yourself launching into an upsetting tale you've told yourself over and over—either in your head or to others—have the guts to admit that you're story fondling. If the story makes you happy, that's not a problem (although experiencing the present moment might prove even more interesting). If your story focuses on things that make you sad, angry, and afraid, however, fondling it all day is definitely unhealthy. You'll stay stuck in the ring of fire, neither enjoying the simple pleasures of the shallows nor seeing from the magical position of the Stargazer. You'll keep hurting as long as you hang on to those thoughts.

Unfortunately, many people use therapy as a place to go over and over well-worn versions of their painful histories long after this has ceased to be cathartic. Instead of releasing pain and moving on to new adventures, they retell the tale until it wears a rut in their minds, keeping them from seeing other options. A good therapist will help you talk through negative experiences, heal your heart, and move on. If you've been recounting the same tragic events to the same counselor for decades with no significant improvement in your quality of life, that kind of storytelling isn't working for you. In a moment, I'll tell you what will. But first we should take a quick look at failure mode number two.

Focusing Only on the Future: Fire Fleeing

"I don't see that it does any good to sit around talking about problems," Ray told his wife, Helen, when she asked him to accompany her to therapy. "All that touchy-feely stuff never did any good. If you're not happy, just suck it up and get back to work; that's what I say."

This philosophy had functioned quite well throughout most of Ray's life. In fact, it had made him very successful in sports and in business. But the reason Helen was in therapy was that the couple's only child had been murdered, shot for no apparent reason on a college campus. The killer had never been caught. Naturally, this event shoved both Ray and Helen into the ring of fire. Helen grieved, wept, sought consolation from friends, and found a good psychologist. Ray? He "just sucked it up and got back to work." He also started smoking like a chimney, developed chronic insomnia, and began having frequent outbursts of violent anger at home, at work, and everywhere in between.

Ray was a fire fleer. Like Clarice, he avoided feeling any part of the ring of fire—the grief process—except denial. Whenever events shattered the surface of his life and pulled him toward the core of peace, he fought like crazy to stay in the shallows. He made bigger goals, planned bigger conquests, hurled himself full force at whatever material success could hold his attention. After his son's death, Ray fled so obsessively into the future that, as we'll see in a moment, he nearly died himself.

The Problem with Fondling or Fleeing

Both being mired in the past and living solely for the future can have short-term beneficial results. Caressing tales of past victimization, as Dinah did, can elicit pity responses from others—and it's a wonderful way to convince ourselves not to take any action that frightens us in the present. Obsessing about the future, whether our focus is the fear of catastrophe or the hope of getting and keeping more stuff, prevents us from feeling legitimate grieving. Whew, what a relief.

The problem is that story fondling and fire fleeing keep us from experiencing the here and now. Since the here and now is the only moment in which we actually exist, getting stuck in the past and future divorces us from our own lives. Not living in our own lives is equivalent to being dead—it means that, in psychological terms, we lose *everything*.

The Stargazer part of you knows this. That's why it never pretends to exist in any moment except here and now. When we're focused completely on an internal narrative about what has happened to us and what may happen to us, we have no access to the Stargazer's map of our destiny. We pull back from the pure light at the center of our existence, hang on to mental storytelling, and get stuck in the ring of fire, where we're broiled alive by flames for years, decades, lifetimes. Our attempts to avoid unhappiness end up leaving us there far longer than necessary.

The solution? Stop fondling your stories or fleeing your feelings and dive right into the flames. "Past and future veil God from our sight," wrote the Sufi mystic Rumi. "Burn up both of them with fire." Here are a couple of methods for doing this, whether your failure mode is story fondling or fire fleeing.

Strategy for Story Fondlers: Stop Talking and Start Doing

Story fondlers are chockablock full of disappointment and anger about the bad things that are present in their lives and the good things that are absent. By talking about this constantly, they get help and sympathy from others. This affords them just enough well-being to endure life, as long as they keep complaining (thereby venting their emotions and getting people to do things for them).

If you have a tendency to story fondle, *pick something you complain about often, stop discussing it, and take action to change it*. If you're underpaid, ask for a raise or quit. Stating clearly to your boss, "I won't continue to work here unless I get a ten per cent raise by March," is very different from telling all your coworkers how bad the boss is and how miserable it is for you to be paid so little. Similarly, if a certain friend mooches off you, stop saying yes—say no and mean it. If a loved one is addicted and it's ruining your life, stage an intervention or go to a codependency group where you'll get help making changes *in your own life*.

I once worked with a client who was preparing to divorce her husband because he wouldn't paint their house. She'd been asking him to do this for over ten years. They'd had endless arguments about it; she'd put pressure on him in every way she could devise. She had dozens of well-rehearsed stories about the various extreme ways she'd tried and the ways in which her husband squiggled out of his house-painting promises. My suggestion? *Paint the damn house—now*. Or, if the house-painting argument was just her way of justifying a divorce, then *get a divorce—now*.

If you need encouragement doing this, get a very proactive therapist or a life coach like me who emphasizes action over storytelling. Whatever it takes, whatever your complaints may be, stop talking about them and start doing something to change them.

Strategy for Fire Fleers: Stop Doing and Start Talking

Ray—the man whose son was murdered—fled his feelings about this terrible loss for almost three years. He worked and smoked virtually nonstop, lost too much weight, and began feeling physically unwell. Finally, as often happens to fire fleers, Ray's body gave out. He had a heart attack. While doctors were treating him for it, they found he also had lung cancer.

Fortunately, both conditions were treatable, but the stress of surgery and chemotherapy finally weakened Ray until he could no longer cling to the shallow levels of his life, which housed his obsessions. He reluctantly attended a cancer support group, where he began noticing and talking about his emotions for the first time in his life. You might as well have thrown him into the heart of a volcano. So much pain erupted into Ray's consciousness that he could barely keep breathing. But he also learned by experience that the emotional anguish of the grieving process is the only way to stop hurting. Once you've sustained any sort of loss in your outer-limit life, the single way out of the ring of fire is through it.

If you characteristically run from feelings or if there are a few awful things in your life that you've never allowed yourself to think about, stop running. In fact, stop doing *anything* for at least a couple of hours a week. Stop smoking, drinking, eating, working, drugging, jogging, cleaning, gossiping, reading—halt all activity that distracts you from your felt experience. Find a compassionate witness who's willing to listen and then *talk about the things in your history and your heart that you least want to talk about.*

By all means, get therapy to help at this point—the talking cure can be a pitfall for story fondlers, but it's a great place for fire fleers. If you can't afford therapy, go to a twelve-step group or a wise friend. Stop distracting yourself with constant doing and verbalize your pain. You'll find that once you're willing to open up, only a few iterations of a story are necessary to burn through those terrible feelings.

Doing the Thing You Think You Cannot Do

The advice I've just given you is the opposite of the usual logic that people adopt when something goes wrong and the flames start licking at their toes. Creating change, causing a ruckus, facing up to bullies, rocking the boat, *taking action* is the last thing story fondlers want to do. Sitting still and feeling grief or fear, while *not moving at all*, is the last thing fire fleers want to do. As Eleanor Roosevelt said, "You must do the thing you think you cannot do." This turns up the heat in the ring of fire so that your limiting beliefs, your outer-limit identities, your mental dungeons burn like tinder.

You may have noticed that every chapter in this book has given you a different approach to the issue of fear. Chapter 1 is about jumping over all the things you're afraid to do by going straight to the end. Chapter 2 has strategies for coping with the lizard fears that are part of your physiological heritage, and Chapter 3 was about dissolving the false beliefs that scare you into feeling trapped. This chapter's instructions about fear are by far the most radical: Instead of skirting it or soothing it or processing it, you might just want to walk right into whatever you fear most. If you're afraid to take a certain action, take it. If you're afraid to feel a certain emotion, feel it. *The only way to the Place beyond Fear is to do the thing you fear most. This is how to surrender to your best destiny.*

Should you choose to accept this option, it will explode huge chunks of your limiting beliefs. It'll incinerate your identity, shock your social circle, hurt like you cannot believe. The advantage of this approach is that in such extreme circumstances, you have the necessary motivation for uniting with your Stargazer self. You're one short step away from more joy, peace, bliss, excitement, and fulfillment than your shallows-obsessed ego can imagine.

Say Yes to the Mess

Since you're old enough to understand language, I'm going to assume you've had at least a few experiences of unexpected physical pain. Maybe you once hit your thumb with a hammer or got stung by a bee or grabbed a pot handle before you realized it was scalding hot. If you look back on such an experience, you'll remember that no matter what you were thinking about when this happened, *all* your attention instantly focused on the pain as soon as it hit you. Whether you were brooding about mortality or composing an ode to long-lost love, in the instant you grabbed that red-hot handle, you let go of all your thoughts and became fully present in the here and now.

That's the brain's reaction to extreme threat or stress: It lets go of perceived time—past and future—and concentrates one hundred per cent of its attention on the present moment. If you've ever been in a car accident or other life-threatening situation, you may have had the odd sense that time slowed down or sped up, that you didn't track time at its normal pace. That's because the part of your brain that handles time sequencing isn't active when you're reacting to an emergency. Likewise, when you "do the thing you think you cannot do" and head straight into the situation you fear most, you'll be so overwhelmed by the experience that you begin detaching from past and future, just focusing on handling what's happening at the moment. At that point, the only thing you have to do to become the Stargazer is to *allow that moment to be, without any resistance whatsoever.*

I call this "saying yes to the mess." It's what I did instinctively when I was skiing in frightening conditions or speaking before thousands of people. I was so scared that I truly believed any slipup would have disastrous consequences, so I absolutely released all thought about any moment but the present one. At the times when I'd experienced relief from emotional suffering, I felt that the unavoidable future was unbearable, so I pulled my attention to the here and now and gave in. What was happening was happening. There was nothing I could do to prevent it, so I stopped resisting.

Life without Time

Twelve-step groups advise members to take life "one day at a time." I find that incredibly ambitious. At my best, I can handle about an hour of life at a time. In the ring of fire, that shrinks to five or ten minutes. And when I'm facing something so scary I have to push fear aside, I can't take life in any time increments at all. I can only handle *now*. You can handle it, too. No matter what's happening at this moment, whether you're dying or grieving or being victimized by terrible injustice, you can handle it. See? You just did. *Now* is over in the time it takes to say the word.

I find that once you're headed into the ring of fire, doing the thing you think you cannot do, just saying the words "I allow this moment to be exactly as it is" will finish the process of surrender and unite you with the Stargazer. You can say this even when you're actively working to make the next moment better (believe me, when you're skiing a steep slope, "allowing this moment to be as it is" includes very high levels of physical activity).

There are several variations of this basic idea that I use as mantras when I'm scared or when I'm in pain (in other words, most of the time) or when I meditate. One that works well for me is what Eckhart Tolle, author of *The Power of Now,* heard during a life-transforming awakening: "Resist nothing." I also like the statement, "There is nothing I need to do now except this," which I shorten to "Just this." You can also use any variation of "yes." "Okay," "All right," "No argument," "This is fine," whatever you like, so long as it conveys the concept of nonresistance to this present moment. Not nonresistance to what might happen tonight at 6:00. Not what will happen in half an hour, ten minutes, one minute from now. *Now.*

The Star Chart

Every time I have managed to eliminate *all* past and future thoughts from my brain and then accept the present moment absolutely, I've experienced the Stargazer's incredible bliss, the feeling I can't possibly describe and you can't possibly imagine unless you've been there yourself. When it occurs in the ring of fire, there's an explosion of joy that permanently destroys large chunks of the mind-dungeons that lock me into unhappiness. But reunion with the Stargazer self doesn't happen just in moments of great pain or alarm; you can also get there by totally dissolving your thoughts or by being totally present, in the absence of any pain.

Hooked up to that brain-mapping computer, I learned that just remembering times of great fear and then repeating my "surrender mantras" brought my anxiety-related beta waves down, down, down. Gradually, this taught me how to calm myself. After all those hours of brain-training, hooked up to the mapmakers' computer, I'm less anxious overall. Considering where I started, that may not be saying a whole hell of a lot, but still, I find it very cool. Much, much cooler than the ring of fire.

The exciting thing about all this is that by constantly surrendering past and future and saying yes to the mess of my life, I may have changed the physical structure of my brain. We social-science groupies who were trained in the twentieth century always believed that the brain was a rigid structure, at least for adults. Now brain maps are showing that we can change our brains by thinking differently. We can literally redraw the map, make it a friendlier, easier, more inviting territory. That's the idea behind every technique I've said will "reunite you with the Stargazer."

If you've come this far, the map of your brain may already be changing. You may have left your old, earthbound routes behind forever. From now on, the strategies you'll learn will help you clarify and then follow your star chart, where something deeper than your mind has already plotted the course of your destiny.

CHAPTER 5

Dreaming Your Star Chart

O nce again, Noah is dreaming of the forest. The bear is back, as he usually is when Noah's worried about his career. The bear has found a beehive hidden in a tree trunk. He's breaking through the wood with his huge paws, ignoring the bees as they defend the hive, slurping up draughts of honey with his long, dexterous tongue.

Then, of course, the Land Rover drives up with all those annoying drunken teenagers. Noah almost runs away, but then, for some reason, he gets into the car with the frat boys, just like he always does. Someone has vomited in the backseat; it smells disgusting. Noah tries to open the door but finds that there's no interior handle. He's stuck in the Pukemobile. The frat boys offer him beer. He takes it because he figures getting a little buzz going might help him tolerate the situation. But before he can take his first swallow, WHAM! Bits of glass smash into Noah's face. He turns to see the bear's massive front feet, its huge claws tearing at the air, destroying the car window.

Noah wakes up in a sweating panic.

This recurring dream has been popping up in Noah's slumber for years—though lately, the storyline is changing. In the past, before he began searching for his right life, Noah's forest dream always ended with his climbing into the Land Rover and driving away with the frat boys to an enormous, loud, disorienting keg party. He always got away from the bear. Certainly, the animal never broke the car window. Noah is unsettled by this part of the dream as he describes it to me.

I'm taking a lot of notes, which is unusual. Ordinarily, my coaching requires watching and listening to the client with all my attention, and writing just distracts me. But Noah has been letting go of many limiting beliefs, burning up in the ring of fire, for some time. He's very close to a clear view of his destiny, though it hasn't fully broken through into his verbal mind.

You'll go through this stage too, if you decide to steer by the light of your own North Star. The earthbound maps of your life, those that were drawn for you by your social circumstances; your parents' hopes; and the status, wealth, or approval needs of your conscious mind, can't possibly contain all the details of your entire destiny. In many cases, these maps will chart a course directly contrary to your happiness. Your conscious mind will be the last part of you to read the map that is drawn for you in the stars.

For this reason, the stage of self-realization I call "mapmaking" usually begins with unusually vivid or unsettling night dreams. In your sleep, you let yourself know things about your future that would never occur to your conscious mind. This is what's happening to Noah. His black-bear dream has been recurring every few nights lately, and it's changing. He's unnerved and unsettled. I'm thrilled. The bear dream has all the signature characteristics of a true "star chart," the Stargazer's innate map of Noah's destiny. Noah is entering the Dreamtime.

Entering the Dreamtime

The indigenous people of Australia believe in two parallel streams of time: the ordinary material world and a metaphysical reality that is actually more real than the world of form. English speakers often call this metaphysical realm the Dreamtime, though indigenous Australians say that "the Dreaming" is a more accurate title, since this state of existence flows infinitely through the present, rendering the notion of "time" nonsensical. (For variety and because I love both terms, I'll use them interchangeably.)

The anthropologist and historian W. H. Stanner described this realm of being as "the Everywhen." A direct translation from the Australian indigenous people calls it the "All-at-Once Time," a convergence of past, present, and future that exists side by side with linear time. We see linear time as objective and the Everywhen of dreaming as a subjective construction of the brain. Indigenous Australians believe the opposite, that reality is "all-at-once," and linear time a mind-construct. You may mock and call this "primitive" if you choose to put your version of objectivity up against that of Albert Einstein, who famously said, "People like us, who believe in physics, understand that the distinction between the past, present, and future is only a stubbornly persistent illusion."

In the traditional wisdom of many premodern cultures, eternity is seen as a time-free zone where things exist in perpetuity while fading and disappearing from the material world. Beings and objects enter and exit the physical world temporarily, like waves forming in water, then fade back into the sea of timelessness. But all these things exist permanently—have always existed—in the Dreaming. And the most obvious paths between the two worlds, as the name implies, are the ones our brains travel while we're asleep.

As you dig through or burn up the various thought-dungeons in your mind, you'll feel a subtle but intensifying change in your inner life. Where you've lived in a world bordered on every side by confining walls, you'll start to glimpse bits of the sky, flashes of starlight. You'll notice this even when you're awake, and it will often come as a surprise. You'll walk into the bar you visit every day after work and think, "What am I doing here? I don't even like this place." Your partner will toss out a passive-aggressive comment, meaning to trigger a fight, but the words will float by without bothering you. You'll get the promotion you've been gunning for, sit down in your new corner office, and suddenly see that corporate America is nothing more than a flimsy stage on which your ego has been playing different roles, and the drama holds no further interest for you.

At the same time, things you've never really noticed become strangely magnetic. A book you had to read in college (and hated at the time) will nudge itself into your awareness, and when you read it again, every word will sink straight into your cells. You'll pass a dance studio that's been on your commute path for years and notice that while you thought you were headed to the supermarket to buy tabloids and Oreos, the dance studio was your real destination from the moment you got in the car.

Symptoms of Dreamtime Progression

During your night dreams, you'll subconsciously unfold your star charts and study them—but your conscious, waking mind (obsessed with its pet lizard and its feverish dungeon-building programme) will see only a jumble of images that make no apparent sense. Your Stargazer self speaks very fluently in the language of the Dreaming, but your waking mind translates your dreams into its own earthbound experience. It's virtually always wrong.

In this chapter, we'll look at a method of dream analysis that can help bring the meaning of your night dreams into conscious awareness. It's interesting any old time, but when you begin breaking through the walls of false ideas and starting steering by starlight, it can be especially valuable. Here's a list of common symptoms that will happen in your waking experience when you reach Dreamtime phases of your life. (If any of these symptoms sound familiar, start keeping a dream journal by your bed, just in case.)

Symptom 1: Decreased Anxiety

Since we all have such energetic inner lizards, the ordinary feeling-state of most human beings is some form of fear. We worry, we fret, we panic—it's a lifestyle! We always think it's situational, that once *this* crisis is averted, once *this* loved one starts behaving, once *this* weight is lost, we can stop feeling such dread and foreboding. One of the most important symptoms of entering the Dreamtime is that *the fear goes away without requiring any situational change.*

Studies have found that people who meditate—in other words, systematically detach from their inner lizards and observe their own thought-stories—don't have "normal" fight-or-flight responses to sudden loud noises such as gunshots. They notice the sound and take appropriate action, but they never get the sinking stomach, racing heart, soaring blood pressure, or frozen brain that afflicts folks operating from fear. Remember, you can't force this kind of calm; pressuring yourself to feel no anxiety merely creates more anxiety. Just be attentive and kind to your own frightened reactions, melt down your false beliefs, or (on a brave day) lean into the ring of fire by doing the scariest thing possible. If you persist, your fear's days are numbered.

Symptom 2: Fading Addictions

Almost all of us use some form of shallows-related distraction to keep us from noticing our pain. Maybe for you it's drugs or alcohol or nachos. Maybe you fill every moment either working or complaining about how much you have to work. Maybe you obsess about your children's lives; what they'll be when they grow up or what they should have been now that they've grown up all wrong. Perhaps romantic love is your addiction, or driving fast, or even organic gardening. None of these is wrong in moderation; in fact, they're all good. But *even good things, when used to distract us from our pain without investigating and dissolving the cause of that pain, will glue us to the shallows of our lives and keep us off the path of our best destinies.*

A telltale sign of reaching the Dreaming, then, is that your old habits and compulsions lose their zing. This can be conscious and triumphant, as when you attend your first AA meeting and deny the demon rum forever. But it's usually slow, sometimes almost imperceptible. Obsession turns to ordinariness and then to boredom. One of my clients who dealt with the first half of his life almost exclusively by staying stoned on marijuana remembers looking at the smoldering joint in his hand and saying, to his own vast surprise, "I'm sorry, Mary Jane. I haven't been attracted to you for a long time." He felt bad about it for the joint's sake, he told me. "I'm sure it hurt her feelings, but it had to be said." He gave the joint to a friend and never had any interest in smoking pot again.

Symptom 3: Decreased Tolerance for Social Façades

People who've burned up a considerable number of limiting beliefs often get excited about their newfound freedom and lightness. Many of my clients are eager to share their insights with their families of origin. "I can't wait to tell Mom and cousin Buck and my sister Petunia about this!" they exult just before heading to the yearly family reunion. "I'm going to explain that they've been trapped by their own thoughts. Once they get it, we'll all be so much healthier, and we'll finally be able to bond!"

These people invariably return from their reunions wearing the expression of a bird that has just flown full-speed into a plate-glass door.

"They, uh, weren't interested," the clients tell me.

This is a nice way of saying that when they questioned the family's usual thought and behavior patterns ("Gee, Dad, you sure have a lot of unrealistic fears. Would you like me to help you examine your belief system?"), their families reacted as if they'd announced, "I have genital herpes, and I want to share it with each and every one of you!" False beliefs are almost always shaped by socialization, and the people who socialized you—not only your family but anyone who matches them in attitudes or demographics—are likely to treasure most the very false assumptions you've found most damaging. They'll want to keep the old ways going.

You will find that this becomes harder and harder to enjoy, and one day, you simply won't be able to play your old role in the familiar group drama. Your mother will launch a timeworn speech about her difficult second marriage, and instead of cooing over her, you'll just keep reading a magazine. Your sister, shocked, will whisper, "Aren't you even one bit concerned about poor Mom?" And you'll say, without any rancor or hidden agenda, "No, not particularly."

This kind of faux pas—recognizing the scene, knowing your lines, and blurting out the truth instead—is a sure sign that you're beginning to steer by starlight. There's no anger involved; the truth just slips into the space where you know the polite lie should go. Or you may catch yourself on the verge of speaking honestly, then push your true self back in line and force yourself to mouth the "courteous" falsehood. You'll be surprised how poisonous this starts to feel. You'll begin experiencing it as affliction. The less attached you are to the shallow region in which others are operating, the more alienated you'll be, and the less you'll fit in. All of which contributes to . . .

Symptom 4: The Empty Elevator

"I've got no friends left," says Alicia mournfully. "I used to spend all day on the phone. Now, none of my old friends call me much."

"Do you ever call them?" I ask.

Alicia thinks for a while. "No," she says. "There's no one I want to call."

"Why not?"

"I don't know," she says, brow furrowing. "They just don't get me any more. Honestly, I find them kind of boring. I mean, I love them to pieces, but . . ."

Alicia has entered what I call the "empty elevator." If an elevator door opens and it's crowded with people, small children will often try to run aboard anyway. This can't work; the elevator has to empty before it can take on a new load of passengers. When you dissolve the false beliefs that once held you prisoner, people around you can't stay connected with both the New You and their old patterns of behavior. Without meaning for it to happen, you may find that many of your relationships simultaneously fall away, leaving a space for new loved ones you haven't yet encountered. The elevator is going up a level. For a little while, you have to ride it alone, or nearly so.

Alicia, for example, just couldn't keep reciting lines in the familiar scenes of her life, with her old familiar characters. When loved ones called to initiate the drama, Alicia would feel as though she were watching reruns on TV. She could join the soap opera again, but it would mean deserting her own truth, and that was no longer an option for Alicia. When her mother called to say, "Marjorie is out of control! Do you know she refuses to go to PTA meetings?" Alicia knew that her line was, "I just don't know why Marjorie is so selfish." But what she said was, "So?"

As long as Alicia continues to connect with her deep self, her loved ones will find conversations with her increasingly unsatisfying, then threatening. They'll sense that they have to choose to either join Alicia's process by questioning their own thinking or move away from her psychologically and emotionally. Most people—in Alicia's life and in yours—will choose to stay where they are and let you move on. You can hardly blame them, since you know how daunting thought-dungeons can seem. Digging out is hard work—and why in the name of all that's holy would any sane person follow you into the ring of fire?

So Alicia's loved ones will drop out of her daily life, freeing up her time and leaving her mind more spacious. "I don't know what's wrong with her," they'll say to one another. "She used to be so hip [or fun or smart or reasonable], but now she's just weird [or serious or silly or irrational]." They may enjoy many more years of their familiar soap opera. Meanwhile, Alicia will escape the dungeon and begin steering her life toward her own North Star.

Wonderful things will happen along the way, and she won't find herself alone. Quite the opposite. From the Stargazer's perspective, she'll realize that no matter how distant her loved ones may seem, it's impossible for her not to be intimately connected with everyone she apparently "left behind."

Symptom 5: The Affection Connection

When you first experience it, this is the most startling and unfamiliar symptom of entering the Dreamtime. Actually, "affection connection" is much too tame a phrase to describe it—but so is every other phrase. As the Stargazer, you see that you are absolutely continuous with the rest of creation. You therefore love everything as yourself and have no doubt, none whatsoever, that you are infinitely loved in return by the entirety of which you are a part.

Many of the most articulate folks in history have tried and failed to describe this, often sounding almost frustrated. "Why callest thou me good?" Jesus said in the King James translation of Mark 10:18. "There is no one good save One, that is God." In Sunday school, I was always told that Jesus was being humble, deflecting praise onto a humanesque narcissistic God, who stood in his heavenly abode wearing very excellent sandals and approving of Jesus' self-effacement. Now, as a grizzled apostate, I believe Jesus meant, "You can't separate me from the single, unified thing that is God—the only thing that exists and the only thing that I am or that you are." It seems Jesus' followers were a little slow about this one. "God is love!" Jesus kept protesting. "God is within your hearts! God is all, and all is one, and you are one with God! I mean, Me H. Christ, stop gazing at my navel and start gazing at *everything*!"

This same set of ideas emerges from the writings of mystics from virtually everyplace, at any point in history. Scan a thousand such accounts, from a thousand cultures, in a thousand dialects, and you'll hear one voice singing one song. Centuries before Jesus, Chuang-Tzu wrote, "The universe is the unity of all things. If one recognizes his unity with all things, then . . . death and life, end and beginning, disturb his tranquility no more than the succession of day and night." In the thirteenth-century Middle East, the Sufi mystic Rumi described it like this:

> *I am the life of life,*
>
> *I am that cat, this stone, no one . . .*
>
> *I see and know all times and all worlds,*
>
> *as one, one, always one.*

Five hundred years later, Walt Whitman penned a description of the core of peace that would shock my Sunday school teachers to the toes of their crepe-soled shoes:

> *And I know that the hand of God is the promise of my own,*
>
> *And I know that the spirit of God is the brother of my own,*
>
> *And that all the men ever born are also my brothers,*
> *and the women my sisters and lovers . . .*

What causes this sensation of ecstatic oneness? Is it a meaningless neurological spasm, as many scientists believe? Or have mystics stumbled across a reality that eludes normal experience? We'll talk more about this later, but here's the short answer I suspect you'll agree with once you feel the core of peace for yourself:

Who cares?

How to Fully Enjoy Losing Touch with Reality

When Noah began dreaming his forest dream every night, he'd experienced all the waking-life "symptoms" I've just described. He first consulted me when he developed severe insomnia. It seemed likely that his sleeplessness was connected to the stress of his job as a police officer. Noah was one of the most idealistic humans you could hope to meet, an absolutely committed "good cop" who'd set out to make the world a place of kindness and justice. This left him ill prepared to spend most of his time cleaning up the nasty messes created by the *least* idealistic humans you could hope *not* to meet.

"It's demoralizing," he told me during our first appointment. "Sickening. I've taken children away from parents who had beaten them, maimed them, used them for sex. I've seen kids steal shoes from a murder victim they found on the street. Once my partner and I tackled this couple who were waving knives at each other. We got them both calmed down. A week later, they killed a convenience-store clerk for cigarette money."

"Wow," I said. "Well, let's find a place where your heart can get some rest."

There was a long silence. Then Noah said in his stiff, formal, cop voice, "Ma'am, I believe if I were a woman, I'd be crying now."

It was one of the high points of my coaching career.

So Noah let go of the shallows and leaped into the ring of fire. He took a leave from his job and started dissolving the terrible "truths" he'd come to believe in his worst moments. There came a time when, macho man though he was, Noah wept for his lost idealism and raged at the people who had demolished it. Because he'd witnessed such horrors, suffering pushed him at rocket speed right into the core of peace. He felt more and more continuous with the rest of reality, an ephemeral wave in an infinitely benevolent sea. Noah had entered the Dreamtime.

Apparently, this is not something your typical cop chats about with his partner during a stakeout. Noah was befuddled and scared by all that limitlessness, all that joy. So, briefly, he scrambled back to the shallows. He returned to his job and focused his leisure hours on manly things like rebuilding car engines and going bowling with his girlfriend. Anyway, his insomnia seemed to be cured; he slept long and hard almost every night . . . until he started to dream of the forest.

The process Noah had started didn't want to stop. Since he was no longer moving toward the Dreaming, the Dreaming moved toward him.

Analyze This!

Vivid night dreams often accompany the waking transitions that occur as you begin to emerge from your dungeon of thoughts. Writing them down as soon as you awaken will give you a star chart, a map of the next steps toward your destiny—but the map is drawn in symbols the waking mind won't understand. I've never analyzed a dream of my own that didn't turn out to have useful information I'd missed entirely before the analysis. What's more, decoding the dream message, because it comes from your own core self, packs a powerful psychological punch. So now I'd like you to learn the method of dream analysis that's been most effective for me and my clients.

I agree with science that dreams are probably produced by the brain as it synthesizes data it's accumulated during the day. I don't believe that dream objects always symbolize the same thing. For example, I disagree with Freud's assertion that snakes or skyscrapers—or for that matter, anything longer than it is wide—are necessarily phallic symbols. Sigmund seems to have been a tad preoccupied by everything going on inside his underwear, but perhaps you are less so. When you dream of snakes, it might be because of an Animal Planet snake-wrangler who reminds you of your jolly uncle: Dream-Snake symbolizes Uncle Bob. When I dream of snakes, I might be thinking about hiking through the desert: Dream-Snake symbolizes Danger.

On the other hand, I don't completely buy into the idea that dreams are simply brain chaos. I've had precognitive dreams myself—night dreams that later came true in the real world—so it would be disingenuous for me to reject all claims that dreams may sometimes be a conduit to the Dreamtime. Whether your dreams are just data processing or messages from the Force, analysis often reveals knowledge you've been holding just outside consciousness or a message that has profound insights for your waking self.

Dream Analysis, Step 1: Keep a Dream Journal

We all dream. Even hibernating animals periodically raise their body temperatures—at a high energy cost—enough to create dream states. However, most of us forget the majority of our dreams. Keeping a dream journal right by your bed is the best way to remember dreams, even if you think you aren't having them. If you do remember a dream when you wake up, write it down immediately. Be as detailed as you can, because even if the dream is intense, you'll probably forget it. I used to wake up in the middle of the night, thinking, "Boy, I'll never forget that!" and write a few key words down on a notepad. In the morning, I'd have no idea what made me scribble "Bus stop peanut butter shoes!" or "Fuzzy bagpipes. Lady Bird Johnson?" in my dream journal.

Dream Analysis, Step 2: Act Out All the Parts

My dream analysis technique is based on the theory of Carl Jung, Freud's wacky, mystical renegade disciple. Jung believed that every part of a dream represents some aspect of the self that has been "split off" from consciousness, and he often used role-playing to help unify the self. To analyze a dream, you "play the part" of every symbol in that dream. You must *become* the symbol; *think, act, and express yourself as the symbol, not the dreamer.*

For example, one night, my client Jessica, who was on leave from being a field medic in Iraq, dreamed she'd gone fishing and was attacked by a purple sea monster. "I think it means I shouldn't go fishing with my dad next week," she said. This seemed logical, but I didn't see it ringing Jessica's chimes the way an accurate dream interpretation does. To find out what the symbol meant from her Stargazer's perspective, she had to *become* the sea monster and speak with its voice.

Jessica initially resisted doing this because it seemed silly. You'll probably feel the same way about "becoming" the symbols in your dreams. But if you can push past this resistance and actually do the exercise, you'll learn much, much more about your destiny than if you insist on analyzing the Dreaming only from the position of your material mind.

"Okay, I'm supposed to *be* the sea monster in my dream," Jessica said. "It was sort of—"

"Stop," I interrupted. "If you want this to work, you have to say *I am*. You have to *be* the sea monster."

Jessica rolled her eyes but complied. "Okay. I'm the sea monster. I'm scary and elusive. I come from a dark, cold place. I want to destroy everything in the—wait a second! I know what I am! I'm Osama bin Laden!" Jessica's jaw dropped, and I knew she'd understood the symbol accurately.

"That's so weird!" said Jessica. "I don't know what to make of it."

"Let's work with some aspects of the sea monster," I said. "Be purple. Be the colour of the monster and describe yourself."

"Uh, okay." Jessica was more willing to play along now. "I am purple, the colour of the sea monster in Jessica's dream. I am dark, like coagulated blood. I'm what's left when tragedy has struck—Oh, my God! I'm like the stains on Bobby's boots! I'm sadness. I'm loss."

Jessica started to cry as she remembered a soldier she'd befriended in Iraq. He sustained a disabling head wound, which effectively ended his life as Bobby. Jessica had seen his boots spattered with blood and brain matter, and in her mind, that image became everything terrible about war.

"So in your dream," I said, "Osama bin Laden, the monster, is the colour of grief and loss."

Jessica looked thunderstruck. As she absorbed this, the dream opened her mind to a shocking insight: She had something in common with one of the worst mass murderers in history. Her anguish about Bobby was so great that Jessica might have channeled it into overwhelming hostility, as Bin Laden did. Her other option was to acknowledge and accept the damaged part of her own psyche until she finished the grieving process, burned up all her disproven concepts in the ring of fire, and arrived at her core of peace. Jessica suddenly knew that the potential for evil existed in her as it did in her worst enemy.

After analyzing this dream, she had to cope with the knowledge (very strange to her mind) that in the Dreaming, she and her enemy were alike, connected by their common capacity to choose good or evil. It was a message from the Stargazer, the only force in the human psyche that genuinely makes peace.

It's impossible to convey the power of a dream analysis like this if you're not the dreamer. Because the symbols are so deeply rooted in your subconscious mind, and because the feeling of the dream is so much more intense than words can describe, simply reading another person's dream analysis is interesting but not earthshaking. Many of my clients (not to mention myself) have experienced major psychological breakthroughs after analyzing a single dream. It doesn't always happen, but it can.

Jessica's sea-monster dream analysis was one of these life-changing insights. This small, seemingly meaningless dream, once it made the jump to her conscious mind, changed Jessica permanently. She became gentler, wiser, more compassionate. She turned into the kind of soldier who goes to war not with the naïve enthusiasm of a child playing a video game, nor with the blind rage of a revenge killer, but with thoughtful, genuinely noble intentions. She realized that she couldn't create peace in the world if her inner life was a place of hatred and war. On the other hand, by healing herself, she would become a source of peace in the world. In the material world, Jessica was primarily a soldier. In the Dreaming, she was first and foremost a healer.

Dream Analysis, Step 3: Fill Out the Form for Dream Analysis

Reading about Jessica's dream won't have the same effect on you that having it did on Jessica, because her Stargazer consciousness created it especially for her. Likewise, your dreams are designed specifically for you. To help you get the most from dream analysis, I've created a form you can either check as a reference or photocopy and use as a template until analyzing your own dreams becomes second nature. (You can also download this form at marthabeck.com.) Once you've written down a dream in your journal, you can use this form to get the message from your Stargazer self.

First, make a list of every object, action, person, or place in your dream. These are your symbols. You have to fill out an entire form for each symbol, which can take some time with long dreams, but it's well worth it. One by one, write each symbol in the appropriate space on a form. Then "become" the first symbol and answer the questions *as the symbol, not as yourself.* If you think of a symbol as "it," you won't get a useful analysis. You must think of it as "I." Sometimes you'll get a rush of answers, sometimes very few. *Don't force or think about the answers. Just write down whatever occurs to you.*

Form for Dream Analysis

After writing as much as you remember about a dream in your journal, list each object, person, place, or compelling image in the dream. Then, process each symbol on your list by answering the questions below as they relate to that symbol.

Symbol #1: (For example, Noah's symbols include "the forest" and "the bear.") _____

_____

As Symbol #1, write down three adjectives or phrases that describe you. (Noah's examples: "I, the forest, am dark, fertile, and mysterious" or "I, the bear, am strong, curious, and invulnerable to harm.")

First descriptive word or phrase: _____

Second descriptive word or phrase: _____

Third descriptive word or phrase: _____

As Symbol #1, please answer these questions with whatever comes to mind.

QUESTION: What is your purpose, Symbol #1? (For example, the forest in Noah's dream might answer, "I am here to give shelter and permit life to thrive." The bear might say, "I am meant to find honey and protect my cubs.")

Your purpose as Symbol #1: _____
_____
_____
_____

QUESTION: As Symbol #1, how are you trying to help the dreamer? (For example, the forest might say, "I am trying to give Noah shelter and a place to hide his vulnerability until he is strong enough to act on his own behalf.")

How you, as Symbol #1, are trying to help the person dreaming: _____
_____
_____
_____
_____

As Symbol #1, do you know what aspect of the dreamer's waking life you symbolize? If so, write it here. (For example, Noah's forest represented his life as a whole. The bear symbolized his heart, which became clear when Noah analyzed the symbol of honey and found that it represented love.) _____
_____
_____

Repeat this process for each symbol in your dream.

If you have a short dream, a dream fragment, or a dream symbol that doesn't want to "describe itself," you can use the analysis form above on any *aspect* of the symbol, such as its colour or shape. (For example, "I am the purple colour of the sea monster" or "I am the sound of the monster roaring.")

Dream Analysis, Step 4:
Retell the Dream with the Symbols "Unveiled"

Once you've done the analysis for each symbol in the dream, rewrite the description of the dream in your journal. This time, replace each symbol in the dream with the thing that symbol represents. For example, when Jessica "became" the symbol "fishing," she described herself this way: "I am fishing. I am something wonderful and fun that Jessica does with her loved ones. I am *family*." So, when she retold her dream, instead of saying, "I went fishing with my dad and a purple sea monster attacked us," she said, "I was enjoying life with my family until the grief and loss of Bobby's injury made me feel disconnected from everyone."

Because it helps to have more than one example, the descriptions below will show you Noah's black-bear dream as he wrote it down at first and as he rewrote it once he'd decoded each symbol individually. The symbols he chose to "decode" and the interpretations he got when he "became" each symbol appear in bold type. Please read through both versions carefully to get a feel for the way new interpretations come to light as the symbols from the Stargazer are translated, one by one, into the pedestrian, earthbound language of the conscious mind.

Noah's Dream (as in Journal)

I'm in the **forest**. There's a big **bear** trying to eat **honey** from a **beehive**, but it's hard to get the honey out of the **tree trunk**, and the **bees** are stinging him. I feel like helping the bear, but then a **Land Rover** drives up. Several **young men** are inside. They annoy me, and I want to run away, but instead I get in the car. The boys are drinking **beer**, and somebody **threw up**. The **smell of vomit** is disgusting. I try to get out, but there's no **inner handle** on the **car door**. The boys offer me beer, and I'm about to drink it, but I turn around to see that the bear is smashing the car **window**. I wake up scared.

Noah's Dream (interpreted)

I'm in my **life (the forest)**. My **heart (the bear)** is trying to get **love (honey)** from my **childhood (the beehive)**, but it's hard to get **love** out of **my father (the tree trunk)**, and **my mother's criticism (the bees)** is stinging my heart. I feel like helping my heart, but then **my role as an adult man, the hard, cold shell I adopt to be masculine (the Land Rover)**, arrives. Several **versions of masculinity (the frat boys)** are inside. They annoy me, and I want to run away, but instead I get into **the hard shell of my masculine role (Land Rover)**. The versions of masculinity are drinking **a potion to make them feel numb so that they won't need anything (beer)**, and **part of me (one of the frat boys)** got sick from the poison of the role. The **beliefs my mind threw up, like "a real man never cries" (the vomit)**, are disgusting. I try to get out, but there's no **implement for leaving my hard shell (handle)** on **the armour I've closed around myself (the car door)**. The **different versions of masculinity (frat boys)** offer me **numbness (beer)**, and I'm about to take it in, but I turn around to see that my **heart (the bear)** is smashing **the shell I've put up around me (the Land Rover window)**. It scares me, but it's actually coming to rescue me and help me learn to live safely and powerfully in **the place where my heart was meant to be (the forest, my right life)**.

Dream Analysis, Step 5: Let It Stew

As you can see, Noah's dream was really about his heart (the bear) breaking through the hard shell of machismo (the Land Rover) in which Noah was trapped. He had no conscious idea that this was the dream's message until he decoded each symbol and retold the dream.

This is more art than science. I've done interpretations of short dreams that ran to many pages of decoding, and I was never sure that I was "doing it right." But even a rough analysis can bring powerful messages from your core of peace. You'll be amazed at the economy of the Dreaming, how it packs a huge amount of intellectual and emotional meaning into a brief, strange story. *Generally, the more frightening or upsetting the dream, the more healing the analysis will be.* (This is because nightmares bring together deeply fragmented aspects of your true self and burn up a lot of scary beliefs in the ring of fire.)

If your analysis seems to make no sense, just let it stew a bit. Write down the interpretation and then let it go. Very often, this starts the process of decoding in your brain, and when you're least expecting it, an insight from the dream will burst into consciousness like a name you had trouble remembering. For example, Noah initially couldn't figure out what the bear meant. He struggled to understand it, then let it go and went on to other symbols. A few minutes later, he burst out laughing.

"I know what the bear is!" he said. "I'm the bear, and I'm Noah's heart, and I'm stronger than all those guys in the car put together! I love the forest—it's my home! I want Noah to come live in it and eat honey all day long!" He kept laughing off and on for the rest of our session. Not long afterward, he resigned from the police force and became—really—a forest ranger. He's married now, happier and more relaxed than at any other time in his life. He spends most of his time protecting habitat and wildlife and has a special, respectful fondness for bears.

When the Dreamtime Invades the Daytime

Most dreams don't come true as literally as Noah's. Jessica, for example, is unlikely to meet a real purple sea monster on her next rotation in Iraq. But like Carl Jung, I've seen enough correspondence between the Dreamtime and the daytime to convince me that sometimes, night visions are more than just interesting brain-burps.

Jung believed in something called "big dreams," which he thought intersected with the real world. On one famous occasion, a patient told Jung he'd dreamed of a large scarab beetle. As they were talking about what it might symbolize, they heard a tapping sound at the window, and a large scarab beetle flew into the room. Jung called such events synchronicity. You can call them coincidence, if you prefer. But if you're like most people who begin steering by starlight, you'll find such coincidences happening to you more and more often. As you get closer to aligning with your Stargazer self, the map of your waking life often becomes so full of "coincidences" that material reality begins to seem as improbable as the Dreaming.

I'll give you an example from my own life because that way, I can be sure the story is neither invented nor exaggerated. I spent the last half of my twenties doing psychological work, burning up innumerable belief structures that had trapped me in a life I didn't want. One thing I dropped was my chosen career. As a faculty brat, I'd always assumed that I'd become a professor. I spent many years and many, *many* dollars getting a doctoral degree. But when my fellow graduate students at Harvard went to give "job talks," or when my professors urged me to publish my term papers in academic journals, I'd laugh and say, "Oh, I'm not going to be a sociologist. I'm just learning social science so I can write self-help books and live in my pajamas."

I thought I was joking, but in fact, I never did go out to give job talks, nor did I submit those papers to journals. I really did want to write for a popular audience. This was a directive from my Stargazer self, mapped out clearly on its star charts all along. But even when I said the truth right out loud, I didn't let myself embrace it—or even fully know it—because in the region of the shallows known as the Ivy League, writing self-help books is about six notches below pole dancing on the scale of respectable professions.

In my early thirties, I quit my job as an assistant professor and began querying literary agents and editors, trying to get my writing published. I'd fielded all sorts of negative feedback on my academic writing with nary a qualm, since I really didn't care about it. But every time my creative writing got a "No" from yet another agent, it felt like being gutted with a dull stick.

Each day, I went further and further out on a career limb where I had no colleagues, no mentors, no encouraging hints, nothing but: "Dear author, We regret to inform you that your writing does not fit our list; in fact, we hate it so much we've taken out a restraining order forbidding you to come within fifty feet of a word-processing program, a pen, or even a crayon."

Okay, I made up that last clause. But it was always implied.

One day, when I was about ready to give up on writing, I was suddenly seized by an obsessive desire to write screenplays. It hit me so hard I literally burst into tears of longing. I rushed to the library to look for a book on screenplay composition. There, on the bulletin board at the library, I saw it: a sign-up sheet for a new screenwriting group! My hands shook as I wrote down the address and meeting time.

If you're thinking (as I did) that my destiny lay in screenwriting, you're wrong. The ways of the Dreaming are usually indirect, rarely obvious. My screenwriting fever lasted exactly long enough to get me to the first—and, as it turned out, the last—meeting of that group. Four people showed up, including me. Two of them (who already knew one another) appeared to have recently escaped from some kind of high-security asylum. They smelled strange and talked incoherently about how cinematic reality was the only place where they could express their true selves, by staging depictions of mass decapitation. But the third person—a woman named Dawn— was a lot like me: a hopeful, ridiculously persistent wannabe book writer. Moreover, she lived less than a mile from my house. My screenwriting urge left as suddenly and absolutely as it had overwhelmed me. But Dawn became my first writing buddy.

That was Dreamlike Event #1. Dreamlike Event #2 followed soon there-after, when I attended a book signing in the wistful hope that it might motivate me. I don't remember anything about the reading except that throughout the whole thing, I really, really had to pee. When the presenta-tion was over, I rushed to the restroom. It was out of order. Aagh! I sprinted for my car, headed home. But weirdly, something seemed to be resisting me. It was like running through a combination of quicksand and a high headwind—something literally seemed to want my body to turn around and go back into the building.

"There's someone you have to meet," said the Force—not in words but in *feeling*.

"Gotta go," I said, climbing into my car.

"No! Turn back! There's someone you have to meet!"

"Listen," I told the Force, "you clearly don't understand these things, being a mysterious disembodied entity and all, but *I really have to pee.*"

All the way home, I wanted to turn the car around. I was seized by a terrible sadness, as though I'd lost a loved one. I had no idea what the feeling meant. But it remained with me until two days later, when I was having coffee with a friend, and a woman with merry brown eyes sat down beside us. "I know you!" she said. "I'm Annette. I saw you at the signing the other night." I felt a rush of intense relief, as though I'd been let out of an emotional chokehold. This, I somehow knew, was the woman I was supposed to meet. She mentioned she was working on a novel. Annette became my second writing buddy and one of my life's all-time dearest friends.

Not long after this, Dawn and I decided to form our own four-person writing group. We agreed that I would recruit Annette, and Dawn would bring another novelist friend of hers, Thora. The night before our first meeting, I had a brief but very powerful dream. I found myself in the Arizona desert near a Navajo hogan. Standing before me was a beautiful old woman, dressed in the flowing velvet skirt and turquoise jewelry favored by her tribe. Her intense brown eyes gazed at me from a soft, weather-beaten face. She spoke a single word. I didn't quite catch it, so the old woman repeated the word twice.

"Dineh. Dineh."

I remembered that in Navajo, *dineh* (pronounced din-*ay*) means "the people." It's the name the Navajo use to refer to themselves. The old woman seemed to know that I'd figured this out, because she gave a barely perceptible nod. Then she took my hand, turned the palm up, and pressed an object into it. It was a stylized butterfly carved from blue stone.

"*Dineh*," she said one more time, curling my fist around the stone.

Then I woke up.

I wrote the dream down, then forgot about it—until I arrived at our first writing-group meeting and met Dawn's friend Thora. Then I almost jumped backward with surprise: Thora was the woman from my dream. Though she wasn't Navajo, she had the medicine woman's face, her regal bearing, brown eyes, and olive skin. I tried not to stare as we sat down, exchanged some small talk, and began reading one another's pages. But I kept sneaking astonished peeks at Thora. She didn't just look *like* the Navajo woman: *It was the same face.*

Then it was my turn to get feedback on my writing, and I stopped thinking about dreams. My pride was about to undergo a spanking it hadn't had in all my years at Harvard.

"Why do you write like such a prig?" said Thora, my newest acquaintance. "What's with all the five dollar words? This is boring."

I felt myself bristle. Once upon a time, I'd written in simple, direct prose. But in graduate school, this had proven to be the equivalent of exposing my tender tummy to a pride of ravenous lions. My professors mocked my "literary" style and taught me to write social-scientese, like this: "The paradoxical role-definition-in-praxis of de facto proletariat existence does not, in fact, lead to Marx's ideal of the superfluous and ultimately withered state, nor the differentiated pragmatism of Weberian functionalism, but to the blah blah blah blah blah."

I thought I'd stepped this style way down for the book I was writing, but my three friends didn't agree.

"It is pretty abstruse," said Annette, "and I'm a fan of five dollar words."

"Like abstruse," grumbled Thora.

Now I was beyond bristly and into angry. "Listen," I said, "I'm writing nonfiction, not a novel. It has to sound reasonably competent."

Dawn jumped in, playing the diplomat. "Martha, it's just like my twin sister Denae was telling me. You have to use language your audience will enjoy."

I stared at her. "Your twin sister who?"

"Denae." She pronounced it *dineh*. The word, combined with Thora's familiar face, brought my dream back so forcefully I forgot to stay in defense mode.

"You guys, this is so weird . . . " I said.

And I told them about my dream.

When I got to the part about the blue stone butterfly, Annette began to laugh. She reached into her commodious designer bag and pulled out—I kid you not—a small butterfly carved from dark blue lapis lazuli stone. She put it in my hand and closed my fingers around it.

"Write to the people," she said. "Not to your critics at Harvard. The people. *Dineh. Dineh.*"

So this humble person went home, ate a massive portion of crow, and started trying to write like a human being again. Which is the only reason you are reading this now. As you take in these words, your mind becomes interwoven with the tapestry of my life. We are standing on either side of a night vision that led me to meet you here, on this page. Your attention, in this moment, is the continued unfolding of my Dreaming.

How can I not believe in magic?

Off the Known Charts, onto the Star Charts

Speaking of writing for reasons other than impressing Ivy League intellectuals, I am now going to get disreputably free about using M-words like *magic*, *mysticism*, and *miracles*. When I see people's psychological obstacles fall away, and they begin experiencing the Dreaming in broad daylight, I'm at a loss to find more accurate terms. As I've said, I don't technically believe in magic or miracles; I think everything has a rational explanation. It's just that I've seen many, many events that lie outside the bounds scientific knowledge can explain at the present time. There's a very high probability that you, too, will begin experiencing such things as you begin receiving the map of your future, the Stargazer's carefully drawn chart of your best destiny.

Our culture—which denies anything it can't explicate in purely material terms—has given you very few tools for understanding the part of you that lives, experiences, and creates in the Dreaming. Other cultures have gone much further and developed much more useful techniques for dealing with the mystical forces and experiences that help us become conscious of destiny. Until now, almost everything you've read in this book has at least some sort of rationalist justification. For the next few chapters, we're going off those particular charts. I won't ask you to share any of the speculations in the upcoming pages, but I will ask you to suspend disbelief just long enough to check and see if the ideas and procedures work for you. If they do, you'll enter the truly astonishing part of claiming your right life. You'll become the Mapmaker who draws charts for your future, steering purely by starlight. Brackets up, please! It's time to do some magic.

CHAPTER 6

North Star
Mapmaking

Last summer, my friend Logan, gifted massage therapist, yogi, and all-around radiant human being, gave me a recording of a guided meditation called Yoga Nidra, which I believe is Sanskrit for "instructions that aren't supposed to make you fall asleep but invariably do." This is my kind of yoga; the most physically challenging part of it requires sitting with your hands on your face. After that, to my great relief, you get to lie down. "Form the clear intention to remain conscious," the instructor on the tape says. So I form just such an intention and then plunge immediately into a depth of unconsciousness rarely observed in organisms capable of voluntary motion.

It took me about fifty Yoga Nidra sessions to stay awake through the entire recording. Nevertheless, I persisted. This was not because of diligence or commitment but because the dreams I had when I fell asleep to Yoga Nidra were absolutely fabulous. They were boring to talk about, just reruns of my everyday life. I'd dream about doing errands, walking the dogs, eating.

But these ordinary situations had an extraordinary quality. Everything in them—the errands, the dog, the food—was incredibly vivid. Colours glowed so intensely that in my dreams, the desert dust and cacti looked like a carpet of opals strewn with emeralds. Flowers were almost too beautiful to look at; if I hadn't been dreaming, I think they would have made me faint. Please don't ask me to talk about how dazzling *people* appeared in these dreams, because it makes me cry.

For several weeks, I looked forward to my nightly Yoga Nidra dreams the way I imagine an LSD addict must anticipate a really good trip. Then one morning, as I was driving along wide awake, I caught a glimpse of some distant mountains, and for a moment the receding rows of peaks glowed like amethysts. Then they went back to their usual flat lavender, which was pretty enough for me, thank you. But all that day, everything flickered in and out of the crazy, delirious, juicy colours of my Yoga Nidra world.

I became concerned. Was this supposed to happen? Was my intense enjoyment of Yoga Nidra a bit beyond the healthy zone? Did falling asleep when I wasn't supposed to mean I was over-Nidracating myself?

I asked Logan, but all he said was, "Cool."

One day, I was pondering this issue when I got an unexpected call from a casual acquaintance I'll call Pam, who told me she'd just given me a quick buzz to say howdy. We chatted for a few minutes about this and that; I told her I was doing a little yoga, but I didn't tell her what kind, and I didn't mention my strange dreams. Then, as we were saying our good-byes, she said the strangest thing. "You know what I think?" she said. "I think the world you've started visiting at night *is* the real world."

Then she hung up.

This is the kind of thing that starts to happen when you're steering by starlight. Honest to God, after a while, you'll start to take it for granted. When all the detritus of your thought-dungeons is gone, when your inner lizard is napping and your social self has detached from anyone poisonous to your soul, your life starts taking excursions you never expected, setting its course to places you wouldn't imagine in a million years. The map of this adventure is what I've been calling your "star chart."

Making a Star Chart

We saw in the last chapter how, as your consciousness becomes ever more closely aligned with the Stargazer, dreaming grows more intense, in a way that informs your life—but living also becomes more intense, in a way that informs your dreams. Charting the path determined by your own North Star resembles dreaming more than it does thinking. However, the "dream state" you must access to feel out the future heightens consciousness rather than diminishing it. This can be so intense and strange that it's a little scary. People (like Pam) show up in startling ways. Obstacles you thought insuperable may change or vanish as you approach. Just when you're wondering how to cross a stretch of difficult terrain, you'll discover you can fly.

I meant that last sentence metaphorically, of course.

I think.

The plain fact is that human beings are far more magical than most of us allow ourselves to believe, and at this point in my life, I'm not sure how far our mystical abilities can go. I do know that you can't fulfill your best destiny without experiencing your own magical side. I think that's why books like *Lord of the Rings* and the *Harry Potter* series have been so wildly popular; something in millions of people resonates—intensely, ecstatically, even obsessively—to the idea that we can educate ourselves to utilize metaphysical abilities. When *Harry Potter* hit the shelves, the young wizard found millions upon millions of readers, in all age groups, who'd been wishing they could go someplace like Hogwarts.

Unfortunately, whatever your mystical talents, you certainly didn't learn to manage them in school. Instead, you were repeatedly taught to deny their existence. Nor are you likely to have learned any practical magic from religion, where only the anointed few are supposed to work miracles and working them yourself can get you excommunicated, sometimes with firearms.

So this chapter contains instructions to connect you with whatever level of mystical talent you may have. If you're a skeptic, treat it as a straightforward placebo effect: It works just fine that way. If you're of a mystical bent, that's fine, too. Either way, the practices in this chapter can bring some wondrous experiences your way. You won't just be steering by the light of the stars. You'll be flying between them.

Caveat Magus

Before we go any further, I must tell you another story I heard from a reputable source, who assured me it was true. It concerns a young Tibetan monk whose teacher fled the Chinese invasion, leaving the monk to seek enlightenment on his own. Not long after his teacher's departure, the young monk started having all sorts of wild experiences: visions, astral travel, premonitions of the future. He was even more stunned by this than I was by my Yoga Nidra dreams, and like me, he decided to get some advice.

Not having a phone, the young monk set out to find his master on foot, walking from his monastery in the Himalayas in the general direction of Nepal. He trudged over impossibly tall mountain ridges and through steaming jungles, across raging torrents and endless barren plains. At one point, he got so sick he had to stay in a little village, gathering his strength, for eighteen months. Four years after starting out, he finally reached Nepal and found his teacher. They embraced joyfully. The young monk told his master about the visions and magical powers he'd developed.

"Oh, yes," said the old man. "That's completely normal. Doesn't mean anything in particular. Just watch it happen and stick with your meditation practice."

So the young monk walked home, and that is what he did.

I love this story because it clears up so much confusion about a category of experience that's been horrifically distorted by literally millions of people since human history began. The young monk's endless hike to question the master was worth it because most people would have given him very different—and very bad—advice.

There are two typical errors people make when it comes to mapping the Dreamtime, and they can be equally destructive. The psychological work you did earlier in this book will render you much less vulnerable to these dysfunctions. But because they're so common and because fulfilling your destiny may involve such astonishing experiences, you should be aware of both classic errors as you map out the star chart of your future.

Dreamtime Error 1:
Making Too Much of Magic and Miracles

Historically, people who experience "supernatural" things—who predict the future, see visions, read minds, or whatever—have been viewed with fear and awe by folks who live exclusively in the material world. The word *charisma* actually means the ability to tap into the spirit world, and "charismatic leaders" are people who get social authority by claiming to be the mouthpiece of God or the dead or other supernatural entities. The idea is that if everyone believes you've got a pipeline to the divine, you can get them to do whatever you want.

Some charismatic leaders gather little knots of followers. Others form entire religions, transferring their godlike authority to dogmas and successors. Either way, the special ability to speak to God or channel the dead or define right and wrong has all too often been used as a tool to gain power in the shallows. With suspicious frequency, charismatic leaders claim that God has commanded them to kill people, have sex with whomever they choose, own large fancy vehicles, and/or treat their followers like slaves.

From cultists to religious inquisitors, people seen as "magical" are very often deceitful and tyrannical.

Some of the cleverest mechanical devices of the ancient world were built by Roman priests to convince their followers that they could do magical things, such as causing a mechanical horse to move "by itself." Today, people with a little psychic talent often try to parlay it into a product they can trade for power, wealth, and status—but because miracles never happen with mechanical regularity, even people who really are very intuitive often begin manufacturing pseudo-magic to keep the pot boiling (much to the dismay of ethical intuitives).

So a high level of rational skepticism is absolutely appropriate—in fact, essential—to avoid being duped by either religious power mongers, delusional True Believers, or fly-by-night con artists. However, totally denying everything but material reality swings the pendulum too far in the opposite direction and into the second type of dysfunction.

Dreamtime Error 2:
Making Too Little of Magic and Miracles

Modern rationalism is in many ways a reaction to centuries of exploitation inflicted by supposedly "spiritual" leaders. In most developed societies today, thank God, you can't just lock someone up because the local religious authority claims he was casting the evil eye on somebody's goat. When Einstein contradicted Newton's physics, he wasn't branded a blasphemer and drowned in a pond. Modern nations don't wage "holy wars" designed to impose their version of "rightness" on unwilling others—oh, wait; yes, they do. So there are still a few bugs in the system. But at least I can sit here in my Arizona home and write that last sentence without being denounced as a witch or threatened with prison or accused of consorting with demons. To get that reaction, I have to go to Utah.

My point is that our society ditched mysticism for good reasons, and I'm heartily grateful. However, in order to keep religious zealots and spiritual pretenders from distorting the truth, rationalism often . . . uh . . . distorts the truth.

Documented Dreamtime Effects

Scientific skeptics often claim that there is no verifiable, well-controlled, testable evidence that any humans ever have "paranormal" experiences. This is simply untrue. For example, according to an overview of published, peer-reviewed studies of double-blind laboratory tests that meet or exceed the controls used in most academic psychological experiments, ordinary human subjects can communicate telepathically, not with the absolute certainty of face-to-face conversation but at a level of statistical significance that is a million billion to one against chance.

Other so-called psi phenomena have also been rigorously studied. It turns out most people have a dash of the psychic in them. Tests reveal much better-than-chance success with skills such as remote viewing (mentally observing situations at distant locations), telekinesis (the ability to affect physical matter with attention alone), precognition (seeing or knowing things before they happen), field consciousness (the apparent synchronizing of energy in areas where groups of people are all focused on a single event), and a number of other zany powers. Psychics really do occasionally help police solve crimes, in ways that defy purely material explanations. Researchers have studied many cases in which people are able to describe in precise visual detail the personnel and procedures marshaled to resuscitate them when they were clinically dead—even when the nearly dead person was (at least in life) completely blind.

Situations don't have to get this dramatic to yield evidence of psi experiences. In fact, paranormal abilities seem to be pretty normal. According to one Cambridge study, over ninety per cent of the general population have experienced the "telephone effect"—thinking of a person just before that person calls on the phone or knowing who's calling the moment the phone rings. When one group of scientists designed a study to test whether any old person could do this, they found that the answer was yes. Randomly chosen subjects could sense who was calling them—again, not with one hundred per cent certainty but at a rate of accuracy that differed from odds against chance by a thousand billion to one.

I've watched scientists bend Occam's razor into a pretzel trying to explain away such events. (Occam's razor is the core scientific principle stating that the simplest explanation is probably the right one.) It seems to me that the most parsimonious explanation for the fact that "paranormal events" seem to happen is that they *do* happen. Not always, but quite often.

This kind of ability isn't like eyesight; it's more like a batter's ability to hit a pitched ball. If a major league player hits three out of ten pitches, he deserves a spot in the Hall of Fame. That doesn't mean you should stake your life on the assumption that he's going to hit every pitch. Likewise, many people have accurate psychic flashes, and some people have a lot of them. But that doesn't mean you should give these people your retirement savings or surrender your rational skepticism. It's just something to observe with an open mind. If you do, the odds are very good you'll discover that you yourself often do things you consciously deem "impossible."

The Secret to *The Secret*

Remember Pam, the acquaintance who told me out of the blue that I was visiting the real world in my Yoga Nidra–enhanced state? Well, my next call from her was equally strange. Someone had just given me a copy of a book called *The Secret*, which had been on bookstore shelves one week and had, at that point, sold eight zillion kajillion copies. In case you were confined to an isolation tank throughout 2007, let me fill you in: *The Secret* by Rhonda Byrne is a brief, beautifully packaged little book about the "Law of Attraction." The whole message of the book boils down to this: Everything you think about happens, and if something happens to you, that's because you're thinking about it.

I respect and appreciate the many impressive people who contributed to *The Secret*. I love the hope it brought to so many readers. The only tiny quibble I have with the book's basic message is that I don't believe it. Did Anne Frank "attract" the Holocaust with her uncontrolled pubescent thoughts? Do babies who die in hurricanes create the weather? And how come so many people who really, truly believe they're going to win millions or become movie stars or live forever end up leaving this world with nothing but a vinyl purse full of losing Lotto tickets? Some coaches I've trained have told me grim stories of *Secret*-reading clients who manically spent themselves into irredeemable credit card debt, announcing, "I have to live as though I can afford everything I want! The checks will just start coming in the mail if I expect them! The bills will stop coming if I never think about them! That's the Secret!"

I read the little book on an airplane, and by the time my flight touched down, I was aghast. It alarmed me that the entire American population seemed to be embracing ideas like this comment on disease: "You cannot 'catch' anything unless you think you can," or this one on weight: " . . . look for, admire, and inwardly praise people with your idea of perfect-weight bodies. . . . If you see people who are overweight, do not observe them." Thinking of how this could affect, say, efforts at AIDS prevention or attempts to end social discrimination against overweight people, I felt like a parrot I once knew who could speak only one English word. He'd stand stolidly on his perch as people cooed "Pretty bird" and "Hello!" until he'd had enough. Then he'd scream, in an absolutely flabbergasted voice, *"What?"*

That's what I was thinking as I lugged my bags through the airport, brooding about *The Secret*. Then my cell phone rang.

"Hello, Martha," said the voice on the other end. "It's Pam."

"Pam?" I thought. Then I remembered: Pam, the spontaneous intuitive acquaintance.

"Well, hello," I said.

"I'm just calling on a whim this time," she said. "Everyone's been trying to get me to read that book *The Secret*, and earlier today it sort of jumped off the shelf at me, and when I got to the part where the author mentions you, I thought I'd give you a buzz."

I stopped and set down my bag. "Me?" I said. "*The Secret* doesn't mention me."

"Yes, it does," Pam told me. "The author recommends one of your books."

"No, I promise," I told her. "I just read it—I mean, literally minutes ago, cover to cover—and I'm not in it. I would have noticed."

To make a fairly short story a tad shorter: Pam had picked up *another* book, also called *The Secret*, which was written by a rabbi named Michael Berg and which does (thank you very much, Rabbi) recommend one of my memoirs.

After chatting with Pam briefly, I sat right down on my luggage in the middle of the airport and gripped my hair with my hands. This, you see, was the thing that really bothered me about *The Secret*: Though I really, truly don't believe that my thoughts make things happen, things very often happen when I think about them. The phone call was a case in point. There I was, focusing intensely on the book *The Secret*, inwardly screaming "*What?*" and "*Thoughts do not create material reality!*" Then someone in material reality (mostly) happened to call me just to mention a book entitled *The Secret*, which had my name in it.

If this sort of coincidence were rare for me, I could've ignored it more easily. But I must grudgingly, reluctantly, peevishly admit that a plethora of highly improbable things have happened to me after I thought about them with particular intensity. In fact, I've taught hundreds of clients about something I call Wildly Improbable Goals (WIGs, for short). I've been making shortlists of these dreams since I was a teenager, and an extremely high percentage of them have come true in the real world, often by means that seemed to go right off the "improbable" charts and onto "impossible" ones.

So on one hand, my entire method of living and coaching is about seeing through thoughts, realizing that they are not the solid dungeon walls they seem but diaphanous mind-stuff, irrelevant, flimsy, and powerless. On the other hand, I completely understand why movies and books like *The Secret* (and *Harry Potter*, *Lord of the Rings*, and all the other magical mega-hits) appeal to so many readers—something in them rings as true for me as it does for the most simplistic lottery-winner wannabe. *So which is it?* I thought that day as I sat on my luggage and pulled my hair. *Are human thoughts nothing or everything, powerless or powerful, worthless or priceless?*

The answer, as far as I've been able to observe it, is this: Yes. Both views are accurate, *but it depends on where the thinker resides mentally*. Thoughts that come from the shallow outer limits of our psyches have a little power— the physical, ordinary power that lets us get up in the morning and slog through another day at an office we dislike or bicker with an annoying neighbour or drag ourselves through a grueling bout of unpleasant exercise. But thoughts that come from the core of peace? They're pure magic.

The Mapmaker's Studio

Here's where all the hard psychological work you did in the first chapters of this book—all the self-questioning, ego-dissolving, and letting go of concepts—pays off. It not only frees you from the dungeon of your worst nightmares, it allows you to create, and then follow, your star chart.

When you live from the shallows' perspective, you have only a pale mental version of the future you want to create. Once your false thoughts burn away, and you abide in the core of peace, you'll see the Stargazer's rich, vivid version of your life, which will be so wonderful that your mind's version will make you laugh. You'll begin to map out your Dreamtime destiny while wide awake, and the very act of creating the plan seems to conjure it from the metaphysical realm to the physical (this, at any rate, has been my very convincing experience). North Star mapmaking doesn't just draw your best destiny in your mind's eye or on a paper; it draws it into being.

Here's how this logic might apply to a pragmatic problem—say, oh, I don't know, figuring out what you'll do with the rest of your life.

Let's suppose you've been fairly happy for the past seven years stacking crates in a bong factory, raising your triplets, and working toward your taxidermist's license. Then one day, while heaving one more box, scalding one more gopher pelt, or watching Brittany smack Brian and Brendan one more time with the Whack-a-Mole mallet, you surprise yourself by thinking, "It's time for a change." Your life was meant to be more.

Now what?

Now What?
(The Rational Mapmaking Approach)

Most teachers, advisors, and how-to books recommend the rational approach to life change: Realistically assess your resources, skills, training, and background; type up a résumé; begin networking with potential business associates; take out a loan; go back to school. Within that framework, of course, you should consider your likes and dislikes—the reasonable ones. You may like food, for example. More specifically, good food. You might even want to recall your (reasonable) childhood hopes and dreams, such as having nice hair.

Once you've assessed your present situation and your attainable goals, you might want to take a few highly reasonable personality tests to find out whether you're an introverted task-oriented emotional problem solver or an extroverted relationship-oriented psychopathic solution doodler or whatever. Then, simply adopt several habits of highly successful people and badabing, badaboom! You're well on your way to becoming an assistant inventory clerk at the local Shop-N-Struggle, with possibilities for advancement in less than five years!

Now What?
(The Irrational Mapmaking Approach)

Here's why the life-planning methodology I've just described sounds lame: It is. Sensing this, you may decide to go in another direction. For example, you could play an encouraging self-help book-on-tape, talk to a wise friend, or—wait, I know!—hire a life coach! Generally speaking, life coaches are the most genuinely optimistic, positive, eager-to-serve professionals on the planet. Many of us become so excited about our clients' potential that we must be medicated with horse tranquilizers to get any sleep at all.

Anyway, you may get so fired up by your book-on-tape or your friend's support or your life coach's infectious enthusiasm that you decide to think big, go for the gold, ignore the naysayers!! Should you sell your doublewide trailer home and use the money to bet on the ponies? Absolutely!! If you really, truly think you're going to win, it *has* to happen!! Plus, just because you're seventy-three, that doesn't mean you can't start learning to play the bassoon right now, then make big money on the classical-orchestra circuit!! And who cares if so far, all the popes have been male? You go get 'em, sister—make yourself a big fancy hat and start blessing stuff from your apartment balcony—you'll attract whatever you think about!! Guaranteed!!

Or not.

Now What?
(The Stargazer's Mapmaking Approach)

What I want you to notice about the uninformed "Everything I think will come true" belief system is that it comes from the shallows. It focuses on lack-and-attack avoidance, material items, easy success, and social approval. It has a grasping, desperate quality. There is power in this, but it's tepid, physical power. It can make things happen by dint of hard work, a little luck, and absolute commitment.

I have many clients who use this approach with apparent success. Ben fought his way to the top of his law firm by putting in eighteen-hour days, kissing up to his boss, subtly undermining his coworkers, and doing whatever it took to get high-paying clients, no matter how unethical or unappealing they were. Cindy, divorced with a young son, set out to marry a rich older man for his money. It worked. She was more than willing to be unhappily married for several years before her husband succumbed to a heart attack, so that she could surround herself with opulence and pass her time with the very best friends money could buy.

These folks, and countless others like them, succeeded by mapping out an ambitious future and then forcing it to happen, come hell or high water. You may be able to do this, too, though frankly, the odds are against you. But the process will wear you out physically, emotionally, and spiritually; isolate you from real love; and never, ever make you genuinely happy. North Star mapmaking, by contrast, is deeply enjoyable in itself, will make you feel good immediately, and from everything I've observed (brackets up, remember), really will begin rearranging the material world to help you.

Making Your Real Star Chart

To make a star chart that will be in harmony with your best destiny, you'll need all the skills you've learned so far in this book, plus a couple of others we'll discuss in a moment. The process goes like this: Every day, you'll take some dedicated time (in other words, up to fifteen minutes spent alone, without interruption) for official mapmaking. Then, to chart out your future by the light of your own North Star, you'll:

1. Enter the state of your awareness that connects you with your core of peace.

2. Turn your attention away from the material world and toward the Dreamtime.

3. Do some mental "drawing" of your future.

4. Cast a small, innocuous spell that will cause the things you've just created in your mind's eye to begin appearing in three-dimensional reality.

By the way, if you happen to be a God-fearing Christian, and this talk of magic and spells is horrifying you, please remember these are just words I'm using to describe a certain kind of creativity. You could just as accurately call this process "prayer," though I prefer not to use that label because it has so many preexisting associations in most people's minds. Feel free to call North Star mapmaking a way to do magic or a way to work miracles; in either case, it's a powerful process that sets all sorts of mysterious forces loose, engendering the best possible events in your life and in the world.

One additional note: After I'd been using this method for some time and had already written this book—but before the final edit—a friend introduced me to the work of Jerry and Esther Hicks, who, according to my friend, were "the secret behind the secret." Proofreading this manuscript, I'm stunned by how closely the process I've been calling "mapmaking" resembles the material published by the Hickses, whose work I'd never heard of during the years I'd used the techniques with clients.

I believe that this—along with the popularity of *The Secret* and other "magical" trends—is a variation of something anthropologists call "the hundredth monkey effect" or, at the very least, a "tipping point." The hundredth monkey effect refers to a group of Japanese macaques who lived on a small island and lived mainly on sweet potatoes. According to several published accounts, one particularly brilliant macaque figured out how to wash her potatoes by dropping them into shallow water. This monkey taught her immediate family the trick, and soon it was common practice among all the animals in that particular troupe. At that point, observation (or was it urban-myth rumour?) revealed that *all* the Japanese macaques, even those on separate islands, began washing sweet potatoes in this particular way.

The hundredth monkey is an example of what Malcolm Gladwell calls a "tipping point," a moment in the evolution of a trend when it suddenly seems to spring up everywhere—sometimes through obvious methods of propagation and sometimes mysteriously. Social change has always followed this pattern; slowly emerging theories or paradigms accelerate exponentially, suddenly appearing everywhere. The ideas in this chapter have hit a tipping point in modern American culture. This may be one reason life coaching emerged as a discipline now and why so many of my fellow coaches, even those who have never communicated with one another, have developed similar techniques. I'd advise any star-chart enthusiast to sample any and all sources that sound helpful or even interesting. Again, the proof of the pudding is in the eating: Try something, see if it succeeds, and then—only then—incorporate it into your Stargazer's plan for life.

North Star Mapmaking, Step 1: Go to the Mapmaker's Studio

To enter the proper psychological space for mapping out your destiny, start with a strategy taken from my Yoga Nidra tape: Retreat to a space where you'll be uninterrupted for fifteen minutes and sit down in a comfortable spot where you can feel balanced and relaxed. Rub your hands together a few times, picturing energy flowing into your palms from a spot just below your navel. Then, put your hands on your face. Imagine energy penetrating from the palms of your hands, through your face, all the way to the back of your head. (I don't know if this energy dispersal is real, but brain research indicates that *picturing* it changes your brain state in a beneficial way.)

At this point, I'd like you to use some strategies devised by Princeton psychologist Les Fehmi, Ph.D., who studies brain wave patterns. The following exercises are taken from his excellent book *The Open-Focus Brain*, in which he teaches readers how to create huge positive changes in mood and physical well-being by learning certain attention patterns. If these suggestions sound strange, just try them on to see if they work for you. For me and most people I've coached, they're seriously powerful medicine.

Begin by focusing your eyes on some object in your immediate environment. Then, while continuing to look at this original object, begin to notice the things around it. Without moving your eyes, slowly broaden the focus of your attention to include everything in your visual field to the full extent of your peripheral vision. For example, you might focus on one blade of grass in a field, then broaden your focus to include all the other blades of grass, the earth, the sky, and things like trees or people. Continue to look at the original object but allow the background to be as important as the object. See both the blade of grass and the whole meadow. Then, broaden your attention to sense everything in your environment with all five senses.

Next, vividly imagine the space between your eyes. Picture the full volume of that area, the space taken up by the physical matter between your eyeballs. Then, imagine the space inside the bridge of your nose—the full three-dimensional area above your airway. Imagine that as you breathe, the inside of your nose and the area all around your eyes is filling with air. Picture the space—the nonmatter—in which your skin and bone and other tissues exist. Realizing that every atom contains millions of times more space than matter, allow yourself to imagine that openness, as well as solid substance.

If you notice fear, grasping, anxiety, pain, or any other negative sensation, pay close attention and *exactly locate the sensation of the discomfort in your physical body.* Focus on this area, moving your attention toward it rather than away from it. Imagine bathing in the negative feeling, whether it's emotional or physical. Then, while still paying attention to your discomfort, once again broaden your perceptions to take in everything in your environment, just as you did with the "blade of grass" exercise.

Now, picture the space that fills your head, neck, and upper body extending outward in every direction. Imagine it permeating you and continuing outward infinitely in all directions. Perceive it penetrating and suffusing all objects: mist, earth, stars, galaxies. Just as it fills your body, it also fills the space in which all matter exists. Feel the sensations of your body and mind functioning, but also feel the entire vast stillness in which you dwell, the emptiness that connects your own inner space with all other things.

Continue these exercises until you feel a strong "shackles off" sensation in your muscles. You may also feel as though shackles are dropping away inside your head. These exercises have been found to change your brain state from high-frequency beta waves (anxiety) to alpha waves (calm) and to get as much of your brain as possible working in the same gentle rhythm, a state called synchronous alpha. I actually feel this as a lilting sensation inside my head, a buoyant rise and fall, as if my brain is gently bobbing in warm water. You will have sensations that are specific to your own body, but they will involve a sense of softening, loosening, and growing more comfortable physically and mentally.

North Star Mapmaking, Step 2: Begin to Draw the Map

While paying attention to the space your body occupies, as well as its continuity with the rest of space, notice again that *you lack nothing you need in order to exist at this precise moment.* The reason it's crucial to recognize this is that to create something you want (as we saw in Chapter 1), you must begin with the feeling state you hope to achieve at the end. You're going to create your best life, one in which you have no unmet needs and no fear. So, to begin, recognize that everything in your present situation is collaborating to support you. Your heart beats by itself. Your lungs breathe. Your eyes see. Your ears hear. It is all being done for you. Breathe that in.

Destination Abundant Love

Now, begin to vividly imagine a point in the future when you are enjoying the most wonderful relationships in the universe. Feel the presence in your life of many beings who adore you and whom you adore. There may be a partner, friends, coworkers, teammates, children, animals. Notice the feeling of each loving individual, without grasping or needing. Realize that there is an infinite supply of others who can love you. In fact, you are already loved by people you haven't yet met. You are already connected to them. You can feel them.

If you can't feel them—if trying to feel them brings on sadness, loneliness, or desperation—recognize that these grasping sensations come from your illusions of separateness and that you can't make an accurate star chart from such earthbound signals. Pat your inner lizard on the head, repeat the process of "going to the studio," and continue until your body and mind relax.

Destination Meaningful Work

Next, imagine your perfect work. This doesn't necessarily mean housework, farm work, or office work; it means the *real work of your life,* your soul's preferred occupation. Feel yourself doing this work. When you're engaged in it, you're completely immersed in the process while still being aware of everything happening around you.

Without thinking or forcing, notice what your real life's work is like. Are you connecting with people, with material objects, with ideas? Are you moving or holding still? Are you outside or indoors? What does the area or the room look like? What do you hear, see, taste, touch, feel as you do your work? What kind of problems are you solving?

Notice any specific images or sensations that come up, *without labeling them, thinking about how to make them happen, or even trying to figure out what they are.* You may well envision a work life your mind can't pigeonhole. When I began making my own star charts, I didn't know it was possible to be a "contributing editor" for a magazine based in New York and still work entirely from my home in Arizona. As for "life coaching"—well, that profession didn't even exist. When I drew the map of my future in my imagination, I simply saw myself writing short pieces to publish quickly, while connecting soulfully with smart, funny, deep-thinking people who wanted to improve the depth and fulfillment they got from life.

Destination Fulfilling Adventure

When you've spent several minutes previewing your life's work, do a little freeform mapmaking, just to open your attention focus and allow unexpected ideas to arise. Imagine your body going forward in time, getting healthier, stronger, and more beautiful; inhabiting increasingly inviting, inspiring, comfortable environments. See adventures unrolling around your body and feel your body moving through them, as if your consciousness is riding a river of wonderful events. Allow whatever appears in your imagination to be there without questioning how or why such experiences could happen.

Destination Perpetual Joy

You may find that the events that arise into consciousness from your core of peace seem huge, unattainably grand. Or you might see yourself doing something modest and expected, such as watching TV with your cat. *Notice that the heart's delight in doing things has no relationship to what the mind thinks of as big or small, impressive or unimpressive.* The many exceptional blessings I've experienced—achieving big goals, meeting famous people, travelling to exotic locations—truly are not one whit more fulfilling than "ordinary" experiences like putting on a pair of fuzzy socks, watching a kitten play, or drinking a glass of water, if the ordinary things are done mindfully. And in retrospect, many "bad" experiences seem just as wonderful as "good" ones, since they burned down my inner dungeons. Every experience that's part of your best destiny is beautiful to your soul.

Because I've done it—and seen it done—so often, I believe that just visualizing your future in this way, without any grasping energy, triggers a creative reaction in the entire expanse of material reality. Both your Stargazer self and the world around you conspire to bring about the visions you've imagined on your star chart. However, if you want some physical representation of your destiny, I'd recommend making two things: an itinerary for your life's future travels and a pictorial star chart.

Your Written Itinerary

Below, you'll find a form in which to write down whatever you dreamed up doing this exercise. Once you've filled it in, you'll have a rough itinerary of the life toward which the stars are steering you. Remember, this itinerary isn't a list of what you think you should do or what you think is possible. It's a description of what you see when you contemplate life from the position of the Stargazer, no matter how improbable that may appear.

The Magical Mapmaker's Itinerary for Your Life

In the spaces below, describe as accurately as possible everything that appeared in your imagination as you soaked yourself in stillness, silence, space, and timelessness.

From my mapmaking perspective, I see myself having _____

_____

_____

_____

_____

From my mapmaking perspective, I see myself being loved by _____

_____

_____

_____

_____

From my mapmaking perspective, I see myself doing _____

_____

_____

_____

_____

From my mapmaking perspective, I see myself experiencing _____

_____

_____

_____

_____

The Pictorial Star Chart

The pictorial chart of your future is even more visual; it's like one of those topographical satellite maps that simply show the location without having to list any words or concepts. I suspect this freedom from verbal attachments is what makes it such powerful magic. Go online or browse through magazines looking for pictures that come close to your Stargazer visions. When you find any image that causes a surge of delight, buoyancy, or "shackles off" freedom, print or cut out a hard copy of that image. Then, glue or tape all the images to a piece of paper or a poster board.

The good people in *The Secret* recommend this practice as well, calling it a "vision board." It's worked incredibly well for me and my clients over the years (beginning with a group of IBM executives who'd been forced to make collages for a training and insisted that I include it in a business-school career development course). I recently made a five-year star chart crammed with pictures of all sorts of wild adventures. I thought I'd finished that little task for the foreseeable future, but everything on the board happened within four months, so I had to make a new chart. Another coach I know installed a corkboard wall in her office so she can thumbtack pictures of her imagined best life to be taken down soon thereafter. The things she visualizes come true so fast that she and her husband have to update their star charts continuously.

Remember, *it's not just putting up a picture that works the magic; it's constantly getting past the shallows and residing in the core of peace that creates powerful conjuring juju.* Anything in the shallows relies on force and effort, while the desires from within your core of peace seem to happen almost without your participation. I don't believe I could "manifest" a Mercedes right now just by slapping up a photo, because frankly, my core of peace couldn't care less about cars. But I have a friend who loves cars from the depths of his soul, and he's had a string of cars that first came to him in his mapmaking studio. Whatever your heart truly desires, once you've got your map made—in your soul's eye or physical pictures—it's time to cast the spell that makes it all work.

North Star Mapmaking, Step 3:
Cast the Spell (or, If You Prefer, Say the Prayer)

When you've spent some time in your mapmaker's studio and seen a few images to put on your star chart, close the session with a small statement, which you can call either a spell or a prayer. This ritual has two purposes. First, it helps you drop your natural, reptilian brain clinging to whatever it is you want. Second, it officially broadcasts whatever creative idea you've mustered into the broader atmosphere. Here's how it goes.

Mystical Miraculous Magical Mapmaking Spell

> **Thanks. I quit.**

The first part of this spell ("Thanks") ensures that you begin at the end, as all magic and miracles must, with gratitude for what you've received (in the future). Saying "thank you" presupposes the fulfillment of your best destiny, which, as we saw in Chapter 1, helps you operate in the ways most likely to help bring it into physical existence.

The second sentence, "I quit," helps you release any effortful, stressful, or needy emotional energy you may be expending. "I quit" is an acknowledgment that you aren't trying to *force* your destiny to occur, any more than you *force* your lungs to breathe. It's not a statement of defeat but of trust, an acknowledgment that your destiny lives you, not the other way around. Resigning yourself to this fact, "submitting your resignation" is a powerful act when it comes from the fearless core of peace rather than from any clinging to the shallow side of life.

The philosopher Bertrand Russell wrote, "There are two kinds of resignation, one motivated by despair and the other by unconquerable hope. . . . Nothing is more fatiguing nor, in the long run, more exasperating, than the daily effort to believe things which daily become more incredible. To be done with this effort is an indispensable condition of secure and lasting happiness. . . . The attitude required is that of doing one's best while leaving the issue to fate." *In other words, don't even bother trying to believe in what you've just conjured.* Climb out of the driver's seat, settle into the passenger side, open a bag of nachos, and relax. Allow the stars to align on your behalf rather than trying to align them yourself.

To Infinity, and Beyond!

Here's my challenge: Follow the steps above each day for a month and see what happens. If nothing changes in your life as a result of making your star chart, you have my permission to scoff. Scoffing rights will be your consolation prize for becoming the only person I know who can do this experiment without beginning to see magic at work. But if you plan to disbelieve in the creative power of star-chart making, do it after some legitimate experimentation, not in a preemptive flurry of *a priori* judgments.

However, if your mapmaking has the effects I've found typical, be prepared to enter the strange and vivid Dreamtime world. Expect dust that glows like opals and plants that shine like emeralds. As my favorite Sufi poet Rumi wrote, "Out beyond ideas of rightdoing and wrongdoing, there is a field. I'll meet you there." I'll be the one lying flat on my back with my earphones on, fast asleep. Jostle me gently to wake me up, because I *really* don't want to miss the next stage of our adventures.

CHAPTER 7

Hear, Here

It took me fifteen years to understand the first word my son ever said to me. That word was a simple one I use every day, and Adam said it very clearly, and I really, truly thought I understood it at the time. I even wrote down and *published* my misunderstanding in a memoir about Adam's birth. If you happen to have read that book, I must apologize for inadvertent misrepresentation and beg your patience as I reiterate the story to set things right.

Back when this occurred, I was heartsore and weary from trying to make Adam talk. He was almost three, and I knew that if a child with Down syndrome doesn't speak by his third birthday, chances are he won't be verbal at all. I'd been a maniac for speech therapy all his life, working with him for hours every single day and taking him to many early-intervention specialists, with zero positive results. I mean goose egg. The kid never said a single word.

One day I finally hit bottom, stopped cold in the midst of yet another hour of fruitless speech exercises, cried for a while, and took Adam and his sisters (Katie was five, Elizabeth was one) to the grocery store.

When we got there, I bribed them. I said that if they'd all be good and please not scream or hide or stab anyone, I'd let them have anything they wanted from the checkout counter. Wisely observing that my last nerve was frayed to a thread, they complied, so as I paid for the groceries, I bought Katie and Lizzy their favorite candy. Adam, weirdly, ignored all the sweets. Instead, he picked out a red rose from a carafe of water next to the till. When I put it back and explained to him again that he could have *candy*, he shook his small head and picked up the rose again. So I bought it for him, drove home, and forgot about it.

The next morning I awoke to see Adam shuffling into my room in his little footie pajamas, holding the rose, which he'd put in a bud vase. This gave me gooseflesh, because I hadn't seen him arrange the flower and had no idea he could do such a thing. Think how you'd feel if you caught your dog using the Internet—that's how the bud vase made me feel.

Adam walked up to me, handed me the red rose in the vase, and said, "Here."

At least, that's what I thought.

I often wondered how and why Adam managed to enunciate this one word so clearly when he didn't manage to garble out his next few meaningful syllables until almost a year later. There was no question he knew what he was saying; the direct blue gaze from his eyes and the extreme care he took to speak clearly were absolutely evident. But "here"? Most kids start out with "Mama" or "Dada" or, like Helen Keller at the pump with Annie Sullivan, "wawa." If a guy's only going to say one word to his mom in almost four years, why choose "here"?

The truth didn't dawn on me until Adam was eighteen and I was telling this story to a group at a spa retreat with the winners of a contest sponsored by *Oprah Magazine*.

" . . . So Adam came up to me," I told the group, "and he handed me the rose, and he said . . . "

And that's when the lights finally went on. It hit me so hard I dropped into a chair like a puppet with cut strings.

"Oh, my God," I murmured. "He said, 'Hear.'"

People with intellectual disabilities are sometimes called "delayed," which is richly ironic to me when I consider how delayed I was in my reaction to Adam's incisive and extremely intelligent lesson. After all, from the moment he was conceived until his birth, I'd been conscious—sometimes frighteningly conscious—of living on two planes of reality. I'd had vivid premonitions, moments when I saw, through the eyes of distant loved ones, knowledge of things I had no physical way to have learned. But since that time ended, I'd been almost wholly tuned in to the outer-limit world. That was why I'd been so devastated that my son couldn't talk—and, I believe, why he broke what Buddhists call his "noble silence" just long enough to remind me.

Hear.

He'd been talking to me all along, since before he was born. He'd just been broadcasting on a different frequency.

Listening to that mystical frequency, while staying safely grounded in logical and pragmatic action, is the key to planning the path of your best destiny. This chapter is about elaborating and clarifying your star chart, a process that requires you to tune one ear toward heaven without losing your footing on earth. Think of it as learning to hear, here.

How We Hear Here

One of the first neurologists to study mystical experiences through physical examination of the brain was Andrew Newberg, M.D., Ph.D. Late in the twentieth century, he and his coauthor, Eugene D'Aquili, set out to track the brain activity of an experienced meditator at a "peak moment." Dr. Newberg and D'Aquili injected their subject with radioactive dye and then had him meditate until he reached Nirvana, or his Happy Place, or whatever he called it. At that point, the meditator tugged a cord, signaling the researchers to snap a magnetic resonance image of his brain.

Dr. Newberg and D'Aquili found that at the moment their meditator achieved a sensation of unbounded bliss, the right side of his brain became more active, and an area at the back (the superior posterior parietal lobe) lit up like a storefront in December. This area of the brain allows us to feel the difference between ourselves and our environment. Without it, you'd have no sense of a "me" that exists inside your skin and an "outside world" that isn't you. This brain region is physically situated next to an area that has to do with sexual responses. Dr. Newberg and D'Aquili hypothesized that the ability to drop our body boundaries, to feel merged with another being, evolved in order to facilitate sexual reproduction. In other words, the feeling of mystical experience is not only experientially but also neurologically very close to the feeling of falling in love.

The thing that interested me most about this research was that the authors, after lengthy study, concluded that meditators who experience mystical states aren't more crazy and delusional than others, but saner and more functional. The reason they experienced ecstatic oneness with the universe, the researchers hypothesized, might be that they actually *were* one with the universe. Their sense of a metaphysical realm might be more accurate than the ordinary human sensation of being an isolated physical form. This, thought the researchers, might be the reason their meditating subject and others of his ilk showed fewer signs of psychological dysfunction than people who were wholly invested in the physical world.

Starlight Gliding

Dr. Newberg and D'Aquili compared the human capacity for mysticism to the evolution of flight. At one time, there were no animals on earth that could fly. Today, there are many. Obviously, flight ability didn't evolve in one generation—it's not as if a flightless dinosaur mated, waited for her eggs to hatch, and then shouted to her significant other, "Ohmygod, Fritz—this one totally has wings!" Instead, flying must have evolved from creatures whose limbs gave them a slight capacity to glide. Dinosaurs with flatter, more aerodynamic forelimbs survived better than those with nongliding arms, and these beasts gradually developed more and more gliding capacity until one day, an animal appeared that was capable of flight. (Birds, scientists now believe, are the surviving remnants of dinosaur ancestors, which means that your canary is actually a tiny flying dinosaur.)

Just as the concept and possibility of flying existed before there were animals that could fly, Dr. Newberg and D'Aquili suggest, the capacity to experience a metaphysical reality might exist even though we experience it in only brief moments of connection. To use one more metaphor: If you're sitting anywhere near civilization right now, the air you're breathing is full of radio signals. You won't be aware of them unless you bring in a radio, but with the right equipment, you can tune in to not only one strand of organized sound but many different songs and conversations. The meditators studied by Dr. Newberg and D'Aquili may have been "tuning" their brains to hear something that was there, undetected by most people, all the time. They could sit here in the visible world and hear the signals from the invisible.

Detailing Your Star Charts

Why am I bringing this up as we move toward clarifying the map for your future? Because in order to detail your star charts, you have to walk with one foot in the material world and one in the nonmaterial. You did some of this in the previous chapter, but now we come to the point where you have to trust the reality of your own visions in the *near future or the present*. That means your actual behavioral choices have to be guided by hearing here, a process that requires high levels of intuitive proficiency. You need the skills and talents of a mystical mapmaker.

The pirates of the Caribbean (the real people, not the Disneyland ride) supposedly wore eye patches not because they lost so many eyeballs but because, when raiding a ship, they knew they might have to fight both on the deck, in broad daylight, and in the pitch-dark cabins and storage spaces below. It takes about forty-five minutes for human eyes to make that light-to-dark adjustment. (You've probably experienced walking into a dark movie theater and not being able to see a thing at first. Halfway through the movie, you can count the dandruff flakes of the extremely tall person who's sitting in front of you, blocking your view of the screen.) By patching one eye, a pirate could keep that eye ready to see in the dark at a moment's notice.

To follow the course of your best destiny, to see the next step as well as the distant goal, requires an analogous kind of double vision. While working away in the logical, ground-bound pragmatism of the material world, you must also be ready to see the stars at any minute. You'll feel a dramatic difference when you switch back and forth between these perspectives. *What* you're doing may not change at all, but *how* you're doing it will feel very different.

For example, when I did my son's speech therapy from the material perspective, in which his lack of verbal skills was a tragedy, I was sad and afraid. When I was able to connect with my Stargazer self, I felt intuitively that Adam's inability to speak clearly wasn't a horrible thing at all—in fact, it felt oddly right. Only much later, after studying the inherent dangers of verbal thought and seeing Adam's immunity to them, did this make even marginal sense to me. But every time I leave the world of form and glide briefly into the stars, I feel enormous, indescribable peace about this issue and a thousand others that upset me deeply in the world of form.

You may experience this counterintuitive response to any number of situations. Charlie was unfairly fired from his job, so he should have been angry and upset—but he wasn't. "It feels good," he told me. "I feel free." And he was free—free to take the job that turned out to be his heart's desire. Another client, Daniella, was mugged the day after her beloved grandfather died—on 10 September 2001. Daniella's two personal traumas, combined with the national tragedy of the attacks on the World Trade Center, completely undid her. After a few days of intense grieving, she found herself thinking, "I'm going to die for certain, but I'm only going to live if I do it on purpose." She put all her belongings in her car, drove to New York City, and joined a professional comedy theater group. The last time I talked to her, she simply said, "I've died and gone to heaven."

Deciding to steer by starlight at any moment helped Charlie and Daniella adapt very quickly to change, to find direction and motivation in events that might have fueled despair. The trait that helped them prosper instead of suffer was a willingness to switch from a purely material view of their lives to a mystical one in a heartbeat. The moment Charlie and Daniella experienced their losses, they switched to the part of their inner vision that could see in the dark, like pirates moving their eye patches from the daylight eye to the one they kept ready for night vision.

Does this willingness to steer by starlight work because metaphysical beliefs have a placebo effect, making Charlie and Daniella irrationally optimistic? Or did their optimism reflect that they'd tuned in to some real metaphysical plane, a mystical force that gently guided them to make choices that were best for their souls? I have no idea. But I like to entertain the possibility that these two clients had some "gliding" ability, that when the solid ground dropped out from under them, they were able to soar through the stars on sheer intuition and find that the capacity to fly really does exist.

Whenever one of my clients has several important things go wrong at once, or I notice an overwhelming urge for a new life arising in someone who's always resisted change, or an extremely improbable coincidence occurs, or reasonable plans meet with what seems to be incredibly unreasonable bad luck, I watch carefully for that person's "gliding" ability. Often, the most nightmarish experiences are the ones that force people to experiment with a new way of planning and acting, to launch themselves into the dark and spread their wings. At times when there's nothing left to lose, we often discover that our intuitive talents allow us to win.

This is a pattern that's familiar and respected in many traditional cultures. When it happens in modern Western societies, we have only awkward and baggage-laden conceptual models and vocabulary words to describe what's happening. Borrowing some concepts from other cultures has helped me handle the need to "hear here" with more comfort and less confusion. I think this might be useful for you as well. So let's talk shamanism.

The Shaman of Wall Street

No one could figure out what was wrong with Madison. Extensive medical testing hadn't revealed any definitive reason for the weakness and pain that had almost destroyed her just when she should have had the world by the tail.

A brilliant, athletic, ambitious Yale graduate, Madison had just started a high-profile Wall Street job when something in her body went seriously awry. First she felt tired, then weak, then exhausted. All of her muscles, including her heart, powered down like computers in "sleep" mode, until her blood barely circulated. Her body—every organ, every fiber, every bone—ached unbearably. Once, when Madison forced herself to carry a stack of towels from her laundry room to the bathroom, the resulting pain was so severe she couldn't raise her arms for two days. Madison went from doctor to doctor, getting dozens of conflicting diagnoses. No symptomology fit exactly, and no treatment helped much.

Madison wrote about all this in a preparatory questionnaire before attending one of my seminars. As I read her story, I couldn't help thinking about the something anthropologists call a "shaman sickness." In many traditional societies, shamans (or druids, or medicine men, or whatever) recognize their calling after being struck by a prolonged, inexplicable illness, which heals only after they accept the mystical nature of their vocation and become willing to "shamanize."

Of course, no rational, well-educated American WASP would entertain such primitive ideas. Madison, for example, didn't write any such outlandishness into her questionnaire. She reported only that after two years of wretched illness, she'd started getting better. I watched her closely on the first day of the seminar. She was a lovely person and seemed healthy, if a little frail. On day two, I jokingly brought up the topic of shaman sickness and said that Madison's history matched the typical story of a mystic in a traditional culture. Later, during a break, Madison drew me aside.

"I didn't write about this in my workbook," she said, "because I figured you'd think I was crazy. But I didn't start getting my health back until I started admitting to myself that . . . " Her voice trailed off.

"That what?" I said.

"That . . . my whole life, I've always known I'm supposed to be some kind of . . . healer," said Madison. "Not medically, more, uh, intuitive." She covered her face with her hands. "I've been fighting this for years," she whispered. "I did not go to Yale to become a fruit loop."

"I know," I said, patting her shoulder. "I didn't go to Harvard to become a life coach."

I've always been interested in shaman illness—any chronic illness— because like Madison, I went through more than a decade of baffling, excruciating physical pain (diagnosed as a whole cluster of autoimmune illnesses, all poorly understood) before giving up my "normal" career goals and deciding to spend the rest of my life helping people live their best destinies. At that point, my symptoms went into remission. When I try to do anything different, the symptoms recur.

I'm not saying that what I do is "shamanizing." I don't see dead people or go into trances or make voodoo dolls of my least favorite political candidates. With the exception of an uncanny ability to locate chocolate during one week of each month, I have few and tepid spooky gifts. But listening to people's stories and helping them build their destinies does feel to me like a vocation, not a job, and when I veer away from it, my body seems to fight back. I've seen the same pattern in many of my clients who've been chronically ill. Our bodies gain strength as we steer by starlight. As we begin heading northward, we become more powerful physically, and then (brackets up, brackets up) we become more powerful *metaphysically*.

Coincidence? I Really Don't Know

After Madison and I had our little coffee-break conversation, the seminar resumed. We were doing dream interpretations, so a participant I'll call Linda asked if she could read an account of a dream she'd had the previous week. "I dreamed I was here, at the seminar," Linda said, glancing at the notes in her journal. "I was drawn to one person in particular; she seemed to be a healer of some kind. In the dream, it was this woman's birthday. She was wearing a blue-and-white striped shirt."

Across the room, Madison raised her hand. "It's my birthday," she said. We all looked at her.

"You're not wearing a blue-and-white striped shirt," said Linda.

"I bought one for this trip, and I put it on this morning," said Madison, "but then I took it off. I think it belongs to you."

Madison went to her room and brought back the blue-and-white shirt, which we all eyed suspiciously. It was just a coincidence, of course, but that, combined with the coincidence of Madison's birthday . . . even for the skeptics in the room, it did seem odd.

After giving Linda the shirt (which she received as if it were the Shroud of Turin), Madison shot me a look in which gratitude, wonder, and apprehension were equally combined. "Is my life going to stay this weird if I want to be healthy?" she asked me.

"Well, I can't know for sure," I told her, thinking of everything I've read about shaman sickness, "but it could get a whole lot weirder."

Then I told the group about a theory of mine—the kind of theory that

occurs to you after you combine sleep deprivation with floods of anthropological reading and so much caffeine that people can hear your pulse from
several city blocks away. This particular theory, however, is one that holds
up fairly well even after a good night's sleep and coffee detox. So, trusting
that your brackets are up and suspecting that you've read this far because
you are more like Madison than most of your pragmatic associates realize,
I shall impart it to you. Here it is: I think we may be living in the middle of
a shaman population explosion.

No, really, hear me out.

The Rise in Dreamtime Talents

First of all, anthropologists have long known that shamans, contrarians,
druids, medicine people from all cultures share certain characteristics.
During childhood, they may be sickly, accident prone, or traumatized.
They're extremely sensitive and empathic, frequently suffering from
depression, very high anxiety, and/or emotional overload. They may have
"psychic" impressions or dreams, and this tends to make them fascinated
by spirituality, whatever form that takes in their particular culture. They
also have a special affinity for animals, may even try to communicate
with various beasties, or consider animals their closest friends. Because
these people project high levels of emotional energy and possess an intuitive understanding of others, people often seek their advice. Unfortunately, they have a hard time finding anyone who can understand or
advise *them*.

Shamans must have some useful evolutionary function, because people
with this cluster of traits crop up in virtually every known culture. They
may be like the flat-armed dinosaurs that happened to glide better than
others—accidental adepts who can utilize metaphysical phenomena a bit
better than most people. But in premodern societies, where life expec-
tancy was very low and infant mortality sky-high, an extremely sensitive,

traumatized, depressed, chronically ill person faced lower odds of surviving childhood, let alone the stresses of adult life. To get any shamans in the grown-up population of any primitive culture, you'd have to start with a seriously high percentage of sickly psychic babies.

Now toss antibiotics and plentiful food and Prozac into the mix, and BAM! Suddenly, all those feeble mystical infants who would once have perished in childhood actually survive to become ministers or crystal meth addicts or both (you'd be surprised how often it's both). An unprecedented bumper crop of natural-born shamans sprouts and ripens just at the time when modern science convinces everyone, including them, that they don't exist.

In modern Western culture particularly, this might play havoc with intuitive people's way of knowing. Other cultures—many unrelated ones, who weren't comparing notes with one another—take it for granted that shamans get sick if they don't accept their gift and start functioning as mystics. But in a context where virtually any level of "psychic" activity is considered insane, anyone with even a tinge of mysticism might repress that aspect of her personality and become commensurately unhealthy. Maybe this explains why Madison suffered two years of near-paralytic illness before gagging out, "All right, I'm an intuitive healer!" Maybe it's why so many of us feel a low-level malaise; addiction; exhaustion; or chronic, nagging unhappiness except for brief moments during which we suspend our disbelief in destiny.

Getting Stuck

If you've done the exercises in this book so far, you are probably connecting with part of yourself that exists outside of time and knows things outside of mind. I'm not sure we can look into our own futures, sense our own North Stars, without accessing whatever shamanic ability was born into us. This doesn't mean we throw away the scientific method; it just means that we approach the creation of our lives like a detective who gets useful tips from a psychic and uses those tips along with rational calculation and physical evidence.

Many of my clients who say they're hopelessly "stuck" are just waiting for permission to trust their night vision, their shaman senses. At heart, they already know what their lives are meant to be. Not accepting this knowledge, not making it conscious or acting on it, is draining and weakening them. They feel physically or emotionally, slightly or horribly, ill. None of the magical, miraculous things I've been referencing ever arrive to affirm their convictions or facilitate their progress. Instead of the sense of gliding through a starlit sky, they're quagmired, powerless, unable to make anything work. Madison's condition is just an extreme version of the breakdown I see in the many clients who tell me that in one way or another, they've lost all power to move forward.

Even after you've done all the exercises we covered in Chapter 6 (foreseeing your distant future, creating a star chart of your best destiny), you may feel as though you get stuck in blind alleys. You may sense your ultimate future and purpose but see no way to get there. It's like pointing to a spot on the globe—Paris, Buenos Aires, Timbuktu—and knowing, "Yes! That's where I'm going!" and then finding yourself shackled to the wall of your mother's house or your career as an accountant or the town you always meant to leave.

If you have enormous dreams but can't seem to make them come true, is it because those dreams are too big? Almost never. The impediments that stop people once they're on the path to their right lives are made of false beliefs, just like the dungeon walls that once kept them from finding the path in the first place. But these false beliefs can prove extremely useful because when you've lost sight of the stars, "stuckness" itself offers you a way to move forward. If you feel you're on the right path but have become stuck, don't assume you've got the destination wrong. Consider, instead, that you may be misinterpreting what you hear (here) and therefore *countermanding* your own destiny.

Commands and Countermands

I call this next exercise "flipping the countermand." A countermand is an instruction that another command should not be followed. In this case, it means an unconscious false belief that convinces you there's no way to go any further toward your own North Star. *Feeling deeply stuck is always the result of a stalemate between a command and a countermand from your own belief system.*

Your mind will always deny that you are doing this, of course. It will disguise its own countermands as external circumstance, situations or forces that make it "impossible" for you to achieve your goals. It will convince you that you absolutely *can't* move forward, that you absolutely *have to* stay mired in a boggy part of your present life. It's hard to see countermands before you question them. However, there's a big old red flag that can tell you where to look. It's the word *but*.

When you did the mapmaking exercises in the previous chapter, you suspended disbelief and wrote, "I see myself having [amazing adventures], loving [wonderful people], doing [fulfilling work], experiencing [my heart's desires]." I hope you found it easy to engage in this sort of distant fantasy. Most people do. However, when you ask folks to take the next step toward their dreams, you often discover that they have (no offense) huge "buts." As long they're sitting on those "buts," they'll never move forward.

For example, Hilda wanted to hike the Grand Canyon, but she thought she could do this only if she hired an expensive personal trainer. Greg dreamed of a perfect relationship but was convinced he'd never find the right woman. Valerie wanted her own business but thought she was undereducated. When these people did their North Star mapmaking, seeing from the fearless position of the Stargazer, their goals were clear. But before they could move toward achieving what they wanted in the *near* future, their minds chimed in with the buts.

> "I see myself hiking the Grand Canyon, **but** I can't afford to train for it."

"I see myself with my perfect mate, **but** I don't know how to find that person."

"I see myself running a successful business, **but** I need an MBA."

Warning to coaches, therapists, and helpful people in general: If you or someone you love is countermanding heart's desires with large buts, do not try to help them solve the problem logically. They will have a reflex response I call a "yeahbut" that will drive you to the brink of homicide, if not suicide. Yeahbuts are like mental cockroaches, the most resilient creations spawned by the fearful mind. You can reason, argue, assist, or subsidize all sorts of solutions, but each time you cut down a yeahbut, two more will pop up like heads on a hydra.

"You could train for hiking by yourself or with friends."

"Yeah, but I get bored with any kind of exercise, and besides, I need the time to focus on solitaire."

"Lots of attractive people have expressed interest in you."

"Yeah, but they just pity me because I'm double-jointed, and anyway, they're all boring."

"There are tons of successful entrepreneurs who don't have MBAs."

"Yeah, but they're luckier than I am, and they all have connections to organized crime."

Encountering a yeahbut pattern in someone else leaves you hamstrung, frustrated, and utterly stuck. *Realize that this is what happens to the magic of creation when you countermand your own heart's desires.* No matter how desperately you try to "manifest" something, a conscious or unconscious countermand will stop the process. Flipping the countermand is the only way to open the channel, in your own imagination and perhaps in the outside world, that will allow your desire to be fulfilled.

How to Flip the Countermand

Think of anything in your life that has you feeling "stuck." Are you trying to lose weight but unable to stick to a diet? Have you long intended to learn French but found yourself falling into a sound sleep whenever you run your "Parlez-vous français!" computer software? Are you overdue for a change in your career, your living space, your underwear? Pick a stuck spot and use it to practice the following steps.

Step 1: Go to an Issue Where You Feel Stuck and State Your Countermand

The countermand can always be phrased like the "but" statements in the examples above from Hilda, Greg, and Valerie: "I see myself . . . but . . . " Your countermand might be "I see myself publishing a novel, **but** I have writer's block" or "I see myself snowboarding like a champion, **but** I'm afraid to ride a ski lift" or "I see myself training bats to fly surveillance for the CIA, **but** I'm allergic to all mammals." Whatever your stuck state may be, record it by filling in the blanks below.

My Stuck State in a Nutshell

   I can't [condition A] _____

   _____

   because [condition B] _____

   _____

Step 2: State the Real Problem

In the sentence you've just written, condition A is the command you're sending out, and condition B is the countermand. Together they neutralize one another, creating nothing but the maddening sense of "stuckness."

Teacher Byron Katie is an excellent resource if you've countermanded yourself into a stalemate. She chooses the side of the command/countermand dynamic that is distressing (the disempowering thought that says, "I can't" or "I have to") and "turns it around." Katie's "turnarounds" often fit this template, which I'd encourage you to memorize—it's awkward at first, but once you master it, you'll find that it's liberation on steroids. In the stalemate between condition A (the thing you want) and the countermand B (the stopper), a scrupulously accurate way to phrase things is: "My mind is choosing not to have condition A because it believes condition B is a problem. My true nature can have condition A because it knows condition B is not the problem—my beliefs are." Since this is fairly complex, here are some examples of works from our friends Hilda, Greg, and Valerie.

Hilda's Countermanding Spell

"I want to see myself hiking the Grand Canyon, **but** I can't afford to train for it."

Hilda's Reality Check

"I'm choosing not to hike the Grand Canyon because of the belief that I have to hire a personal trainer. My true self can hike the Grand Canyon because it knows that my having to hire a trainer isn't the problem—my perception that I can't afford to train is what's stopping me."

Greg's Countermanding Spell

"I see myself with my true love, **but** I don't know how to find that person."

Greg's Reality Check

"I'm choosing not to let myself have my true love because my mind believes it doesn't know how to find that person. My true nature can create the perfect relationship because it knows that finding that person isn't the issue—my belief that I can't find the right woman is what's making me suffer right now."

Valerie's Countermanding Spell

"I see myself running a successful business, **but** I need an MBA."

Valerie's Reality Check

"My brain is choosing not to let me have my own business because it's been taught that not having an MBA is a problem. My true self can create my own business because it knows that not having an MBA isn't the problem—my beliefs about education are."

Your Countermanding Spell

I see myself [condition A] _____

But [condition B] _____

Your Reality Check

"My mind is choosing not to have [condition A] _____
_____
because it believes [condition B] _____
is a problem. My true self can create [condition A] _____
_____

because it knows [condition B] _____ .

_____

isn't the problem—my beliefs are."

Step 3: Discredit the Countermand

Remember, the countermand (condition B) is the belief that has closed your mind to the possibility of gaining your heart's desires. Once you've stated that your mind, not external reality, is the real cause of your "stuckness," you're more likely to focus on changing your belief system rather than feeling like a victim. As you map out the path of your immediate future, instead of trying to fight outward obstacles, spend your time simply imagining what you would do if condition B did not exist.

Fill in the blanks below, and you may find that fulfilling your dreams is easier than you think. Or you may not have to fulfill them at all—the moment you free your mind from countermands, the Force will do the job for you. Thinking of things you might do if you disbelieve your "stuck" thoughts is a powerful magic spell. It sends you on a brief glide through the stars, and all of nature, including other humans, will respond to help you take your next steps.

Discrediting Your Countermand

First thing I would do if I did not believe condition B: _____

_____

Second thing I would do if I did not believe condition B: _____

_____

Third thing I would do if I did not believe condition B: _____

_____

You'll notice that I haven't given you much space to describe the things you'll do without your countermand. That's because the next steps on your star chart are always simple. The psychological work you did to connect with your Stargazer is quite a lot of work. But this step, the actual manifestation of your dreams, is usually just that—a step. Not a thousand steps. One. One step—the next step—is all you ever have to take. And since it's a step in the direction of your own North Star, it will match your desires and your talents. There may still be moments of feeling bogged down, in which you can repeat the exercise above. But most of the time, you'll have the eerie, wonderful sense that you're gliding through the Dreamtime.

For example, one day, Hilda let go of the belief that training to hike the Grand Canyon was necessarily an expensive proposition, and do you know what she did? She just drove on out one day, all by herself, and hiked the Grand Canyon. "I don't know what got into me," she told me later. "I just slipped into believing I could, so I figured I'd better do it right then, before I stopped thinking I could." Was the hike easy? No. Could everyone do it? No. Would I advise *anyone* to do it alone and unprepared? No. But Hilda could manage this and did. So there you go.

In Greg's case, releasing the belief that he couldn't find his true love changed his entire personality. He became less needy and impatient, began to relax around people in general, and started attracting the women who matched his real personality.

Valerie, once free of the belief that she needed an MBA, simply started charging people for event planning, which was something she'd always loved. Before long, she had a thriving business, using her street sense to great effect where many MBAs, with their awkward book-learning, would have crashed and burned.

These examples are representative of what happens when we get "unstuck" in our minds rather than insisting the problem is in surrounding conditions we can't control. If you think I chose atypically successful examples, you're wrong; in fact, the results I see when my clients flip their countermands are usually quicker and easier than those experienced by Hilda, Greg, and Valerie. They often seem to happen by themselves, with stunning speed and in ways that make it hard not to believe our consciousness is sending out radio signals to the rest of creation.

Abracadabra

One reason I prefer working with groups rather than individuals these days is that I like to watch the magic of destiny-fulfillment happen right in front of me. When one client in a group dissolves a countermanding idea, other people in the room almost always *immediately* offer information, connections, physical equipment, and any other resources necessary to help that person's dream come true. In the astonishingly few cases where no solution arises within the group, it usually pops up within a few hours or days of the "countermand dissolution" process.

One of my favorite examples is a client (I'll call her Susan) who discovered during her seminar that she longed for just one really close friend, someone who understood her new path and was savvy enough to help guide her along it. Now, Susan had brought a copy of her favorite book to the seminar, a well-loved volume filled with marginalia, underlining, and dated references to events in Susan's life. After she returned home, she was horrified to realize she'd somehow lost the book in transit. She could buy another copy, sure, but all her notes, all her moments of insight, were lost. "I thought it was a bad sign," she told me later, "but that felt like a 'shackles on' thought, so I let go of my preconceptions and thought maybe someone else was supposed to have that copy, or maybe I needed to go on information from my own heart instead of any book."

The reality, as it turned out, was much more benevolent even than that. A few days after arriving home, Susan got a phone call from someone she'd never met, a woman I'll call Alexa. She lived 3,000 miles away from Susan. Alexa had just taken a flight on the same aircraft Susan had ridden home from my seminar. Though the plane must have made several flights in between, Susan's book was still in the magazine pouch. Alexa found it, began leafing through it, and found herself resonating deeply to the passages Susan had underlined and even more to the comments Susan herself had written in the margins.

Then Alexa found something else: Susan's boarding-pass slip, which she must have stuck into the book as a marker. The pass bore Susan's name and her destination city. Alexa began calling everyone with Susan's surname in that city, and before long, the two women were chatting. You know the rest of the story, right? Sure enough, not only did Susan get her book back, but Alexa became the close, inspiring, supportive friend Susan had seen as she mapped the path to her destiny.

From Mapmaking to Pathfinding

In the next chapter, we'll talk about how you can swing into action once you can see your own North Star, your distant goals are clear, and you've begun to let go of the beliefs that are getting you stuck. But as you can see from Susan's story, this level of detail in "mapmaking," though it happens in our heads and hearts, often segues seamlessly into what I call "pathfinding," or achieving your objectives in physical reality. Once you've tuned your equipment to the frequency of the magic realm—once you can hear here—fulfilling your best destiny becomes a matter of continuously working miracles. Fortunately, since you've already done the hard work of becoming a Stargazer, you'll soon realize that miracles are right up your alley.

CHAPTER 8

Working Miracles:
The Pathfinder's
Progress

I t was the actor's nightmare, times a number so large it is purely theoretical. I wanted to be anywhere but where I was: in a small bookstore
in Switzerland, surrounded by kindly Swiss people who were expecting me to address them any minute now.

In German.

Which I don't speak.

During one of those ghastly, endless moments that yawn open under
conditions of utmost dread, I contemplated the boneheaded way I'd gotten
myself into this situation. Four months earlier, a wonderful German author
named Werner (Tiki) Küstenmacher had visited Phoenix and invited me
out to lunch. Tiki and his handsome teenage son, with their perfect
English and genteel Continental manners, were so charming that when
Tiki asked me if I'd like to come to Germany to join him on a book

tour that would promote both our books, it sounded like a wonderful idea.

"The only problem," I'd said, "is that I don't speak German."

"Well, yes," said Tiki, "but you *read* it, right?"

"Trust me," I told my new friend. "I'm American. When I say I don't speak a language, I don't speak it, I don't read it, I don't understand it. At all."

Tiki looked troubled, but only for a moment. "Well, we'll work something out," he said.

Then he showed me how he gives lectures, not only speaking but drawing cartoons on an overhead projector, because in addition to being a madly successful self-help author, Tiki is a brilliant professional cartoonist. Also a famous minister. I was too intimidated to ask, but I suspect he's also a heart surgeon, a concert pianist, an Olympic gymnast, and the principal engineer for the Space Shuttle. So, caught up in the reflected glory of Tiki's genius, I agreed to go to Germany. I'd say *Guten Tag*, sign a few books, share a few European-sounding laughs with polyglot Germans—it would be fabulous.

I ordered some "learn German" CDs to play in my car and a similar program for my computer. For four months, I happily studied the language in these modest ways. But I never actually interacted with anyone who, you know, spoke German.

When I arrived in Frankfurt, disheveled by many sleepless hours on a plane, my German publisher's representative met me and handed over a list of my speaking engagements. There were nine of them. Beside the last two listings I saw the words "translator available."

"Um," I asked my chaperone, "does this mean I'm supposed to give speeches at all these venues? Without a translator?"

"Exactly," he nodded.

"And I'll give these speeches in English, right?"

"Mmm . . . no, it would be better if you spoke German," he said. "I've lived in Canada, but it's hard for most Germans to follow American English."

"I don't speak German," I said.

"But you *read* it, right?"

That was about twenty-six hours before the hideous moment in the Swiss bookstore. I'd been awake the entire time, trying desperately to think of a plan, scribbling cartoons that might illustrate some of my ideas the way Tiki illustrates his. Now, here I was, facing a cheerful German-speaking crowd, not understanding one damn word of the gentle hubbub. I'd read that the fear of public speaking is more common, and more paralyzing, than the fear of death. And now, oh, I knew why.

After a few eternities, a man—the bookstore owner or whoever—stood up. The crowd grew silent. I became so terrified I exercised the only option I had left: I retreated inwardly to my core of peace.

The bookstore owner (or whoever) started to talk.

And I understood everything he said, as if he were speaking English.

"Heilige Scheiße!" I thought, nearly jumping out of my skin. *"I speak German!"*

Immediately, the words of the bookstore owner (or whoever) dissolved into a meaningless string of alien sounds.

Shaken, I returned to my core of peace.

I understood everything the bookstore owner (or whoever) said.

Unfortunately, whatever shamanic dispensation allowed me to understand German didn't take things so far that I could actually speak coherently. But with no trouble understanding, I found that a combination of slowly spoken English (Tiki translated) and live cartooning (I'd learned while teaching art at Harvard that people love to watch others draw) added up to a presentation that the kind crowds seemed to enjoy. With Tiki doing all the heavy lifting, we worked up a dog-and-pony show that ran along pretty well for the whole time I spent in Teutonic lands.

That was a weird, wonderful week. I never did speak any decent German, but as long as I stayed mentally ensconced in my core of peace, I understood things my mind couldn't possibly comprehend. Once, when I ran out of transparencies (indispensable to my new sub-verbal presentation style), I found an office supply store and found myself blurting out a sentence in German that I didn't know I knew. ("I need those things that are like sheets of paper, but made of clear plastic" is what I said. I think.) Though Tiki bore the brunt of our co-presentations, I stumbled along by drawing my own cartoons, speaking English while he translated, and staying in my core of peace, which apparently speaks German even though I don't.

Along with this strange verbal comprehension, I experienced the Stargazer's sense of falling in love. I felt addicted to German, to Germany. My brain seemed to be *eating* the language, ravenously. I bought German books-on-tape and played them while I tried to sleep, delirious with the joy of understanding. A woman in Berlin took my hand and said, "We don't speak the same language with our heads, but we do with our hearts, don't we?" I watched my brain translate her German words into English—*after* I understood them. Don't ask me how I did this; I *can't* do it, any more than I can make three human infants with a few simple tools anyone might find around the house. All I know is, it happened.

Amazing Space

This is the way life unfolds when you remember to steer by starlight. What you think will be easy proves impossible; what you think is impossible happens by itself. Insuperable barriers arise in the material world, only to vanish once you look at them from the realm of the Stargazer. The more of this I see, the more I identify with the poet Mary Oliver, who wrote: "All my life I was a bride married to amazement." If you allow it, your life will flow into zones of astonishment you could never invent.

This doesn't mean you won't have to work if you follow your own North Star. This chapter is all about work—specifically, how to approach and complete the work necessary to bring your envisioned destiny into material reality. Since only you can find the path of your destiny, I can't advise you here about the particular course of action you should take right now. However, I can teach you the process of establishing your position, checking your star charts, and deciding what to do next, no matter what your situation.

As you'll see, you may work harder when you start steering by starlight than you've ever worked before. But if you're on course, travelling in a way that's guided by your Stargazer self rather than a set of socialized ideas or fear-based assumptions, you'll find the work unbelievably fulfilling. Especially since, no matter what kind of work you're doing, you'll also be working miracles.

Miracle-Working 101

"I can't believe it!" Sarah exulted when I visited her home city some three years after we'd finished working together. "Everything I wrote down on my star charts has come true! Miracles really happen!"

The thing is, Sarah had been working flat-out to build her coaching practice, lose thirty pounds, get her children raised right, and maintain her many friendships. At one point, she'd taken out a second mortgage on her house to send her daughter to a high-ranked performing arts high school. She'd spent two years of her nonexistent "spare" time writing a book, then another year submitting it to a string of agents, all of whom had said no. Then she'd self-published the book and marketed it herself, until a publisher took note and decided to buy the rights. Sarah had labored and sweated and stayed up nights making her dreams come true.

And yes, miracles really had happened.

The perfect business partner had arrived in Sarah's life through a chance encounter at a bookstore, and they'd built a practice that had, in turn, given her ideas for her book. Even so, her best writing ideas seemed unintentional and even external to her intentions; they'd popped into her head as if someone were whispering them to her. The editor at the publishing house that eventually bought the book focused on it through a string of small coincidences: He found a copy lying on a park bench; then met one of Sarah's best friends, who sang the book's praises; then received a copy as a birthday present, all in the same week.

This is how miracles operate: If you stay connected to the Stargazer and do everything you can think of, you'll find yourself being assisted by things you *can't* think of. As the Sufi poet Rumi wrote, "Be helpless, dumbfounded, unable to say yes or no. Then a stretcher will come from grace to gather us up." This doesn't mean that we just have to lie around waiting for divine stretchers to lug us toward our North Stars. It means that when you're steering by starlight, the place of maximum delight is an exquisite combination of practical challenge and magical assistance.

The Satisfaction Zone

Another fabulous current brain researcher whose work I love is Gregory Berns, M.D., Ph.D., whose book *Satisfaction: The Science of Finding True Fulfillment* is (as the title suggests) a most satisfying read. Dr Berns's research establishes quite clearly that humans need challenge—really difficult challenge—to reach a brain state that creates the feeling of happiness. As it turns out, people to whom everything comes easily just can't get no satisfaction. In fact, they can't get no more satisfaction than people who are horribly overchallenged.

Part of your destiny is to live in the zone of maximum satisfaction. That means that if you steer by starlight, you'll choose goals that require lots of work. However, that work should always—or pretty much always—feel fulfilling. The place where you're happiest lies at the edge of your ability envelope; in other words, the journey to your own North Star at its best will be almost too difficult, almost too fast, almost too complicated. *Almost.*

In yoga, they call this "staying at your edge." My friend Logan, the yoga instructor, always asks his students, "Does it feel delicious?" Deliciousness was what I experienced in Germany, that strange sense of my brain gobbling up words, licking its fingers, then looking for more. It's what Sarah felt as she built her practice, engaging so totally in her clients' lives that she'd forget how hard she was working. It's what you'll feel when you set out on your own starlit path. All you have to do is site your course by starlight, envision the map of a future that makes your body hum with agreement, then move forward in a way that's almost too difficult to manage. Here are the rules of North Star pathfinding in a nutshell.

Finding Your Perfect Path through Life

1. Go to your core of peace and stay there, dissolving any thought that tries to dislodge you.

2. Focus on a goal from your star chart.

3. Take the step toward your goal that feels most delicious.

4. Repeat steps 1 to 3 over and over until you're dead.

What to Do in Case You Feel Lost

You can't get lost for long when you steer by starlight; at the very worst, you'll notice yourself feeling foggy and out of sorts. Then you stop, find the thoughts that are causing the unhappiness or confusion, and dissolve them. This will allow you a clear view of the stars again, and you'll feel your next step forward as a falling-in-love connection with some form of action.

For example, Daniel wanted to start a martial-arts program for at-risk youth in Los Angeles but kept running into a brick wall when it came to renting a studio. After months of effort, he finally questioned the thought "I need a studio." Since this wasn't true, Daniel started teaching kids at outdoor basketball courts and generated far more interest among the kids than he would have indoors. Jody dearly wanted a cat but lived in a rented house whose owner didn't allow pets. She longed for a furry friend for years before questioning the thought "No one will let me have what my heart desires." Once she confronted and dissolved that belief, she cheerfully, relentlessly, and successfully persuaded her landlord to become a cat lover. Well, a cat tolerater.

Staying connected to your Stargazer self allows you to think your way past almost any obstacle. When my kids were little, they used to watch a short cartoon on *Sesame Street* that was meant to teach them prepositions. The cartoon showed a fish swimming past a sunken ship, while the narrator said, "Over and under, around and through/ The wreck of the good ship Mary Lou." This is my mantra whenever I'm coaching myself or my clients around apparent obstacles that arise on our starlight paths.

Staying in the almost-impossible zone of maximum satisfaction is a good thing. However, there may be times when you set out to do something you've clearly seen during your mapmaking exercises, only to find yourself hating the process. It's not just hard; it's *icky*. Difficulty, fear, opposition from others, danger—none of these should stop you from forging onward. But *ickiness* is a sign that you should change either your target or your way of breaking the trail ahead. If ever you find yourself hating the path to your own North Star, there are three possibilities to consider.

First Possibility: You may be working toward the wrong goal

If the destination you've targeted isn't right for you, you'll feel increasing aversion to everything related to the goal as you work toward it. Fear—fear of failure, success, the unknown—is often part of your starlight path. But *aversion*, the sense of being poisoned, of shackles going on, is a sign you should reevaluate your objective. The only reason you chose the wrong goal is that you're trapped in a mental dungeon. Reconnect with your Stargazer self, using the tools in earlier chapters of this book, and melt down your false beliefs until the right goal occurs to you. It will.

Second Possibility: You may be navigating with your mind, not your deeper awareness

Your own North Star will tell you not only where you should go but how you should get there. If the objective you're pursuing passes the Stargazer tests, creating a "shackles off" response in your body and exciting your imagination, you may still have chosen the wrong path if you stopped steering by starlight and decided to go by sheer mental calculation. The mind is a good soldier that will keep marching forward through thick and thin, but you—and by *you* I mean only your Stargazer self—have to lead it.

I can't count the number of clients I've had who assume there's only one way to get to their North Stars. Actually, in today's social and technological climate, innovation—doing things in ways they've never been done before—is the process most likely to yield success in almost every aspect of our lives. If you know you're on the right road to your destiny, but you hate certain components of the work you do, dissolve the belief that "I have to pursue my goals this way." See the possibilities that arise when you open your mind.

Speaking of star travel, there's a catchy story about how NASA engineers spent millions of dollars to develop a pen that could write in zero gravity, while the Soviet space engineers, facing the same problem, sent their astronauts up with pencils. Moral: Don't assume you have to do something fancy and expensive when something easy and cheap is right before your eyes. The truth about the space-pen story, however, is that everyone in space used pencils at first, but the leads broke off and floated into the machinery. So yes, NASA did develop a space pen, which is now used by Americans and Russians alike. Moral: It's okay to use short-term solutions while you're perfecting more substantial long-term processes.

Notice that "We need a space pen to function" and "Damn, the pencils aren't perfect, so we can't use them at all" are two false beliefs that would have interfered with space exploration if the engineers at NASA had believed them. Moral: If you get stuck on the path that feels right to you, revert to dungeon-digging, see through your false assumptions, and notice whatever alternatives arise.

My favorite scene in the movie *Apollo 13* is the one where the space capsule is filling with carbon dioxide, so the engineers in Houston figure out how the astronauts can make a carbon dioxide filter using only what's available in the capsule, such as a cardboard book cover and their undershorts. "Work the problem!" shouts the lead engineer, meaning "Drop all your assumptions and play around with possibilities until a solution arises!" This is how all miracles are worked.

Third Possibility: You may be working against your conative type

Conative type? Yes, that's what I said. *Conation* is one of the least-used words in the English language, but it's one of the most important concepts to understand as you steer by starlight. At least as far back as Aristotle, scholars have divided human consciousness into three aspects: thinking, feeling, and doing. Thinking is the *cognitive* component. Feeling is the *affective* component. Doing is the *conative* component. Of the three, doing is the least studied and most neglected part of human experience. Knowing just a little about your conative style will help immeasurably on your journey to your own North Star.

According to theorist Kathy Kolbe, a leading expert in the field of conation, human ways of taking action vary among individuals rather like eye colour. Kolbe identified four different conative approaches people use to approach any task, whether that task is growing potatoes or solving differential equations. Steering by starlight not only requires that you strive toward the goals that feel most delicious to your true self but also requires that you use the conative style you naturally prefer.

The Four Conative Styles

Think of it this way: Let's say an otter, a squirrel, a mole, and a mouse all set out to find the Ring of the Nibelungen. Which animal will reach the ring first? Depends. If the ring is underwater, where Alberich the dwarf got the gold to make it, the otter will have a huge advantage. If the ring is hidden in a haystack, I'd bet on the mouse. If it's in a tree, the squirrel is a shoo-in, and if it's buried underground, the mole will get to it first. Neither swimming nor scampering nor climbing nor digging is "the best way to go forward." They're all just different ways to reach a goal.

Kolbe calls the four different human action styles Quick Start, Follow Thru, Implementor, and Fact Finder. You can use any of them, but you'll probably prefer some over others. If you want to take a formal test to see your precise conative profile, which will show you the level of preference you have for each action style, visit Kathy Kolbe's Web site (www.kolbe. com/all_kolbe_indexes/all_kolbe_indexes.cfm). If you don't mind imprecision, you can just notice which of the descriptions in the following pages seems most like you.

People who favor a Quick Start action style tackle any challenge by jumping straight into the process, learning by trial and error, working with pure *action*. Folks who happen to prefer Follow Thru behaviors focus on *systems*, either using an established system to move forward or inventing such a system. A person who favors the Implementor pattern works with physical *objects*; engineers, artists, and athletes often favor this action style. Finally, Fact Finder actions are about compiling and analyzing *information*.

Conative Preferences in Action

For example, the way I approached my book tour in Germany had everything to do with my conative preferences. As someone who prefers Quick Start action over all other conative styles, I just showed up in Germany, assuming I'd work something out. If I had a different conative profile, I'd have done the same basic things—but in very different ways. To wit:

If I happened to like Fact Finding best, I'd have done a hell of a lot more research before simply landing in a foreign country—for example, I might have, oh, I don't know, phoned ahead to ask if I'd been scheduled to give speeches in German.

If I were higher on the Implementor conative preference scale, I probably would have found some real live person to teach me German, in three dimensions. I'd also have prepared my cartoon presentations more than a day before I needed them. (Actually, I do have a fairly high preference for the Implementor style, which is why I bought language-learning tapes and CDs and decided to use transparency cartoons.)

Finally, if I had a primarily Follow Thru conative style, I'd have looked for a German book-tour system, taken a language course from an established institution, prepared and polished my speech to a high gloss. Then, upon arriving in Germany and finding that there was no system for doing what I was expected to do, I would have stabbed myself in a way calculated precisely to land me in the hospital and escape my speaking engagements, while getting very little blood on the rug.

Whatever your conative preferences, *do not try to adopt an action style that doesn't feel natural to you.* Any conative style will work for a person who gravitates to it naturally. If I'd tried to learn German systematically before hitting Frankfurt, I'd never have experienced one of the most wonderful weeks in my life. If you naturally prefer Follow Thru work, you'd have nailed the language before you ever reached German soil and had a wonderful time doing that. *The action style you use should be as delicious as your goals.* When process and destination are both tasty to you, the path to your North Star will unroll before your feet. You'll enjoy the journey, and when you fall, a stretcher will come down from grace and gather you up.

Pathfinding Exercise:
Your Life as a House

Finding the next step on your path is always a matter of staying plugged into your Stargazer, finding your zone of satisfaction, and giving yourself permission to work in whatever conative style feels best for you. Now I want you to use those pathfinding skills on a real-world task, one that may seem small but has profound repercussions for all who undertake it. I'm talking about redecorating your house.

Wait! Come back! If you're a very masculine sort of man, or for that matter, a very masculine sort of woman, you may think of redecorating as a simpering or daunting task, one that should be left to people who think all day about duvet covers and sconces and finials and other words found only in *Martha Stewart Living*. But living space is a powerful metaphor for your life. Whether you know it or not, you can't change your life without changing your home, and vice versa.

Every time you make a choice about which objects you bring into your space, where you put them, or whether to remove them, you're following psychological directives that also shape every other aspect of your life. If you feel overwhelmed by tasks and people, your home will be overcrowded with objects. If you care more about your children than about yourself, you'll take better care of their space than you do of your own. If you have a lot of secrets, the physical manifestations of those secrets will be stowed—usually in a grubby, hidden, or suffocating bundle—somewhere in your house.

The Butterfly Effect

The exercise you're about to do works on three levels: First, it's a physical action that improves your quality of life, however minutely. Second, you can't do it without changing your habitual patterns of action. Third, even one tiny iteration of this process has a "butterfly effect" on the rest of your experience. The butterfly effect is a concept based on a 1952 story by science fiction author Ray Bradbury, in which a time traveler goes back to the age of the dinosaurs, accidentally steps on a butterfly, and returns to find that insects, not humans, rule the modern world. Stepping on that one butterfly, seventy million years ago, led to enormous changes over the eons. If you start to pay attention, you'll find that making a change in your living space—say, taking down one photograph and putting up another—can have equally far-reaching effects, sending you down a *slightly* different path that hardly shows in the short term but putting you in a *very* different place at some point in the future.

Step 1: The Walkthrough

To begin the exercise, do a mental walkthrough of your living space. If you're at home as you read this, walking through the space in real time will work even better. As you observe each area of the space in your mind or with your physical senses, notice your body's reaction to each area. Pay attention to your moods as well. We're looking for the part of your house you like *least*.

Step 2: The Place of Least Satisfaction

If you love your home, your least favorite spot in it may be an area that's mildly unpleasant, such as a shelf that tends to get a little cluttered. If you're living in a horrible space, think of the nastiest, ickiest, most awful part of it, the place where no one but the plentiful family spiders ever go unless they absolutely have to.

Step 3: The Homemaking Star Chart

Now, for a moment, forget about your own home. Close your eyes and think about some other space, one spot on earth you find absolutely gorgeous. It could be a room you've seen with your own eyes, a house you saw in a movie, someplace in nature. As you did when you made your star charts, find a pictorial image that reminds you of this beautiful place. Print it or cut it out and put it someplace you can see it.

Step 4: The Three Adjectives

Think of three adjectives that describe the beautiful place you've targeted with your star chart. You can write them here if you like.

Adjective 1 _____

Adjective 2 _____

Adjective 3 _____

Step 5: The Hunt

Go out and find some physical object you can bring back to your home—a paint color, a piece of fabric, a knickknack, a pillow, a photograph—that can be described with at least one of the adjectives you chose in Step 4.

Step 6: The Acquisition

Bring that object into your home's area of least satisfaction.

Step 7: The Disposal

For every beautiful or inspiring object you bring into the space of least satisfaction, throw away something less beautiful and inspiring.

Step 8: The Next Step

Repeat the steps above until you love the space you once hated. Then, move on to the next most unpleasant space.

Ready, Set, Go

So, are you doing your house exercise? Have you started? Do I hear a "yeah-but"? *If you balk or stall out at any point in the process I've just outlined, it's because you are living in a dungeon of false thoughts that is limiting your entire life and keeping you from steering by the light of your own North Star.* You can tell me that's a preposterous claim, that this whole exercise is simplistic—but only after you've tried it.

Once you start using this exercise, you'll find "butterfly effect" changes in the rest of your life, not just your decor. In fact, you can use precisely the same process on any other aspect of your lived experience. Here's a handy-dandy reminder you can use on, say, your social calendar, your daily activities, your physical fitness, your career, or your plans to climb Everest by hopping on one leg.

How to Change Your Entire Life (One Tiny Little Bit at a Time)

1. Mentally or physically "walk through" the part of your life you want to change.

2. Identify your least favorite part of your experience with this area of life.

3. Picture a beautiful life (career, relationship, etc.) you've seen somewhere else.

4. Describe that beautiful life (career, relationship, etc.) with three adjectives.

5. Find a physical change you can bring into that part of your life—a different activity pattern, way of communicating, physical object—that can also be described with the three adjectives you've just chosen.

6. Bring that thing into the worst area of your life.

7. Discard something you dislike that has been occupying the dismal space.

8. Repeat, working through all inner resistance with your star-steering skills, until you are walking the path laid out for you by your own North Star.

Watching the Butterfly Effect Play Out

Whenever I nudge a client through these steps, I see not only hardworking people achieving their goals but also the flowering of miracles. The magic that just won't happen when we're headed for the wrong goal or using the wrong action style comes on like a hurricane when we return to the process of steering by starlight.

Let me end this chapter as we began it, with an example taken from my own travelling life. It's similar to a hundred other stories I've heard from people who began pathfinding with the "change your living space" exercise, but even after teaching this exercise for years, it stunned me like a mullet.

I was nearing the end of a book tour, and I was *fried*. For months, I'd been coaching and speaking to all sorts of groups, nerving myself up for radio and TV appearances at weird hours, accepting interviews not only with bona fide magazine and newspaper reporters but also with the sort of Internet bloggers who have serious emotional disorders and speak only Latvian. All the time, I was writing magazine columns, coaching clients, running seminars, and trying to check in with my children often enough to see if they'd, say, gone off to college or formed a collective and begun subsistence farming in the Balkans.

The maddening thing was, all this exhausting work didn't seem to be doing much good. Whenever I went somewhere to speak, it turned out that the books I was supposed to sell hadn't arrived. Talking to all those bloggers, not surprisingly, seemed to make people *avoid* reading anything I'd ever written. The harder I pushed myself, the harder failure and disappointment seemed to push back.

One day, on a brief visit home, as I picked through my book collection looking for something to inspire me to work harder, I found a little Chinese book I'd read and forgotten long before. It was all about the Taoist concept of *wei wu wei*, "doing without doing." *Wei wu wei* is a concise and elegant way of saying that if you align yourself with your Stargazer and follow the star chart it lays out for you, the whole energy of reality will carry you along like a raft on a river. You'll end up moving with great speed and power, but all that energy is generated by the current, not by you. The only thing you have to do is float.

Talk about a "shackles off" reaction! As I read through this book, a river of peace truly did run through me. It was such a tangible sensation that I decided it was time to walk my talk, stop working so hard, and trust in destiny.

So naturally, I redecorated my bathroom.

I practice what I preach.

The main focus of my new room was a certain art piece I'd owned for years but had never displayed: a large sheet of rice paper bearing the Chinese character for "play." The calligraphy had been done by a play therapist whom I'd met briefly and who believed absolutely in the power of "doing without doing." I'd been inspired by the short time I'd spent with this man and thrilled to receive the calligraphy he'd created. However, I'd stuck it in a storage space and forgotten to display it. Now I dug it up, had it framed, and hung it on a wall where I would have seen it every day, except that I immediately left the country.

The next leg of my book tour took me to South Africa. Once there, I began giving even more speeches, meeting with even more reporters, and having to work straight through many African nights, since they coincided with American days. I'm passionately in love with South Africa, so I thrived on this psychologically, but my body began to give out. One afternoon, while I was being interviewed by an absolutely lovely journalist, the muscles in my torso began to shake with the effort of holding me upright. I wasn't sure how long I could keep sitting up.

Still trying to chat coherently with the journalist, I began to rant inwardly at the Force. *"All right, that's it!"* I told it. *"I am too damn tired to keep going! If life really is about aligning myself with the frigging will of heaven, I want . . . I want . . . a Thai yoga massage! Yeah, that's it! And I want it NOW!"*

A Thai yoga massage, in case you've never had one, is the most sublime and healing sort of bodywork ever conceived. You lie there in loose clothing, and the massage therapist pushes, pulls, thumps, and sometimes throws you all over the place. It's not like other forms of massage, where you basically just get rubbed. Thai yoga massage therapists have to be athletic, smart, sensitive, and thoroughly trained. I'd encountered only one in my life. But that had been such a healing experience that as I sat with the African writer, it was the only thing I could imagine making me feel better.

We finished the interview. The journalist got up to walk me back into my hotel and then, apropos of nothing, she suddenly asked, "Did I tell you I'm also a Thai yoga massage therapist?"

Really.

As soon as I could stop gaping and speak coherently, I asked if she was free to work on me that very day. We quickly arranged the massage. Then she said, "You know, there's one other American author whose work I love. I don't suppose you'd know him . . . "

"I don't think so," I said, meaning it. Book authors rarely run into one another—writing isolates more than it connects—and the United States isn't exactly a tiny neighborhood.

"Well, maybe you've heard of him, anyway," said the journalist. "He's a play therapist. His name is Fred Donaldson."

"Okay," I told the Force. *"Now you're just showing off."*

Fred Donaldson was the man who painted the Chinese character I'd hung on my wall the day before flying to Africa.

Walking the Milky Way

The night after this happened, I went out into the African night and stared up at the sky. The Milky Way shines much brighter in the South African sky than it does over my home in Arizona. I almost fell over backward looking at it, knowing that every photon reaching my eyes had left its star millions of years ago, when the dinosaurs still roamed, in order to register on my tiny consciousness at this particular instant of earth-time. When you begin finding the path of your best destiny, when you begin walking it with your eyes on the stars, mind and heart wide open, the magic you'll feel assisting you is just that vast, just that unfathomable. You can feel the inconsequential, infinitesimal importance of your own ego, and yet (to quote Byron Katie) "if you knew how important you are, you would shatter into a million pieces and just be light." The fourteenth century poet Kabir put it this way:

> We sense that there is some sort of spirit that loves the
>
> Birds and animals and the ants.
>
> Perhaps the same one who gave a radiance to you in your mother's womb.
>
> Is it logical that you would be walking around entirely orphaned now?
>
> The truth is you turned away yourself, and decided to go into the dark alone.
>
> Now you are tangled up in others, and have forgotten what you once knew.
>
> And that's why everything you do has some weird failure in it.

I don't know why it matters that we untangle ourselves from others, remember what we once knew, understand that we are not walking alone. I don't know what it is that seems to encourage this. But I do know that once you join up with your true self, even in tiny, seemingly insignificant ways, you will live the rest of your days married to amazement. The stars will burn themselves out to light your path.

CHAPTER 9

Leading Your Life

At forty, Luke was wealthy, divorced, and raising two small sons on his own. Then Mother Nature smacked him with one of her trademark wallops: Luke was diagnosed with diabetes. The disease was taking a particularly horrific toll on his eyes. Though they did all they could, Luke's doctors told him they were fighting a losing battle to save his sight. They gave him a devastating worst-case scenario: At the current rate of deterioration, he'd be completely blind within six months.

Fortunately, Luke had two big things going for him: his considerable fortune, which he'd earned early as an investment banker, and a close relationship with his older sister, Fiona, and her husband, Leonard. Fiona and Luke had survived a childhood with two alcoholic parents, so Fiona was more like Luke's mother than his sister. After Luke's diagnosis, she and Leonard—who had no children of their own—moved across the country to live nearby and help him raise the boys.

Because this setup sounded close to perfect, my only suggestion for

Luke was that until his eyesight failed, he should see everything he'd ever wanted to see. He'd always longed to travel but had been so busy working and then raising his sons that he'd never gone sightseeing. In addition, when Luke went through the "life as a house" exercise you read about in the previous chapter, he realized that his home was sorely lacking in natural light. It was a gorgeous antique mansion that Luke and his then-wife had restored, but it had only a few small windows with virtually no view of anything.

After our first session, Luke bought a ticket to Paris and left his boys with Fiona and Leonard for three days while he toured the Louvre and bought some antiques for his house. He had a wonderful time, experienced a sense of growing inner peace, and (as often happens when people begin steering by starlight) felt inspired to make larger changes. He hired a contractor to begin carefully carving out windows in the walls of his mansion, bringing in light and allowing gorgeous views of Luke's large wooded property. "I want my kids to grow up seeing everything," he told me.

Though my heart ached for Luke's many losses, all of this seemed very positive, so I was stunned by what happened next: Fiona and Leonard threw a dual blue-faced fit. They told Luke that if he continued to travel, they'd withdraw their emotional support, move away, and cut off contact with him and his sons. As for Luke's putting windows in his home—well, Fiona and Leonard were having none of that.

Fiona began sending Luke long, angry e-mails about how he planned to "expose everything" and "hang out the family's dirty laundry." She was obsessed with keeping people from seeing *into* his home. Luke realized that he'd deliberately chosen a home with few windows because he had a subconscious fear of the same thing. However, he managed to shrug this off. Fiona? Not so much.

Long story short: After two weeks of tension and conflict, Luke managed to get everyone into a family therapy session. There, Fiona revealed that ever since Luke was a small boy, she'd suspected him of plotting to kill her. Leonard shared her suspicions. He revealed that staying close to Luke was one way he and Fiona felt they could keep an eye on him. "Keep your friends close," he said, "but your enemies closer."

During the subsequent weeks, as suppressed conflict exploded into the open, Fiona just unraveled. She was diagnosed with paranoid personality disorder, greatly exacerbated by a truly epic marijuana habit. Last I heard, Fiona was in rehab, and Leonard had filed for divorce, saying he had to get away from a "dangerous situation." As for Luke, he'd found an excellent therapist and started talking about the realities of his very strange family dynamics. He also continued his travel and remodelling projects. I don't think it's a coincidence that his eyes had begun responding much better to medical treatment. He was ready to see everything around him, literally and figuratively.

Road Bandits

Here's what I've learned from clients like Luke: The terrain you must travel if you plan to steer by starlight may be not only rocky but also infested by bandits and pirates, some of whom will launch sneak attacks you never dreamed possible. I'm not trying to scare you, but it would be wrong to pretend that people won't try to stop you, often for strange reasons. Some of these people are merely confused. Others are frightened because as you change, they must either change with you or adapt to differences in their relationship with you. And then there are the folks like Fiona, who are (to use the technical medical term) total freaking loons.

You may be one of the lucky people whose loved ones and associates are all delighted and inspired when you set out to live your right life. More likely, though, you'll encounter some level of resistance. After all, the most common reason we stray from our best lives is that we're socialized to behave in ways that aren't right for us. Our social groups, almost by definition, tend to disapprove when we drop those behaviours.

This chapter is about handling the human obstacles that may loom or leap at you when you begin steering by starlight. You'll find that the skills you learned in earlier chapters are the key to handling opposition. In addition, it helps immensely to have just a little information about why people may resist you and what sort of attack you're experiencing. But in order to use these tools wisely and effectively, you must embrace one pivotal truth: No matter what your social context, no matter how difficult your road, no matter what sort of opposition you encounter or what other people do, *you must approach each situation from the perspective of leadership.*

Lead, Don't Fight

You are responsible for leading your life. If you don't accept that responsibility, whether because others try to stop you or because you're not aware you can, the odds of your fulfilling your best destiny are practically nil. The actions of others are not your fault, but even in situations where you're being treated outrageously, acting as a leader is the way to stay on the path to your North Star.

This doesn't mean that you dominate other people. Quite the contrary. To be an effective leader means staying grounded in the psychological position of the Stargazer, which has no fear and therefore no need for aggressive power. As Lao-tzu put it, "All streams flow to the sea because it is lower than they are. Humility gives it its power." When you're steering by starlight, you lead by acting like the ocean: flexible, transparent, open, yielding—and unstoppable.

The more you feel the power of this position, the more you'll see why leadership, not battle, is the way to handle attack: From the backward view of the Stargazer, everything on the path to your own North Star, including your opponents, turns out to be fighting *for* you. Everything and everyone in your life—whether they know it or not—ends up acting in your best interests.

Low-Level Conflict:
Lizard Attacks from Loved Ones

In most cases, resistance from other people—whether your nearest and dearest or total strangers—comes from the reptilian brain. Remember that most people believe their inner lizards implicitly, and the lizard's job is to pump out a never-ending series of fear responses, all framed as lack ("There's not enough for me.") or attack ("Something bad is going to happen to me."). Every time another person opposes your steering by starlight, you can be sure that person sees you as a lack/attack threat.

The general rule to remember is that when we're scared, we're scary, and when we're scary, we're usually scared. If someone seems strangely opposed to your actions, even though you're motivated purely by good intentions and are doing nothing that could possibly injure him, rest assured that person is afraid. This does not excuse violent or malicious behaviour; it just explains it. A common psychological error you'll find in movies and television is that the evil people on the screen are often depicted as knowing they're evil and feeling powerful in their destructiveness. In real life, people who perpetrate evil virtually always see themselves as victims, forced by circumstances to "defend themselves" by attacking others.

Inner lizards that see themselves as the victims of possible lack or attack sometimes create absolute horror, as when one ethnic group decides that another ethnic group is "threatening" them and uses this to justify war. Usually, though, it just makes people uneasy and tense. Most of my clients elicit some anxiety from their loved ones when they start steering by starlight. José's wife, Marcie, was terrified that if José made a midcareer job change, they'd end up penniless. Laura's parents worried that she was "abandoning the family" when she went to a monthlong meditation retreat. Barbara's husband, Peter, criticized her for not earning enough money, until she started earning more than he did—at which point, he accused her of trying to "damage his masculine identity." All of these people began subtly projecting anger, rattling their interpersonal sabers, hoping consciously or unconsciously to get loved ones to reverse the changes they'd made.

I know one therapist who calls these "changeback attacks." They're actually a good sign because they show that you're beginning to behave in ways that are genuinely new. And, if you can keep your own fear responses from ruling you and act as a leader instead of a reptile, they don't need to cause much trouble.

Reining In Your Lizard

When you respond to loved ones' fears with fear of your own, you create a vicious cycle: Your change scares them, they act scary, you respond by being scared and therefore acting scary, which scares them even more, which makes them even scarier, etc., etc.

Peter and Barbara are a classic case: Barbara had good reason to think that Peter wanted to keep her from succeeding professionally, as he reacted to her professional success by subtly threatening to leave. Peter feared that Barbara was going to fall in love with someone wealthier and that he had to earn more money than Barbara in order to keep her. Their relationship, which began simply as two people in love, became a minefield of suspicion, hidden agendas, and rage.

The way to handle fear-based opposition is to *be the person who refuses to act like a lizard.* Suppose you become happier and less needy as you steer by starlight. If your loved ones believe that your neediness is necessary to sustain your relationship with them, they might find this very threatening. You might hear comments like "I don't know what's gotten into you lately" or "I don't think this 'Do what you love' stuff is really healthy." Your inner lizard might interpret this as an attack on your new, authentic-feeling path and feel scared of having your independence taken away.

This is the point at which you *lead* the relationship by sustaining calm, fearless affection. If you stay connected to your Stargazer self, you'll see your loved one as rattled and afraid, not dangerous. From that place, you won't fight back ("What are you saying? You don't support me? What's your problem?") but simply reestablish calm ("I know I'm acting different, but I feel really good about it. And I love you more than ever."). Barbara and Peter's relationship changed dramatically when Barbara started using this approach. "It's amazing," she told me. "All he wanted was some reassurance."

The more you focus on sustaining your Stargazer attention, the less fear you'll feel in relationships and the easier it will be for you to continue doing what's right for you while projecting the calm, secure energy of a leader. When my clients are changing radically, I often have them practice saying just one simple phrase in response to subtle or overt pressure from their loved ones. You can use it, too, whether you're dealing with your business partner, your ten-year-old, your fiancé, or your grandmother. Look them right in the eyes and say, with the calm conviction of the Stargazer, "All is well."

Don't be distracted by words when you're using this leadership strategy. Remember, people dress up their inner lizards' fears in all sorts of verbal stories. The story isn't the point: Their fear is. Don't sink to the level of epic dinosaur conflict by engaging in word wars. If you keep breathing deeply, feeling peaceful, and offering reassurance, you'll defuse arguments that could become endless, before they even begin.

Midlevel Conflicts: Different Objectives

Chet and Leslie were one of those joined-at-the-hip couples: They worked together at home, coparented, and even cooked their meals together. Then Chet's mother died unexpectedly, and the grieving process uncovered aspects of Chet he'd never known were there. Like many people who've dealt well with a loss, he became less afraid of death, more committed to living every day he was alive. Gradually, he realized that he felt underchallenged. He wanted to go to business school and learn how to grow the business he and Leslie had created. His star chart included travel, adventure, service, a whole smorgasbord of experiences he and Leslie had never even discussed.

Leslie found this very threatening. She launched a series of changeback attacks that rocked the couple's silky-smooth relationship. When I met with both of them, she said, "I just want the old Chet back."

Unfortunately, that was one thing Chet couldn't give her. Trying to cooperate with changeback attacks is like trying to unring a bell or voluntarily grow shorter. You can't forget the view from the Stargazer's eyes without losing what's most important in yourself. People who try this in order to please loved ones become *imitations* of their old selves, and unhappy ones at that. It's never good for the relationship or anyone involved.

What Chet and Leslie needed wasn't a commitment to never changing but a commitment to handle change with creativity and negotiation. As the old saying goes, if two people agree on everything, one of them is superfluous. And if they don't agree on everything, they need a method for sustaining a loving connection no matter where the paths of their best destinies may take them. This kind of connection is easiest to describe in contrast to its opposite, something I call "spider love."

Spider Love versus Real Love

If you went into your garden, recruited a spider, and asked it, "What do you love most?" the spider might answer, "I love flies." This is true: Spiders enjoy a tasty fly the way I enjoy ice cream. And how does this love cause a spider to behave? Well, it makes a sticky web, catches flies alive, wraps them up to keep them from escaping, and keeps them there, conscious but helpless. Then, whenever the spider needs a snack, it scurries over to the fly, injects it with venom to dissolve some of its insides, and slurps up some of its life force.

This is the way many people think of "love." They will say, in all honesty, that they love their children, their partners, their friends more than anything in the world. But their love is *consumptive*, not giving. They need their "loved ones" to feed them emotionally, so they imprison people, trap them in webs of obligation or guilt, paralyze them to keep them from going away. They love other people the way spiders love flies.

Before you set out to lead a relationship where conflict is occurring, remember this: *The goal of real love is always to set the beloved free.* If someone else's "love" requires that you abandon your own soul, it's spider love. If you find yourself trying to control a loved one, you're in the spider's role. Spider love really isn't love at all but a version of fear that creates a perceived need to control.

There are two red flags that will start to wave when real love disappears and spider behavior begins. The first is the deception, by which I mean *saying or doing anything at all that is not honest for you.* The second is the word *make.* When you do something even slightly dishonest because you're trying to *make* someone do or feel something, love is no longer running the show. This is just as true when you're trying to *make* people feel good and loving as it is when you're trying to *make* them follow your orders. People-pleasing and guilt-inducing are as much control strategies as domination.

If you're on the giving end of spider love, you'll feel grasping, desperate, angry, wounded, or all of the above. If you're on the receiving end, you'll feel a desperate desire to escape, often muted by your own rationalizations. "Mom's just trying to make me happy," you might think. "That's why she offered me a house if I get gastric bypass surgery." Or "Coach only screams at me because he's trying to make me achieve my potential." Or "Jesse just needs to make sure I deserve his trust; that's why he's tied me to this chair."

If you find yourself repeatedly convincing yourself someone loves you, check yourself for spider-glue. If your body tenses and your mood darkens when you think of the person who's trying to "make you happy," listen to it. If you feel wretched and panicky with the need to control someone else, realize you may be playing spider yourself. Either way, leave the web behind. Detach. Whatever your role in the drama, drop it and begin focusing on real love, the sort that always frees the beloved. You can think of it as Stargazer love, because at the level where you are truly steering by starlight, you'll do it naturally.

Leading Liberation

To love others without feeling the need to trap or control them requires trust that your needs will all be met, with or without the other person's cooperation. You must be absolutely sure that loving connection can encompass any level of difference without disappearing. *You don't have to trust the other person. You must only trust that your needs will be met no matter what that person may do.*

Neither your social self nor your frightened lizard brain is likely to sustain that kind of trust under pressure. But to your Stargazer self, your safety and the absolutely indestructible nature of love are both obvious. You need that Stargazer perspective to negotiate any long-term connection with other human beings, because someone has to lead the relationship out of trouble. Volunteer to be the first person to give away fear and to communicate from a place of emotional security.

Because Chet was following his own North Star into a different relationship with Leslie, he bravely agreed to lead the path through their conflict. (It would have worked just as well if Leslie had done it—you can act as a leader from any position in the relationship.) To accomplish this, Chet had to be willing to hold the position of the Stargazer and communicate with Leslie truthfully and directly, without trying to *make* anything happen. To do this in relation to someone in your life, first answer these questions.

Relationship Leader's North Star Location Questions

1. How would I *feel* if I knew absolutely that all my emotional needs would be filled forever, with or without the other person in my life?

2. What would I *say* to the other person if I knew absolutely that all my emotional needs would always be met?

3. What would I *do* if I needed absolutely nothing from this person?

4. What as-yet-unspoken things would I tell this person if I knew he or she could not be hurt in any way by the truth?

If it's hard for you to answer these questions, sit down with a notebook and work the problem in your imagination. Get to the point where you can *imagine* feeling that both you and your loved one are completely safe. You'll find that the grasping, angry, needy, or controlling energy you feel toward that person dissolves when you're in a position of emotional security. It's true that when we're scared, we're scary, and by the same token, when we're calm, we're calming. As the general who's leading the mission to follow your star chart, you must accept the responsibility of staying calm. You must keep your eyes on the North Star. If someone else freaks out, you must get even calmer.

Leadership Magic: The Balcony, the Evidence, and the Spell of Power

Once Chet had anchored himself in Stargazer mode by imagining his own reactions and inclinations without fear of losing or damaging Leslie, he moved on to learn the basic pattern of communication that I recommend for all leaders, by which I mean anyone who plans to fulfill his or her best destiny. This is a simple four-step process created by organizational behaviour theorist Al Preble for use in organizational leadership and modified for life coaching by me and Kim Barber, who worked with me training life coaches for years.

Leadership Magic, Step 1: Speak from the Balcony

The first step in leading a relationship out of a tough spot is something conflict mediators call "going to the balcony." Picture the conflict occurring on a stage, like a live-action soap opera. Then, freeze the action and jog up to the balcony. From there, describe the action.

In Chet's case, this meant that he told Leslie exactly what he'd say to a close friend or therapist about the relationship: "Leslie, I think you're feeling threatened because we've always done everything together, and since my mom died, I want to do some things on my own. I'm guessing you're scared of losing me, but I also think you might be worried about not being able to create a fulfilling solo career if I go off in another direction."

Since he was emotionally grounded in his Stargazer self, the energy with which Chet said this was calm, clear, and matter-of-fact. It didn't open the door to an emotional tussle between two scared inner lizards. Still, it was important that Chet go on to the next Leadership Steps.

Leadership Magic, Step 2: Describe the Evidence

After you've led the charge by describing what you think is happening in a relationship, you need to explain the reasons for that description. On what evidence do you base your opinion? This is a very scientific step: It demands that you be rigorous in sticking to observable facts. For example, "I just know you're angry" isn't an evidence-based claim. "I think you're angry because you haven't been saying much and you're frowning a lot" is.

Chet told Leslie, "I think you're scared, because you keep saying things that sound like they're meant to undermine my confidence. That's not like you, and I know you wouldn't do it maliciously. I'm guessing that you're scared."

The reason Chet could be so calm about Leslie's lack of support was that he remained grounded in his own sense of destiny, independent of anything she did or said. By not needing her, he could interpret her actions—even her inner-lizard-based actions—without just swinging back at her out of his own fear. This is one way in which the leader gains power by using humility, staying low and receptive like the ocean, rather than trying to exert dominance. If you can get this far, you're in position for the most powerful leadership step of all.

Leadership Magic, Step 3: Speak the Spell of Power

One of the most powerful sentences in the English language, a sentence that has vastly improved my relationship life, made me more useful to my clients, and helped me in all sorts of professional situations, contains only five simple words. I make all prospective life coaches repeat these words, this wonderful spell of power, until they're mumbling it in their sleep. The spell goes like this: After you've described the scenario from the "balcony" (Step 1) and given your evidence (Step 2), you make this genuine request:

"Tell me where I'm wrong."

For example, you might say:

> "Claudia, I think you just don't want to go with me to the flower show. You look unhappy when you talk about it, and you've lost your ticket six times. I'd be fine going alone, and I just think you're not up for it. Tell me where I'm wrong."

> "Norman, I get the feeling you're angry at your parents. Every time we go to their house for dinner, you're tense beforehand, and we always fight on the way home. You come across to me as being upset, and it seems to be about them more than me. Tell me where I'm wrong."

> "Loretta, I don't think you really like this job. You seem to mess up all the important meetings, and I know you're capable of handling them well. It's almost as though you're trying to get fired, maybe without knowing it. Tell me where I'm wrong."

> "Christopher, honey, I think you like hockey better than Little League. You seem really happy after hockey games, but after baseball, you're grumpy and sad. Tell me where I'm wrong." (This style of leadership works unbelievably well with children, especially teenagers, if it's done *very, very honestly, with no hidden agenda or manipulative intent, as a pure request for information.*)

If you can state your opinion clearly, give concrete evidence for that opinion, and ask sincerely and without resistance to be shown where you are wrong, you'll eliminate the vast majority of resistance you might receive from other people, period. Human beings have an overwhelming compulsion to be validated, to be proven right. Wars are fought over this need. People kill and die to prove they're right. And all along, we all know it's impossible to be absolutely right about everything.

Simply admitting that fact—which is what you do when you say, "Tell me where I'm wrong"—may feel like a terrible risk. Actually, it comes as close as anything can to making you bulletproof. It's a martial-arts move for the mind; because almost everyone is constantly trying to be right, admitting that you know you're wrong (at least about some things) defuses attack and deflates aggression. When you say it sincerely, you'll find that other people are befuddled but thrilled. They feel heard. They feel safe. The level of trust goes way, way up; the level of resistance, way, way down.

This is what happened when Chet said to Leslie, "Tell me where I'm wrong." He wasn't saying he'd gotten everything wrong; he wasn't taking blame he didn't deserve. Having clearly and powerfully stated his beliefs, he was simply a scientist looking for any data that might correct his understanding. This is both a humble and powerful position; when you do it from the position of the Stargazer, it's leadership at its best. Especially if you go on to Step 4.

Leadership Magic, Step 4: Listen

"Well, you're mostly not wrong," Leslie told Chet. This is usually the way people respond when you give them the chance. Leslie went on to describe what she was feeling—mainly a simple fear of change—and apologize for undermining Chet's plans to go back to school. Chet listened closely, without judging or "spinning" what Leslie said. This is the way the Stargazer self always listens. Then he assured Leslie, in almost these simple words, "All is well."

The facts Leslie and Chet exchanged were useful, and the new implicit deal in their relationship—that Chet would change at his own pace while allowing Leslie to respond in whatever way felt right to her—made them both feel relieved. But the real point of this whole interaction was that this basically functional, loving couple now had a way to explore their differences and their mutual plans for the future. *The process of reestablishing trust made their bond much stronger than it would have become by forcing themselves to agree with one another.*

This is the beauty of real love. When you set other people free by allowing them to do and say whatever is real for them, they don't abandon you or run roughshod over your feelings. Instead, they want to have you in their lives, the way they want fresh air or sunlight. You can be as different from one another as night and day, and just as seamlessly cooperative. I suggest trying this communication pattern—state your thoughts, give the evidence, ask where you're wrong—any time you encounter conflict with any person who's significant in your life, from your teenager (teenagers *love* being well led) to your boss to your in-laws. It works with almost everyone.

Did you notice I said "almost"?

Defense against the Dark Arts

Whenever I see one of my clients carrying around a well-thumbed book with a title like *Women Who Love Men Who Can't Love Themselves Enough* or *Tough Love for the Toxic Wounded Healer from Mars*, I brace myself to witness a painful disillusionment. They're almost always reading those books as part of an overwhelming need to understand one person (sometimes more, but often just one) who is driving them stark staring bonkers and has been doing so for years. If their well-meaning attempts to create a happy relationship with this person had been effective, they wouldn't be rereading those books. The reason they're still reading is that their significant other isn't amenable to ordinary relationships. They've run smack into the Dark Triad.

The Dark Triad is the label psychologists have for a certain group of very icky individuals: narcissists, psychopaths, and people with Machiavellian personalities. You can try calm, fair, loving communication with these people until hell freezes over, at which point you'll get very, very cold because these folks are the denizens of hell on earth, and they'll drag you right down there with them. This is also true of sociopaths, many addicts, people with obsessive paranoia—in fact, some psychologists think that the odds of having a healthy relationship with *any* disordered personality are mighty slim. Such people are versed in the Dark Arts. Trying to connect with them will plunge you into a night where the stars never shine.

Remember Luke, the diabetic whose sister and husband thought he'd been plotting homicide from the cradle? Sitting down and having a loving conversation with Fiona and Leonard, which Luke actually tried to do, was a waste of time and oxygen. What's more, Luke instinctively knew this. He'd gotten along with his sister and brother-in-law simply because he was used to their brand of crazy-with-a-side-of-crazy—so used to it that it felt normal to him. But when I asked him how he expected Fiona to respond if he tried to have an honest relationship with her, Luke immediately responded, "Oh, that won't work. Fiona would never go for that. You have to work within her perceptions if you expect her to talk to you at all."

If you feel this way about someone in your life, chances are you're trying to relate to a Dark Arts specialist. You can still lead the relationship, but you can't do it by simply helping him feel calm or opening lines of mutual honest feedback. In fact, this may actually expose you to danger, emotionally and in more concrete ways. Instead, lead by utilizing (thank you, J. K. Rowling) a "defense against the Dark Arts."

Recognizing a Dark Arts Practitioner

Diagnosing personality disorders isn't nearly as clear-cut as, say, recognizing a compound fracture or a case of the measles. Psychologists and psychiatrists spend years haggling over diagnostic details, and they may never agree on any given person's precise condition. I like the *Far Side* cartoon that shows a patient lying on a therapist's couch, gesticulating and ranting, while the therapist sits behind him with a notebook in which he has written, "JUST PLAIN NUTS." You don't have time to learn enough psychiatric nuance to correctly diagnose every nutty person you encounter. So be alert for the following symptoms that indicate you're facing a Dark Arts practitioner.

One general proviso: The mind is easily deceived by people with no scruples and no conscience. To pick up on a nut-bag, you must listen to your trusty body, which has a deep instinctive aversion to the Dark Arts. If you repeatedly, consistently have any of the following experiences when dealing with a specific person (we'll call this individual Person X), pay very close attention.

The Ick

We've already discussed this reaction in more general terms, but it has special relevance and urgency when you feel it in response to someone in your life. There are many reasons you might be nervous around others: You may be intimidated, desperate for their approval, self-conscious, worshipful, hopeful. But when you encounter someone with a Dark Arts disorder, you'll feel the sensation I call the Ick. Your body will feel torpid and out of sorts, as though you've taken a drug that clouded your brain. There will be no inner clarity; the strongest sensation you'll have is a sense of general *wrongness*. You can be sure this isn't about your own mental state if it goes away when you're not dealing with Person X. Pay special attention if you have this feeling in your usual life, but it goes away when you leave for a vacation—or when someone else takes a trip that leaves you free of his or her company.

Truth Slippage

People with Dark Arts tendencies lie the way most people breathe; easily, smoothly, all day every day. However, even the smartest psychopath can't always square up every lie with actual, physical reality. There's a sense of "slippage" around everything habitual liars say. You won't see glaring false-hoods, you'll just feel as though you're not standing on solid ground. Things you thought would happen don't; things you thought wouldn't happen do. Promises will be made, broken, and then never mentioned again, as though they'd never been made in the first place. You'll get increasingly confused and think thoughts like "I don't know what's going on" or "I'm not quite sure what's true." Over time, this grows into . . .

The Crazies

I once had a business associate (Person X) who was in the midst of broker-ing a deal between two small companies. As the two parties reached a consensus and prepared to sign a contract, this woman called all the par-ticipants and told them, "We'll finish this thing tomorrow! Everyone, stay by your phones—nobody talk to anybody else until I give the signal!"

Then, without telling anyone, she left the country.

For two weeks, no one on either side of the deal heard from anyone else. Both sides thought Person X was in cahoots with the other team. If some of the participants hadn't called each other and begun communicating directly, the deal would have imploded. When Person X showed up again, tanned and relaxed, she asked everyone else involved how *they* had enjoyed *their* vacations. The insanity of Person X's behavior is egregiously clear in retrospect, but at the time, all the normal people involved asked themselves the same question: "Am I going crazy?"

Constantly asking yourself this question in relation to one individual is a strong indication you're dealing with the Dark Arts. It may be hard for you to believe that some people brazenly manipulate others into feeling insane—but that's because you're not a Dark Arts practitioner yourself. Psychologists use the term "gaslighting" to describe sociopathic manipulation. The word comes from a movie made in 1944, in which Ingrid Bergman played a woman whose husband (played by Charles Boyer) tries to drive her insane by creating odd incidents—pictures disappearing from the walls, objects showing up in her handbag, the gaslights dimming and brightening—and then telling her *she's* responsible for all these events. This causes another symptom of Dark Arts victimization, to wit:

Shame Storms (Person X Good, Me Bad)

Another sign you're dealing with the Dark Arts is that you enjoy interacting with Person X and see him or her as a very impressive individual but invariably feel like crap after the two of you have spent time together. People with personality disorders are often masters of the subtle stiletto dig, the comment or raised eyebrow that lets you know you're bad—and that if you're very nice to them, they may forgive you for this. If you feel a general sense of "badness" after being around Person X, make no mistake: Person X *wants* you to feel this way. And it has nothing to do with who you really are.

I remember my college Shakespeare professor saying that Iago, the villain in *Othello*, is a flawed characterization because he messes up people's lives with no obvious motivation. Score another one for the Bard: Shakespeare's Iago is a brilliant depiction of a real-life Dark Artist. Sociopaths actually do things like this, though they rarely become serial killers or mass-murdering cultural icons because they usually don't dare perpetrate evil on an enormous scale. Martha Stout, Ph.D., of Harvard, one of the world's leading experts on sociopathy, estimates that as many as one in twenty-five people may have a predisposition to this disorder. So most Dark Artists aren't epically evil; they're just incredibly annoying. And if you happen to run across one, like poor old Othello, you may lose not only your North Star but your basic grounding in reality. Along the way, you're guaranteed to experience . . .

The Numbies

Going numb, emotionally or even physically, is one way your instincts will try to shut down to avoid being totally destroyed by a Dark Artist. Watch out if you don't know what you're feeling around Person X. The truth is that you always know what you're feeling, but Person X has such a strong, disorienting, disturbing effect on you that you stop believing in your own subjective experience.

If you go numb when you think about a certain person, or whenever he's around, or after you've spoken with him, you're actually experiencing an aborted fight-or-flight reaction. Your instincts are telling you to fight or flee Person X, but your social sensibilities won't let you. The only option left is to freeze, and that's what you'll do whether you think it's "appropriate" or not.

Pitying the Perp

In her book *The Sociopath Next Door*, Dr Stout reports that the best indication that you're dealing with a sociopath is that *you consistently feel pity for someone whose actions are harmful to you or others.* Most people don't realize that the dominant emotional state for someone who practices the Dark Arts is a baseline state of boredom marked by swelling, repetitive waves of self-pity.

Dorothy had an extremely distorted view of herself; she felt bad, crazy, confused, and numb all the time. To me, this was a good indication Dorothy had spent some serious time with a Dark Arts practitioner. Most of her pain seemed to radiate from interactions with her father, who routinely sabotaged Dorothy's attempts to build her own life or develop any measure of self-confidence. "But I know he loves me," Dorothy said. "He's a very tender-hearted, sensitive man. He cries all the time about what happened to him as a child— I've never known a man so willing to be in touch with his emotions."

"Tell me," I asked Dorothy, "have you ever seen your father cry about what happened to anyone else during their childhoods?"

Long, long, long pause. "Not specifically," said Dorothy, "but he must . . . um . . . he must have . . . "

No, actually, he mustn't. Self-pity masquerades as "tenderness" in many a Dark Artist. If you can't remember a person showing *empathy*—compassion, understanding, sorrow on anyone else's behalf—you're up against the Dark Arts.

Any combination of these symptoms should alert you that the leadership techniques you can use in your relationships with nor-

mal people will not work with Person X. You can read all the books, visit all the therapists, develop all the communication skills in the world, and *nothing will work*. But this doesn't mean you have to be victimized. You can still lead your life—and you must. If you don't lead a relationship with a Dark Artist, trust me, Person X will. And that will not be pretty.

Leading Yourself out of Crazy Town

Luke told me that when he set out on his trip to Paris—the trip that catalyzed the huge blowup in his family—one of the preflight instructions stuck in his head. It wasn't the old "use your own oxygen mask first" rule, though that always bears repeating. It was the instruction about what to do if the plane encountered an emergency. The exact words that stuck in Luke's mind were "Leave everything behind."

I think Luke's subconscious self paid close attention to those words because he knew he was up against the Dark Arts. Once his sister's paranoia was revealed, Luke's therapist gave him the same instructions about dealing with her. You can lead a Dark Artist, but not if you're trying to salvage some sort of workable relationship, the kind of relationship you long to have with everyone you love. Your first leadership skill when dealing with genuine craziness is to let go of your hope for normalcy. You may get a measure of it, but not if you're attached to the effort.

Dissolve the Lies

You'll need your Stargazing skills front and center all the time when you're up against Dark Arts opponents. Many Dark Artists feed on other people's misery; they'll mess with your head just because they like seeing you suffer. In a way, their detachment makes them excellent observational psychologists: They know that the primary cause of human suffering is believing thoughts that aren't true, so their primary weapon is lying. Because they lie when no ordinary person would, you may never suspect them. "Why would Bill lie to me?" you'll think. "There's no reason for it."

If you're dogged by a thought like this, reread *Othello*. Why does Iago go to great lengths to convince Othello that his wife is cheating, driving the hero to murder and suicide? Just because. Psychopaths don't need a reason to do harm; they do it for its own sake, for the rush of power it gives them, which is as close as they ever get to happiness.

The only way to defend yourself against this level of insanity is continuously noticing thoughts that cause you to feel any discomfort, from mild irritation to anguish. Dissolve those thoughts. Question them, test them, reverse them. If a coworker takes you aside and tells you, "I just want to warn you, there's a lot of negative talk about you going around the office," don't just believe it. Test it against the facts, against your sense of truth. If you're being as kind and loving as you can and someone accuses you of being "hateful," check with your sense of truth before you desperately try to be even more kind and loving. *Question every thought that causes suffering and test it against your own sense of truth.*

Yield to Overcome

"When two great forces collide," says Lao-tzu, "the victory will go to the one that knows how to yield." This doesn't mean that yielding to a psychopath, a narcissist, or a sadist is the way to overcome him. Anyone who practices the Dark Arts wants you to hand over your sense of what is true and right. If you do that, you'll go deeper and deeper into suffering, ultimately to despair, because yielding to lies always weakens you. *What you must yield to, in order to prevail against the Dark Arts, is your own deep sense of what is true.*

This means coming out of denial and accepting the horrible fact that someone in your life—maybe someone you dearly love—is too destructive to engage in any normal relationship. It means diving into the ring of fire, grieving the loss of the friend or parent or lover you thought you had. It means continuing to hold fast to the truth as your illusions burn away and arriving at the core of peace where you can continue loving your Dark Artist without being vulnerable to her insanity.

For Luke, this meant realizing that his sister and her husband were dangerously mentally ill. It meant surrendering an incredibly important relationship, "leaving everything behind," as he would in a plane crash. It meant continuing to love Fiona and Leonard, and trusting them—to keep being lethally crazy. As Luke processed all this with his therapist, I saw him burning up illusions and assumptions he'd carried with him since childhood: that he had to participate in subtle dishonest social posturing, that he had to please everyone, that no one could really be trusted.

All along, he'd known at a deep level that these beliefs caused suffering, that there had to be another truth. The more he yielded to his core of peace, the more calmly and effectively he dealt with Fiona and Leonard, and the less interest they had in engaging with him. Dark Artists don't get much fun out of interacting with people who question lies and remain grounded in their own truth. Your refusal to follow where they lead will ultimately influence them to go away and find other targets.

One more point: If there's a Dark Arts practitioner in your life, there will be damage. It's virtually unavoidable. Don't blame yourself and don't think you should have "handled things better." Remember what Gandhi said: "When I despair, I remember that all through history the way of truth and love has always won. There have been tyrants and murderers and for a time they seem invincible, but in the end, they always fall—think of it, always."

See Everyone in Your Life as Your Teacher

Anyone who comes into your life, under any circumstances, has something to teach you. A true leader is not someone who feels fully informed but someone who continuously receives insight and guidance. When you lead your own life, you become more and more transparent, open, willing to be taught (*"Tell me where I'm wrong."*) but anchored in your own fundamental sense of truth.

The irony of living this way is that you'll learn and benefit immeasurably from your friends, but even more from your enemies. Because you gain so much strength and insight from encountering hardship, because dealing with the craziest person in your life gives you wonderful incentive to find and remain in your core of peace, even a Dark Artist will only push you into the light of your own North Star. In the backward view of the Stargazer, everything an enemy does—everything *anyone* does—can be to your benefit. The brilliant Nigerian poet Ben Okri put it this way.

> *Remember that all things which happen*
>
> *To you are raw materials*
>
> *Endlessly fertile*
>
> *Endlessly yielding of thoughts that could change*
>
> *Your life and go on doing forever . . .*
>
> *So fear not, my friend.*
>
> *The darkness is gentler than you think.*

For someone who lives as a Stargazer, going into the darkness, whether with a friend or an enemy, simply puts you in the place where you can see your destiny blazing away overhead.

CHAPTER 10

The Beginning

Marianna shone like a lighthouse. I can't describe her without succumbing to every cosmetological cliché associating beauty and light; she had glowing skin, shining eyes, a radiant smile. I met her because she enrolled in one of my coach-training seminars, which was ironic, since she was far more qualified to train me than I was to train her. Especially at that particular time.

I was just entering the kerfuffle surrounding the publication of my second memoir, the one that deeply upset pretty much everyone I'd known as a child, plus a lot of people I'd never met. One evening, after the training seminar had concluded for the day, some unexpected visitors from my past showed up at my hotel room. They talked to me for several hours, telling me that if I didn't retract publication of the book, my life would be entirely destroyed. One of these people told me there were "guardian demons" dictating all my actions. Another assured me that I would soon be arrested. "You have no idea," this person said, "of the forces marshaling against you."

I tried to listen without any internal resistance and to genuinely consider all their suggestions. But each time I considered torpedoing publication, I felt a massive "shackles on" sensation. I'd written the book because I was intensely conscious of what Hannah Arendt called the banality of evil, the idea that most historical injustice has been perpetrated by ordinary people who are simply going along to get along with their cultural systems. My sense that I needed to break this pattern hadn't changed, despite the fact that I was facing, shall we say, a variety of socioeconomic pressures.

The visitors left very late, and I spent the rest of the night meditating to calm my skittery inner lizard. In the morning, I found it a delightful contrast to be among the life-coaching trainees, and I thought I handled myself reasonably well. But Marianna saw through me. After we'd dismissed for the day and all the other coaches had gone off to their respective rooms, Marianna returned to give me a precious gift: her story. She'd grown up in a distant country where her family had been part of the nobility for centuries. Though they no longer owned castles, lived off the farming of peasants, or commanded troops of knights, Marianna's people were still oh-so upper crust, oh-so conscious of their indigo blood. She'd grown up accepting her family's sense of superiority, not knowing there were other options.

Then, as a young adult, Marianna went on a sightseeing tour in a Third World country, where she visited a spot venerated by the locals as a place of great spiritual significance. When she walked into this space, without any warning, Marianna was hit by a mystical experience in much the same way a pedestrian might get hit by a train. It literally knocked her to the ground. She had trouble describing it, but in the language of this book, I'd say that her sense of being an isolated small self exploded like a nuclear bomb, and all that was left of Marianna was her core of peace—complete with its knowledge of being connected to absolutely everything.

In that moment and forever after, Marianna left behind almost everything she'd ever been, done, or considered important. She began walking back toward her hotel in a daze, seeing the poor people on the street for the first time, realizing that her family's wealth and power could change millions of lives. Then she began talking to the street people, listening to them, and—when it felt right—giving some of them sums of money that were insignificant to her but monumental and life-changing to them.

Naturally, Marianna's family believed she'd gone insane. If she'd spent millions of dollars on a mansion with gold-plated toilets, that would have been one thing. But mingling with Third World indigents? She must have had a psychotic break, developed the mania of bipolar disorder, begun manifesting latent schizophrenic tendencies. They begged her to get help and start acting like the Marianna they'd always known. She couldn't. For one thing, she didn't want to. She was experiencing pure joy for the first time in her life, locked on to her North Star, and everything about turning away from it felt like shackles, like a return to the dungeon.

Finally, Marianna's family took matters into their own hands and committed her to an asylum. She was heavily medicated and given many, many hours of therapy to help her realize that her love of all things, her newfound altruism, her deep joy, were just bats in her belfry. She tried to be a willing participant, but she simply couldn't deny what she'd experienced nor feel that it was a symptom of mental illness.

This combination of imprisonment and extreme pressure continued for some two years, until Marianna's therapists finally nailed their diagnosis: They decided she was sane. She signed herself out of the hospital, took a bus to a small town, spent a few days clearing her body of psychoactive drugs, and began an anonymous life doing menial labor. But she glowed so brightly—I swear, you could go cave-spelunking by the light of Marianna's presence—that people began asking her questions about their lives, and she became an informal teacher.

"One thing you learn when everything is taken from you," Marianna told me, "is that no time is ever lost, and nothing is ever finished. This moment—every moment—is a launching pad. Every moment breaks you open and begins a new life."

That's what North Star pathfinding is like. Every moment, you're being guided. Every moment, you can feel what puts shackles on your soul and what takes them off. But this doesn't mean you'll get rich quick and have no more heartache. In Marianna's case, it meant getting poor quick and going through devastating heartbreak. But once she had locked on to that point of light, once she'd experienced real joy, nothing that could be done to her could shake her from her connection to it.

And thus we find the path. We live in a time when new things are available to us every day, new possibilities, new perils. We have the ability to do things unheard of even a generation ago—and we face commensurate difficulties. The road that is unique can also be lonely. It's unknown and uncharted; the well-beaten path is the privilege—and curse—of former humans in former times. Following your star chart means you'll be breaking a new trail, the operative word being *break*. You'll break the mold, break the rules, break through barriers, and sometimes, break your heart. Sometimes, it will feel as though the path is breaking you.

Strong in the Broken Places

"Life breaks everyone, but some are strong in the broken places," wrote Ernest Hemingway. In fact, I think we are here precisely because we get stronger only by feeling or being broken.

Every couple of days, to keep my fibromyalgia in check, I go to the gym and work out every muscle in my body. I have to work the small muscles of my fingers and toes, the ones that hold up my head, the ones that open and close my mouth. I do this because I am particularly susceptible to muscle pain, and the fitter and denser my muscles, the less pain I experience. But let's be clear about what I'm doing at the gym: I'm breaking myself. By pushing and pulling and lifting and heaving in every imaginable way, I break down muscle tissue. That's half of the strengthening process. The other half is healing, getting plenty of rest and sleep so that the broken muscles heal—stronger than they were before I broke them.

I see life as a cosmic gymnasium where we have come to be broken and healed, broken and healed, for the joy of the process and because we have decided to become strong. But our bodies are just rented instruments; the part that's here to get stronger is the Stargazer. This is how strength training goes in the soul's gymnasium: Life breaks us. We hurt. We seek healing. We find the path to our North Stars and know instinctively that following them will lead to healing. We act on that instinct. We heal. We learn to trust that the path we've taken is the one we're meant to take. And with every experience taken through to its conclusion, we become more able to experience joy.

Trust is the force we use to become stronger and more joyful, like a weightlifter pushing a barbell into the air. The weight of fear and suffering tires us and makes us submit to gravity, dropping the weight. Then we push ourselves into the zone where we feel what is true all over again. Imagine that an alien from another planet dropped in and found a weightlifter pressing an iron bar over and over again. "Here," the alien might say. "You don't have to keep heaving that thing; let's build a small platform so that the weight stays up in the air, where you are obviously trying to put it. Then, instead of pointlessly trying to lift it up over and over, you could go have lunch. Don't worry; I'll keep that weight up there for you."

Of course, this would be ridiculous. In the gym—and in life—the point of endeavor is not sustaining the apex of achievement. The point is falling from that apex and finding our way back, over and over. We are here to learn something, and that something is trust. "When you trust yourself," said Goethe, "you will know how to live."

The Pathfinder's Plan

Marianna has learned that. As a result, she sees the slings and arrows of outrageous fortune—and ultimately her own death—as more of an exciting, wonderful game than a struggle. She has learned to head due north, whether that means plowing through cranberry bogs or jungles or glaciers. Sometimes, the journey breaks her down, more or less, but she always heals stronger in the broken places. So do we all. And when it is our hearts that break, they are the part that grows strongest. There will come a time when your new, old heart is so strong that it will create things beyond anything you could plan with your mind.

I used to make plans and set goals almost obsessively. When I ran out of goals and plans for my own life, I'd goad clients into making them for themselves. But several years ago, I realized that following my star chart was taking me further north than I could hope or even imagine. I no longer make plans or set goals—well, I do, but I know they're not the point. I know that I can never quite comprehend the places the stars want to take me. Here is my plan for life, the pathfinder's plan: *"I exist in perpetual creative response to whatever is present."* I suggest you try this yourself.

Following Freedom

Marianna left the asylum with no intention except to live free and follow her own North Star. In a strange way, her incarceration was part of her liberation; how else could she have totally disentangled herself from her old life, the family and friends who could not let her be herself? On one day, being in that institution was Marianna's path northward. But on another day, leaving it became the next act to perform in faith. The day after that, Marianna's next step was getting a job as a waitress. Later, it would mean taking vows as a religious contemplative. After that, it would mean becoming a teacher. Every day, Marianna's path was new. Though she had plans and goals, the only one she wouldn't change was the plan to stay in the zone that felt most "shackles off."

If you move toward freedom by saying and doing what is most honest for you, the result may be a beautiful, magnificent life of petting the dog, waiting tables, getting your teeth cleaned. This can be mind-bogglingly wonderful. "Ordinariness," which our culture tends to see as disappointing, is considered the highest manifestation of enlightenment in many other belief systems. I treasure my ordinary days, the ordinariness of my life as a whole. Each day, I list at least twenty things for which I'm profoundly grateful, and my rule is that I can never repeat an item. I've never had to. The variety of an ordinary life is infinite and precious. But because I follow the steps I've outlined in this book, I'm also willing to take leaps of faith into *extra*ordinary experience when my North Star seems to require such leaps.

For example, let me tell you about the week that's happening to me now, as I finish this book. This will show you the process of following one's star chart (the process I've described throughout this book) in a nutshell: aligning with the Stargazer, dreaming, visualizing, acting in faith, expecting miracles, then surrendering to the process through which preconceptions shatter, social connections shift, and unimaginably magical beauty begins to permeate daily experience.

The Dreams

I began having incredibly vivid dreams about Africa during that pivotal time in my life just before my son was born. In the dream, Adam was already a young man, one who did not have Down syndrome but was wearing the costume of his mentally retarded body with a kind of amused detachment. He would show me things in dreams, dreams so vivid that twenty years later, they still make my skin bristle. I had no idea what they meant. But I wrote about them in my dream journal and sometimes drew pictures, since what Adam showed me was visual, not verbal. The things I drew included people, animals, places in nature, unusual rooms.

I didn't realize until much later how many of the pictures I saw in these dreams were scenes in South Africa. I'll tell you what threw me off: the penguins. There were elephants in the dreams and other animals I knew to be African, but I had no idea that in South Africa, penguins waddle around places very close to pachyderms. I thought the Adam dreams were showing me a potpourri of symbols.

When I finally visited South Africa in 2001, I realized that the scenes in my dreams weren't symbolic. They were real. There was the bull elephant I'd drawn, in just that position, after dreaming about him ten years earlier. There were the penguins, toddling around in their small tuxedoes. There, above all, were the people. I returned to Africa six years later. Not only did the realization of those old dreams come back—it came back much more strongly than before. I recognized more animals. More places. A village school full of people I'd dreamed nearly two decades before. These people were more than my friends; they were part of me. Meeting them in the flesh was like getting pieces of myself back from oblivion.

The Star Chart

When I got back from that second Africa trip, some five months ago, I was so in love with South Africa that I made myself a star chart. I covered a large cardboard slab with pictures of more African animals, more African people, more exciting adventures. I thought that maybe, in the next five years or so, I'd get to go again.

The Impulse

During my recent trip, I'd met a brilliant tracker who made a special effort to connect with me because he'd read my work and felt we had some basic ideals in common. He was one of those people who were clearly part of my tribe, so we continued talking by phone when I returned to the States. He offered me free lodging at the game park where he lived and worked. I had only one spot on my schedule when I could work in such a trip—actually, even that time was all wrong, because I had work to do, a book to finish. Plus, even with free lodging, a trip to Africa is a big bite out of my budget.

The Leap

I thought about staying home. It seemed logical. Smart. Sound planning.

It felt like shackles clamping on.

I thought about going. My mind said, "Are you out of your gourd? Travel ten days to be on the ground in Africa for four? You can't do anything in four days, and you certainly can't afford the time or the money." That was the word machine, the inner lizard, the social self. But underneath that, the Stargazer said, "Shackles off, babe. Shackles off." So I decided to go. Yes, it felt insane, in a giddy, happy way—but then, as usually happens when I do something crazy to follow my own North Star, the miracles began. They are all small in and of themselves. But as they add up, they start to feel sort of big.

The Financial Means

After making the commitment to travel ten thousand miles, I had a phone appointment to follow up with a South African life coach I trained. I thought we might have lunch, but as we talked, it became clear Louisa could arrange a one-day lecture that would pay for part of my trip. She agreed to do all the legwork—planning, getting a venue, marketing, taking payment. All I had to do was show up. It felt nerve-racking—and shackles off. Done.

This deserves a brief discourse on money. As much as I hate the facile "do what you love and the money will follow" song and dance, I also have to agree with it—*on the same conditions outlined in Chapter 4*. If you pursue it from a place of fear and grasping, money will elude you. If you melt down your fears and approach money from a place of conviction, you'll get it. Remember my favorite heroin addicts, with their six-figure drug expenses; these people can't come up with rent or food money, but the dollars they're *absolutely committed* to getting—their heroin money—somehow shows up.

In fact, the correspondence between people's financial expectations and their actual income—or lack thereof—is so close it often strikes me as nearly miraculous. Which takes me to my next point.

I'll now switch to the present tense because I am entering the world of the Dreaming, where there is no time and everything is present. But though they're dreamlike, all the events I'll recount actually happened in the "real" world.

The Miracle Timeline

So one fine day last week, instead of finishing this chapter, I climb on a plane bound for Africa. I don't even know the reason. Well, technically I do know the reason—those vivid dreams, that sense of shackles falling when I think about going—but none of these reasons would make sense to, say, a career counselor or the IRS. There is no blank on Tax Form 1040-SS labeled "expenses incurred while following filer's own North Star."

And that's just too damn bad.

My assistant, fellow life coach and master horse whisperer Koelle Simpson is with me. Why? Because she's supposed to be, that's why. Taking her along felt "shackles off." Don't bother me about details. The woman at the counter in the airport is reading a copy of one of my books; she looks at my ticket, recognizes the name, and asks me if I'd mind signing the book for her. To say this is no trouble is a vast understatement. Having a stranger ask me to sign a book is like having her give me a pie for my ego.

"What a cool coincidence!" Koelle says.

"Maybe," I say. "But watch what happens from here on." I don't know what I'm telling her to watch. I only know that whenever you head off steering strictly by starlight, coincidences tend to get thick on the ground.

Flash Forward Thirty-six Hours . . .

. . . which is how long it takes us to wend our way from Phoenix to a game park called Londolozi, in the wild savannah region of northern South Africa. Koelle and I drop off our luggage at the camp and go straight to the village nearby, where the Londolozi workers, mainly from the Shangaan tribe, live with their families. Four months ago, I walked into the village's new learning center and met the headmistress, a lovely woman named Mo. She had just begun teaching literacy and English to everyone in the village who wanted to learn.

From the moment I first walked into the learning center, everything about it—about the whole village—felt weirdly familiar to me. Why did I know this simple one-room building? Why did the monkeys in the trees seem so familiar? Oh, that's right, I remembered suddenly. I'd been dreaming about them. I'd dreamed about them on and off ever since Adam was born, for almost twenty years.

Today, Mo introduces me to Sidney, a gorgeous little boy with huge eyes and a left hand that appears to be affected by slight cerebral palsy.

"I've been working with a few special-needs children just lately," Mo says. "An elephant told us about them."

You'd be surprised how ordinary this sounds when you hear it in a Shangaan village. But even here, the story Mo goes on to tell is remarkable.

Eight years earlier, the game trackers at Londolozi spotted a baby elephant who'd been born with horribly deformed hind legs. The trackers who first saw the baby figured it was lion chow, but that particular herd of elephants reacted in a way no one had ever seen and no one expected. The herd had begun to walk in an unusual horseshoe formation, with the little elephant—named Elvis, though she turned out to be female—in the center. When they reached an obstacle Elvis couldn't clear, the other elephants would lift her with their trunks. The herd slowed to Elvis's pace and became an unusually gentle, peaceful pod of pachyderms.

"One day," Mo tells me, "one of the land owners came and told me he'd seen Elvis's herd. And Elvis told him—I mean, he says Elvis told him—that there were some children in the village with special problems who weren't getting the same opportunities as the others. So we looked, and sure enough," she grazes Sidney's head with a gentle hand, "we found them."

Maybe, I think, I came here to meet Sidney, to talk to Mo, to make plans for helping the learning center move forward. That alone would certainly be reason enough.

Flash Forward Twenty-four Hours

The man I came to meet with at Londolozi is busy digging a well somewhere, but it doesn't matter because I've met someone else at the camp who seems to need some coaching. Life breaks us all, and lately, it's been this guy's turn. We talk for half an hour, do a little dungeon-digging. Then he breathes a sigh of relief and tells me he feels lighter. I can see it in his face and posture; his shackles are looser, if only a little. This is why I love what I do. Maybe, I think, I came here to help free up this beautiful young man. That alone would certainly be reason enough.

Flash Forward Twenty Minutes

As I sit with my new friend, we hear a crackling sound in the brush below the deck where we've been having tea. From out of the brush directly below us, an elephant appears—a small elephant dragging her terribly deformed back legs. Elvis. She lugs herself up onto a huge, broad, level rock until we're only a few yards apart. Then she turns and tilts her massive head, so that one huge, brown, thick-lashed eye seems to look straight into my face. She lifts her trunk toward us. Just in case it's not random, I imagine my arm as a trunk and hold it out toward her in imitation. Her mother comes and stands beside her, to help her back down the rock.

Elvis doesn't look well; her body weight is crushing her poor bandied legs. It hurts me to imagine her pain, but I see no suffering in that great, soft eye. I remember what one of the trackers told me: that no normal elephant aggression has been observed in that herd in the eight years since Elvis was born. She is a broken elephant. Her family is the family of a broken elephant. But they are strong in the broken places.

Maybe, I think, I came to meet Elvis. That alone would certainly be reason enough.

Flash Forward Four Hours

Later that night, after a Jeep trip that has brought us within a few feet of giraffes, leopards, warthogs, hyenas, rhinoceroses, waterbuck, buffalo—utter heaven for animal lovers—we return to find a dazzling surprise: Dinner has been set up in the village. The children have been sternly warned to stay quiet, and the village is illuminated by luminaries made of candles and brown paper. I meet my friends from my last visit, people who throw their arms around me like long-lost family members, because that's what we seem to be.

During my last trip, I dreamed that I woke up in a thatched African house, and I knew I was waiting to be visited by the Ancestors. This terrified me because I anticipated a group of seriously ticked-off Mormons bursting through the door. Then I thought, no, these are the *real* ancestors, the ancient Africans from whom (scientists tell us) all humans have descended. This gave me a moment of relief until I began wondering if they'd want me to kill a goat. I was tense and sweating with anxiety when the air of the dream began to thicken like gelatin, and I knew: They were here. Just as I was about to really freak out, I felt a sweet warmth, like a flannel blanket being tucked around me, and a message filled my mind. Without any actual words being exchanged, I knew what the Ancestors were telling me. *"Martha,"* they said. *"Relax!"*

And then they went away.

Since this dream, I've been curious about African shamans, who are said to receive visits from the Ancestors. It's one reason I decided to use traditional shamanism as a metaphorical vehicle for this book. So I'm startled and thrilled when the village headman calls for the attention of all us feasters, and we turn our chairs around to see a small, timid-looking woman sitting on a grass mat, holding what I recognize as a bag of bones. "Throwing the bones" is a divination technique in many parts of Africa. The woman, who is introduced as Cecilia even though she speaks no English, is a shaman.

The anthropologist in me feels like she's died and gone straight to Paradise—this beats the Discovery Channel hands down. We're told that Cecilia is going to give us a kind of show-and-tell, explaining through a translator some of the traditional religious beliefs.

But she doesn't.

She just sits and stares.

At me.

Flash Forward Five Minutes

Cecilia is still staring at me. I've read that if two people lock eyes for over ten seconds, they're going to either kiss each other or kill each other. I'm not sure which way Cecilia is planning to go. Aside from a few quick glances at the rest of the group, she hasn't taken her eyes off mine for a good five minutes. It feels like eternity, there in the crackling firelight in front of the small, silent crowd.

My head begins to spin. The jet lag, the firelight, the half-glass of excellent South African wine I've just drunk already make the night surreal. But Cecilia's eyes go beyond surreal. I've looked into thousands of people's eyes, and I'm more comfortable doing it than most people, but I've never met a gaze like Cecilia's. Later, I'll learn that she fled here from Mozambique, where decades of civil war led to widespread atrocities so horrific I literally can't force myself to read the details. That would explain the strangeness of Cecilia's eyes. I see in them a terrible intimacy with horror and an absolute commitment to battling that horror; the utter fear of a hunted animal and the utter ferocity of the hunter. And deep, deep down, below all of that, there is a soul crushed by unimaginable forces into something as clear, sharp, brilliant, and piercing as a diamond, or a star.

Finally, Cecilia speaks in Shangaan. The translator tells us, "She says she isn't here to give a speech. There is one person here who has come to this place to see the *sangoma*. The bones wish to speak to this one person."

As the translator speaks, Cecilia's eyes keep boring through my head, and everything starts spinning again. Of course, she means me: Whoever fetched Cecilia undoubtedly pointed me out, helped her Google me, and told her to give me a good show. But no one could fake that stare. Every time Cecilia looks at me, I feel pierced to the bone by the mighty spirit in that timid little woman, the brilliant star in that broken body.

I say nothing. Silence. To break the tension, one of the camp trackers jokingly suggests that she tell him whom he is to marry. The tracker is at the top of the social pecking order; Cecilia is at the bottom. She tosses him the sort of glance an empress might give a mosquito and shoots out a terse response. "This is not for him," the translator says. "The bones choose the person with whom they wish to speak."

Cecilia goes back to staring at me, and I finally confess that yes, I may have come to see a *sangoma*, but out of anthropological interest, not to, like, get a reading.

Cecilia nods as though I am a slow child who has finally caught on and throws the bones. They "talk" to me for a good half hour, continuing even when I protest that this focus on me is stealing time from everyone else. The bones tell me (according to Cecilia, according to the translator) to shut the hell up and listen.

If Cecilia did Google me—which I am still by no means ruling out—she did a thorough job. She talks about my children, my career, my sense of connection to Africa (all very Googleable). Then she starts to talk about the book I'm writing. She doesn't say "book," she talks about what I am "telling many people." At this point, Cecilia actually seems confused and uncertain, as though she can't imagine how I might be telling so *many* things to so *many* people. Despite this, the bones seem to be quite conversant with the unfinished document I'm wearing on the four-gigabite flash drive that hangs on a lanyard around my neck. Okay, she could be guessing, cold-reading me like a stage magician. But if she is, she's damn good at it.

The whole time, when the translator speaks, Cecilia keeps fixing me with those laser eyes, set in the beautiful coal-black face of a small, broken body. Maybe, I think, I came here to encounter Cecilia. That alone would certainly be reason enough.

Flash Forward Twenty-four Hours

Now I'm dressed in a suit, teaching a group of city dwellers in Johannesburg, worrying that this highly educated audience will find my talk of "North Stars" and "visualization" too unscientific. During a coffee break, a woman named Elizabeth sets me straight.

"When South Africa became democratic, when we ended apartheid, everyone was positive there would be a wholesale bloodbath," she says.

Now that she mentions it, I remember reading about that as a student in America. Elizabeth goes on to tell me how, in the weeks prior to the first democratic South African election, journalists poured into the country practically licking their lips as they prepared to videotape the inevitable gore.

"We were so afraid," Elizabeth tells me, "and so absolutely committed to not following our fear." She describes to me how every day in many workplaces, South Africans of all colors would spend their lunch hours gathering to join hands and visualizing the country moving gently into democracy, without wanton slaughter.

"This stuff you're talking about isn't new to us," Elizabeth says. "We've staked our lives on it. We've staked our nation on it." I look around the room and see these quiet warriors, each of whom has faced fear and refused to bow to it. I think that maybe I came here to learn from them what courage is. That alone would certainly be reason enough.

Flash Forward Eighteen Hours

A group of Africans have gathered in a paddock to learn from interacting with horses. Koelle is working with a horse named Zorro, who has been rescued from one of the enormous "townships," or ghettos, where he's been used and abused in every imaginable way. Zorro is small, gaunt, covered with scars, and clearly traumatized. Koelle is trying to win his trust, projecting the body language and energy of a matriarch mare. She's signaling him so strongly—speaking so "loudly," in the silent language of horses—that other horses have come from a hundred yards away and gathered by the round pen where Zorro is shivering, sweating, pawing the ground with anxiety.

Horses are generally better people than people, and Koelle is a world-class expert at healing traumatized animals. Damaged as Zorro is, he begins to respond to her signals. Then it's time to pitch in one of our life coaches. The work of "horse whispering" is so similar to the work coaches do that I wish everyone I train could experience it.

This particular coach is intellectually brilliant and physically brave, but I know enough about her to call her a "wounded healer." Zorro, similarly wounded, is acting out emotional pain Louisa has felt since childhood; he is her fear on four legs. So it's especially magical when, under Koelle's guidance, Louisa is the one Zorro accepts as his matriarch mare. After who knows how long a life of trembling in terror, he decides to trust. Zorro relaxes, lets out a long, snuffling breath, and walks up—

without rope, without coercion of any kind—to rest his head against Louisa's shoulder. When she moves, he moves; when she stops, he stops.

And from both of them, the broken-and-healed woman, the broken-and-healing horse, great waves of gentleness radiate to every two-legged, four-legged, six-legged, and no-legged creature in that wide pasture.

Maybe, I think, we came here so Louisa could help heal Zorro, and Zorro could help heal Louisa. That alone would certainly be reason enough.

Flash Forward Thirty Hours

I'm home in Arizona, typing this, wondering if I've had another long, complicated dream about Africa. But I know that couldn't be true because even in my wildest dreams, I never would have imagined everything that just happened.

The Path Forward

This hasn't exactly been a typical week for me, but it isn't atypical either. I no longer have typical weeks. I am steering by starlight, thank you, and I haven't had a typical week for years. Einstein said that there are two ways to look at life: as though nothing is a miracle or as though everything is. I choose "everything."

To wake up is a miracle—how has this strange beast I call "my" body survived another night? To drink coffee is a miracle—think how it got here, from some hill in South America all the way to my hand! I sit down at my computer, a miracle anyone in the African Ancestors' day would have recognized as magic beyond magic. I go online (miracle), and in a few minutes, I realize there are no programs for learning Tsonga-Shangaan dialect. So I download a program (miracle), and within a few minutes, my computer is well versed in Zulu, a closely related language. It begins to speak Zulu to me (miracle), and I start studying.

Because miracles, unfathomable as they are, must be worked.

This particular work is very hard for me. There are sounds in Zulu I've never even heard. Tongue-clicking is involved. The word for "no" is so difficult to pronounce (it combines an aspirant Chinese "ts" with a gutteral Germanic "ch") that as I try to mimic it, my dogs gather around me in alarm, convinced I'm having a lethal asthma attack.

Now, there are many things I could be doing at this moment. I could be finishing this book, which, thanks to my African adventures, is well overdue. I could be answering infinite e-mail, badgering my broker about my retirement account, cleaning my laundry room, double-checking my children's homework. But I am learning Zulu instead, because at this moment, that's what feels most like freedom, most like falling in love. I'll work like a pack mule to do something no one wants me to do, something I'm bad at, something impossible, if I feel my own North Star steering me in that direction. If I don't follow that star, no matter where it leads, I'll lose it. And that's just not an option.

The Fellowship of the Stars

After writing that some of us "become strong in the broken places," Hemingway took his own life, becoming the last magnificent living being he would shoot in a lifetime of shooting magnificent living beings. I like to think that if he'd focused less on killing and more on healing, something else might have happened. Maybe he would have been guided and helped by other souls that had been broken and healed strong, like Sidney and Elvis and Cecilia and Zorro and all the people who, over the ages, have faced fear by choosing to join hands and hope instead of doing the logical thing and bashing each other's brains out. Maybe Marianna would have walked in, glowing like a lighthouse, to tell him nobody walks through the darkness alone.

There are so many ways to lose the perspective of the Stargazer. Maybe, right now, your inner sight is clouded by the opinions of others or the horror stories of your inner lizard. Or maybe you're sun-dazzled by a perfect-looking surface, projecting all the trappings of enviable success and hiding the sense that you're lost, directionless, hollow. It could be you're reading this because life has given you a chance to walk into the darkness, and you've been staring terrified at the ground in front of your feet, trying to see your way by finding some well-beaten path. And maybe—quite likely, in these days of dizzying change and unprecedented possibilities—no beaten path exists.

Look up.

No matter how clouded, sunblind, or terrified of the dark you may be, your Stargazer self is always gazing calmly at your destiny. Follow it forward expecting to break things—rules, conventions, precedents, your own vulnerable heart—but knowing that you'll heal strong. The strength itself, the joy of finding it, using it, testing it, and feeling it grow, is the purpose of the whole adventure.

One night in Africa, I watched the full moon rise huge and orange over the savannah. Giraffes walked in front of it like movie stars. A leopard huffed somewhere. One of the men in our group said he was afraid to look up; the stars were so bright he felt he was falling into them. "It makes me think too much," he said, sounding genuinely scared. I know what he meant. If you see the stars too clearly, they make demands of you, throw out rude, intrusive questions. The poet Mary Oliver did this in one of her poems, brazenly asking, "Tell me, what is it you plan to do with your one wild and precious life?"

If you're afraid you've come to this question too late, you are wrong. Ask your Stargazer self. It will tell you what my fallen-noble friend Marianna told me in one of my darker hours: that the world is re-created in every instant of time, and this moment is always your life's beginning. No matter how many years have been stolen from you by your own ignorance, by cruel fate, or by the acts of others, you have a clean, broad slate before you. In this instant—*this one now*—you can begin steering by starlight, and if you do, the rest of creation will conspire to guide, teach, and help you.

Our African guide knew this. As the last of the sunlight faded and the moon cleared the horizon, he read us one of his own favorite poems.

Live while you are alive . . .

Learn to be what you are in the seed of your spirit

Learn to free yourself from all things that have molded you

And which limit your secret and undiscovered road . . .

Never forget that love

Requires that you be

The greatest person you are capable of being,

Self-generating and strong and gentle—

Your own hero and star . . .

Be grateful for life as you live it,

And may a wonderful light

Always guide you along the unfolding road.

He finished reading, and we sat in silence. How amazing, I thought, to have come so far in order to find myself at home, among loved ones. How many other homes have I not yet seen? How many loved ones have I not yet met? I can't count them, waiting out there. But I can feel them.

Maybe you can feel them, too, if you try right now. Maybe you can't. No matter; they're still there. As soon as you get your night vision, you'll see them. No other person will ever walk the path that destiny has laid out for you, but along that path, you'll come home to a thousand different places. You will meet your mother, your father, your twin, yourself, in a thousand different bodies. Even on the loneliest night, when it seems there is no one else on earth willing to travel such a strange and magical road, you will find your tribe out walking among the stars.